C & O #3025 2-10-4 Type. Class T-1 leaving Russell yard, Ky. with 13,500 tons of coal for Toledo, Ohio. Many of these heavy trains totaling 160 loads leave daily behind these great locomotives forty of which were built by the Lima Locomotive Works. Courtesy Chesapeake & Ohio R.R.

RAILROADS AT WAR

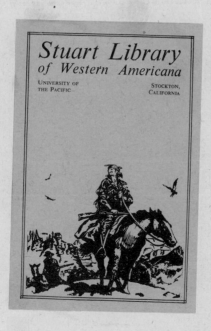

Books by S. KIP FARRINGTON, JR.

ATLANTIC GAME FISHING

BILL, THE BROADBILL SWORDFISH

PACIFIC GAME FISHING

RAILROADING FROM THE HEAD END

GIANTS OF THE RAILS

RAILROADS AT WAR

Dedicated to the locomotives of the United States and Canada, steam, Diesel, and electric, in every class of service, that are hauling the trains that are helping to win the war.

Oil for the people and ships along the North Atlantic coast. Eastbound New York Central oil train hauled by engine 3130 4-8-2 Type Class L-4 built by the Lima Locomotive Works scooping water at East Palmyra, N. Y. on the Syracuse division. Courtesy N. Y. Central R.R.

S. KIP FARRINGTON, JR.

COWARD · McCANN, INC.
NEW YORK

RAILROADS AT WAR

Designed by Robert Josephy

CONTENTS

ix

INDEX OF PHOTOGRAPHS

NOTE: The picture described will be found in the group of pictures immediately following the page number given.

xii

xiii

INTRODUCTION

This brief introduction affords me an opportunity to express the Navy's appreciation to the American railroads for a job well done. Two of the Navy's Bureaus maintain an intimate working contact with the railroads. The Bureau of Naval Personnel under the direction of Vice Admiral Randall Jacobs, USN, handles Navy passenger traffic, and the Bureau of Supplies and Accounts, under the direction of Rear Admiral William Brent Young, SC, USN, handles freight traffic of the Navy.

I have observed with satisfaction the mutual respect which has marked the relations of these Navy organizations with the railroads, and the manner in which the substantial, and sometimes difficult, transportation needs of the Navy have been met. I do not recall a single instance where any Navy operation has been embarrassed through a failure of rail transportation—and the railroads have had some difficult deadlines to meet.

The reader of this book will be impressed by Mr. Farrington's description of the physical and mechanical operation of America's railroad transportation machine. I share the admiration everyone must feel in this accomplishment, and have been equally impressed by the planning and teamwork evident among shippers, receivers, governmental agencies, and the armed services. Without this teamwork the finest operating and mechanical power, capacity and skill might have been frustrated.

Effectiveness of railroad transportation in World War I was to a considerable measure nullified by serious congestion, particularly in and behind eastern port areas. This congestion was primarily caused by inability of consignees or transshipping activities to unload shipments from railroad cars, thus, in effect, utilizing railroad rolling stock for storage rather than transportation. The Navy has considered the prompt unloading of railroad equipment so important that by order of the Secretary, naval activities must report daily any cars on hand which have not been unloaded within the brief free unloading period. The reasons therefore must be good ones. In consequence, the Navy has established a record for the speed with which it has unloaded and released railroad equipment, both at its continental shore establishments and at its major transshipping activities over which millions of tons of material have moved to the Navy's overseas bases and units.

The Navy's stake in railroad transportation is enormous. The Navy's rail freight bill in the early months of 1944 averaged nearly forty million dollars per month. This includes only direct payments by the Navy, and not the many millions more in which payment was made indirectly. If the Navy's present annual shipments of petroleum products alone were loaded into one train, this train would stretch from the Atlantic to the Pacific Coast and back again.

In no field have the Army and Navy worked more closely and harmoniously together than in the field of transportation. Examples of joint cooperative action are numerous; e.g., Army-Navy Consolidated Car Service, under which both services consolidate less-carload shipments in heavy production areas and move them in solid cars and even solid trains to points of use or export; plans for port capacity and utilization; pooling of military police and shore patrol activities; and joint action on rate adjustments and schedules.

Unselfish teamwork has made possible the achievements described in the following pages. Mr. Farrington has written an absorbing story of industrial America at war.

JAMES V. FORRESTAL,
Secretary of the Navy

Washington, D. C.,
July 17, 1944.

FOREWORD

America's railroads made the union of the states a physical fact, a practical reality. Today they are the great inner lifelines of that union's survival in the holocaust of world war: an indispensable base behind the tremendous charges under which the tyrant attackers across both oceans are now crumbling.

Farseeing Americans in the early days of the republic, looking from the westward side of the Alleghenies only as far as the Mississippi, thought it might take five or ten centuries to settle those vast stretches. Railroads brought population and statehood all the way to the Pacific in a matter of decades.

World War II loaded our railways with a job whose hugeness and complexity almost baffles imagination. Failure could have been fatal. They have succeeded magnificently.

In 1943 the transportation systems of the United States moved inter-city freight equivalent to a billion-ton load hauled a thousand miles—in transportation language, a thousand billion ton-miles. Of this tremendous total the railroads moved nearly three-fourths: 730 billion ton-miles. That was six times the load of the next largest freight carrier, the Great Lakes ships; more than seven times that of the pipe lines; more than fifteen times that of all the inter-city trucks combined; twenty-nine times that of the barges and boats on inland waterways other than the Great Lakes. Besides hauling their great burdens of ores, fuels, building materials, finished armaments, and home front essentials, the railways have carried an unprecedented load of passengers, military and civilian, whose mobility, as much as that of war goods, is an essential of mobilization.

From December, 1941, through June this year 23,300,000 troops have been handled domestically in organized movements —2¼ per cent by highway and 97¾ per cent by rail. A total of

173,400,000 tons of Army freight and express have been moved by domestic railroads and less than 8½ per cent as much by truck. More than 4 million troops have been transported overseas and, with them, more than 63 million ship-tons of supplies.

In the last two years it has been my privilege to ride both the locomotives and the various types of trains they haul, over forty-one Class I railroads in this country; and I have spent much time on the property of several others. The very skill of their accomplishment has tended to veil its drama from all but those directly involved. This book represents a conviction that the indispensable is worth a good look.

I am grateful to the railroads for their many kindnesses to me in aid of this project. I particularly wish to thank The American Locomotive Company, the Baldwin Locomotive Works, The Electro-Motive Corporation, the Lima Locomotive Works, the Union Switch and Signal Company, the Railway Age Magazine, and J. M. Nicholson and O. L. Gray, assistants to the operating vice-president of the Santa Fe Railroad, for their courtesy to me.

I am also much indebted to Olive Flannery, Herbert Worthington, and Charles Tyler for their work on the manuscript.

Preston George, Richard H. Kindig, Otto C. Perry, and H. W. Pontin of Railroad Photographs, four of America's master railroad photographers, have generously allowed me to use their excellent pictures.

S. KIP FARRINGTON, JR.

East Hampton, New York,
July 25, 1944.

RAILROADS AT WAR

CHAPTER I

THE IRON WARPATH

The Railroads Gird for Battle

The backbone of America is a steel rail. Never was there a time when this was more fully demonstrated than during the grim days that followed the Japanese attack on Pearl Harbor, and the United States was forced to meet emergencies created by involvement in the greatest cataclysm the world has ever known.

A steel rail and the iron-fisted monsters that ride it. Peaceful steel and friendly engines, passing your back door and mine. Sunday morning. The kids poring over the funnies; dad buried in the sports pages; mother looking for bargains. Folks going to church. A lazy day—Sunday. God's day.

And then a hand in the sky, writing words in red. December 7, 1941!

Almost in a twinkling the steel rail, glinting in the sun, was turned into an iron warpath. Before the last red-dotted carrion hawk had made its homing on those Japanese carriers, skulking in the distant mists of the blue Pacific, American Railroads were springing to attention. In a matter of hours, trains were wheeling out of the East with vital supplies for our exposed and vulnerable West Coast, and they were traveling fast, with great, iron-lunged locomotives shouting their battle cries of freedom.

Tojo's war fleet was on the prowl. Our own Pacific defense was a shambles. Many of our proud battle wagons were smoking hulks; scores of our planes had been ruthlessly smashed on the ground. The air waves were alive with dark rumors: Japanese submarines were at the Golden Gate; hostile planes were over San Francisco—threat was stalking everywhere.

In that black hour, the railroads rushed to battle stations. The

1

railroads, with the decks cleared for fight, were ready. War transport was on the move.

Railroad men everywhere were quick to accept the challenge. A telegraph operator in Cajon Pass; a track walker in the Rockies; a Mexican section hand on the Mohave; a conductor on a coal train in the Alleghenies; a yardmaster at Blue Island; a brakeman in the Berkshires; a train dispatcher in South Station, Boston; an engineer on the Coast Line in Florida; a switchman on the Pennsy—every mother's son of them knew a quickening of the pulse, a tightening of nerves, as they braced themselves for war.

A broadcaster in Honolulu was still crying news of the rape of Hickam Field into his microphone, people of America were still crouched before their radios when the first war train began to move. The full import of the horror at Pearl Harbor had hardly been hammered home in the mind of the average citizen before war cargoes destined for European fronts were being swiftly transferred from Atlantic port docks to cars making up for the West Coast.

Special trains were made up, crews were called, big, pulsing engines were assigned, and by midnight of December 8, 1941, freight was rushing westward over every transcontinental system in the country.

The railroads of America tightened their steel belts and began gearing for their mightiest effort of all time. Soon there was under way the greatest movement of men and supplies known in all of the world's history.

As this is written, day and night, somewhere in these United States, a special troop movement starts every six minutes. A freight train, loaded with vital war goods and food stuffs, highballs out of a make-up yard every four seconds. Put that down!

No institution in America has been more thoroughly damned as a soulless corporation than the railroad; no American institution is more deserving of praise, now and forever more. The Goulds and the Harrimans and the Hills may have been renowned tycoons, but they gave us as our heritage the steel rail, and not a mess of pottage.

And because of this steel backbone, old Uncle Samuel today

2

stands ready to fight the Hitlers and the Tojos from hell to breakfast.

A steel rail carries iron ore from Mesabi to the blast furnaces, and from the blast furnaces to the arsenals, and from the arsenals to the Army camps. Put a gun in the hands of the American boy, and he will lick any fighting man on earth. He knows, too, how to use his fists, and from an alley on the New York East Side to Europe and Asia, he is the toughest barehanded scrapper that this or any other war has seen. He will battle for fun, money, or eyeballs. God love him!

The steel rail is the first link between our farms and our factories and our sons on the battle fronts. It is the first line in America. And one day the steel rail will bring the boys home again, to Oshkosh and to Brooklyn.

Down the lean, tough depression years, the railroads of America were readying for war. Though, perhaps, they did not fully realize the extent of the danger around the bend, their courage and their foresight, nevertheless, prepared the way for the rush of war transport that was to come.

As great as has been the burden thrust upon them by World War II, the railroads were far better prepared to carry it than they had been back in 1917. And this in spite of the fact that 1941 found them with fewer engines and fewer cars than they had had in service in World War I; fewer miles of track. Two-thirds as many cars as they had in 1920; almost half as many locomotives. And yet in 1942 American railroads carried 638,000,000 ton-miles of freight. Nearly two million troops are moved every month. The marvel is that there has been surprisingly little congestion.

In the following pages, we shall attempt to show how the railroads have met and whipped this tremendous transportation problem. The subject, however, is far too great and too complex to be covered in one book. The best we can hope to do is to draw a rather sketchy cross-section of a few vital railroads, attempting to show the enormous task they have performed.

Free private enterprise has arisen to meet a great national emergency, and when we write of the Southern Pacific, the Santa Fe, the C.&O., the Milwaukee, and others, we are simply writing the story of every railroad in the United States—the New York Central, the Illinois Central, the Pennsylvania, the Louisville & Nashville, to mention but a few, as we salute them all.

The writer has ridden thousands of miles in cabs of freight and passenger locomotives, in cabooses, coaches, Pullmans, and business cars. Days and nights on end, he has had a front seat. He has talked with engineers and firemen and conductors and telegraph operators; with railroad officials, with roundhouse men and trackmen, with women railroad workers in overalls. In all humbleness, he approaches this task of attempting to set down a little of what he has seen, feeling that the best he can do is well-nigh futile and inadequate, as compared with the enormity of the subject of railroads at war.

Not long ago we were listening to a short-wave broadcast from Tokyo. The honey-voiced speaker said in perfect English, "If only Mr. Roosevelt could see with his own eyes what Japan has done for Greater Asia."

We only wish that Tojo—yes, and Hitler—could see Centralized Traffic Control in operation on an American railroad. Just that and no more. Dollars to doughnuts, this pair of starry-eyed maniacs would turn to clabber and start talking to the crickets.

And small wonder. For right there is a piece of magic that has made more than one solid, sober American citizen gasp. And this in a country where men perform miracles and do the impossible as a warm-up for the day's work.

Centralized Traffic Control is just one of the tricks the railroads and Uncle Sam have up their sleeves. And it is not a military secret. Centralized Traffic Control provides a single-track line with 75 per cent of double-track capacity, and this in territory where bottlenecks have existed is of vast importance.

It is told that a desert rat, or prospector, on the Mohave saw two trains racing toward each other on a single track. He closed his eyes against the sight of a frightful head-on collision. When he opened them, the two trains had miraculously passed each other and were speeding on their respective ways. The old desert rat and his burro lit ashuck for the Funeral Mountains, bearing tidings of an all-time rip-snorting mirage.

The weathered nomad of the Mohave could not know, of

4

course, that this was neither a mirage nor hocus-pocus, but just a little thing that the boys at the Union Switch and Signal Company had cooked up to expedite railroad traffic and keep train dispatchers from getting gray-haired before their time.

Centralized Traffic Control made its bow to the railroad world back in 1927, and since that time has had widespread acceptance by the railroads of the country. Briefly, C.T.C. places at the tips of a train dispatcher's fingers complete control of switches and signals over extended distances of track. It eliminates train orders and time lost by trains "in the hole," and has proved a vital cog in many of the Nation's strategic rail lines.

Interstate Commerce Commission figures show that at the close of 1929, two years after its introduction, there were twenty-six installations in service. During the next three years, this figure was almost tripled. By the end of 1935 there were 160 installations. Since Pearl Harbor, C.T.C. has been constructed on a scale that dwarfs all previous years.

Centralized Traffic Control systems installed in 1942 and 1943 alone totaled approximately sixteen hundred miles, or about sixty per cent of all mileage completed prior to 1942. The reason for the intensive construction of C.T.C. as a wartime measure will readily become apparent as the discussion of this method of train dispatching receives our attention in a subsequent chapter.

Through the lean years of 1930 to 1941, the Southern Pacific spent more than $195,000,000 for new equipment, additions and improvements. In the two-year period before Pearl Harbor, this road ordered $64,000,000 worth of cars and locomotives alone.

Right here we find one reason why the railroads of the country were immediately able to shoulder the enormous load of war materials flowing to the war theaters.

The railroads had faith in the future of America, and they backed that faith with hard American dollars, and at a time when all around them factories, farms, mines were wallowing in the bog of depression. Everywhere the cry was retrenchment. A man with a dollar squeezed it until the eagle would have screamed if it had the strength.

Those were the years when crops were being plowed under and buzzards were eating American beef. Those were the years when

5

railroads of the Nation were building for war. Those were the years when American Railroads were investing every dollar they could lay their hands on in "Tomorrow!"

Those were the years when the Louisville & Nashville, "Old Reliable," unveiled its famous l.c.l. fast freight, the *Silver Bullet*, when the Pennsylvania Railroad expanded its program of electrification between Wilmington and Potomac Yard, employing a construction force of 11,000 men, recruited from furloughed employees.

Those were the years when the Burlington brought out its famous Zephyrs, and the Union Pacific introduced its first dazzling Diesel-electric streamliner. Those were the years when the new speed queens of the rail were born, and steam locomotives waltzed down the rail in aluminum jackets and skirts.

Low-cost coach trains appeared, and a man and his wife could go from here to yonder, traveling in the style of a nabob. Poor people walked out of the sooty old day coach into the last word in de luxe, air-conditioned trains.

Main-track manifest trains started courting shippers, trains like the New Haven's *Speed Witch*, the New York Central's *Merchandiser*, covering 429 miles in ten hours and fifty minutes. Preference freight boomed to new heights on the Pennsylvania. The big brother of the streamliners, Diesel-electric freight engine No. 100, made its bow on the Santa Fe.

Yes; the railroads were getting ready for war while they were fighting a war. Old Man Hard Times hung on like a hobo to a boxcar. The Defense Program went into effect and traffic started to roll. The railroads took it in stride. Came Tojo and Hitler with their sneak bombs and their submarines. It was then that those American dollars spent to whip the depression, truck competition, and the fiddle-footed automobile started paying dividends.

There had to be cars, and there had to be the locomotives to handle them—and there were. Not enough, it is true, but they managed to do the job. The American railroad system immediately proved itself to be a mighty instrument of war.

Since 1918 more than ten billion dollars have been spent for improvements to the railway plant. Since World War I, the

6

railroads, for every dollar of additional stocks and bonds issued, have spent ten dollars for additions and betterments. Despite increases in wages, taxes, and other costs of producing service, the railroads are receiving now an average revenue per ton-mile very little higher than that received twenty-five years ago.

The capacity of the average freight car during World War I was forty-two tons. In 1942 it was fifty-one tons, or twenty-four per cent more. There are over half a million fewer freight cars in service at the present time than in 1918, but they are bigger, stronger, tougher. Locomotives now travel farther in a day than ever before—fifty-six per cent farther than in the first World War. The tractive power—the load that a locomotive can pull—has been increasing steadily.

More remarkable has been the increase in average brute horsepower, which not only measures the power to start a heavily loaded train but the power to keep it moving at high speed over long distances. Today's high-wheeled, high-horsepower freight locomotive is a different breed of animal from the Iron Horse of twenty-five years ago.

The thing called "utilization" of locomotives has increased tremendously down the years, and today is of major importance, and is vital in the handling of war transport. An example of this is shown in the chapter dealing with Santa Fe locomotives.

The average freight train does more than twice as much work in an hour than in those distant yesterdays. Many a Red Ball train in America today can, and does, fan the breeze down the railroad at close to passenger-train speed, and not in isolated instances, but in day-in and day-out performance.

The list of arranged fast freight schedules on the Pennsylvania reads like a list of thoroughbreds at the starting barrier on a glorified Derby Day.

Better track, improved signals, Centralized Traffic Control, modern engine design—all have played a part in the increased, all-time-high performance of our modern freight train.

The railroads are handling the unprecedented traffic of this man's war with a minimum use of critical materials for new cars, engines, and other equipment. Although the total increase in traffic during the three-year period of 1940-42 was six times as

7

great as the increase in 1916-18, the railroads have been permitted to purchase less than one-third as many new engines as they did in the first World War period, and less than three-fourths as many new freight cars.

In 1921 there was only 32.4 miles of travel in the average passenger dollar. In 1942 that dollar carried the average passenger 52.1 miles—carried the passenger faster, more safely, and in far greater luxury.

Railroad passenger traffic in 1942—measured by passenger-miles—was more than one-fourth above the peak of the first World War. In the first three months of 1943, it was virtually double the traffic of the corresponding period of 1918. Troop movements are more than four times heavier than in 1917-18.

About one-half of all Pullman sleeping cars and one-fifth of all railway coaches are required for the transportation of troops. Throughout 1942-43 more than two hundred troop trains were operated daily on American railroads, not to mention large numbers of troops moved in regular trains.

"The railroads have more than justified the confidence reposed in them by Army men," said the Chief of Army Transportation, Major General C. P. Gross.

"There could be no Navy without land transportation to move the tremendous quantities of materials required to build, equip and supply our ships. Virtually every mile of railroad is a vital part of the transportation system on which the Navy depends." —Rear Admiral William B. Young, Chief of Bureau of Supplies and Accounts, U. S. Navy.

When Uncle Sam was crying for land transport, the American Railroads delivered. Not a ship has been launched, not a soldier or sailor sent overseas, not a single item of Lend-Lease food and equipment shipped to our allies without first having begun the journey, as raw material or finished product, somewhere, sometime on a steel rail.

A huge naval gun bound for the west coast via the Santa Fe in the yard at Wellington, Kansas on the Middle Division. Photo by Delano, Office of War Information.

On the way to the fighting fronts, these iron-clad land cruisers and other wartime equipment in boxes are part of the ceaseless stream of weapons, supplies and munitions that are flowing over the American railroads to training camps, supply depots and ports of embarkation. Courtesy N. Y. Central Railroad.

Back to the mines with the empty ore cars. When the lakes are open this parade never ceases. D. M. & I. R. #224 2-8-8-4 Type is one of the three most powerful steam locomotives operating in the United States and have created a remarkable record not only over their own lines but also on the other roads to which they are loaned during the winter months to aid in the war effort while the lakes are closed to navigation. Courtesy D. M. & I. R.

High and wide wartime loads on the New York Central. One of the greatest jobs that this country's railroads have achieved is in carrying and expediting heavy wartime shipments on and in freight cars. Train LS-1, New York to Chicago, pulling into East Cleveland, Ohio with Engine #2995, Class L-2D 4-8-2 Type. Cleveland Division. Courtesy N. Y. Central.

CHAPTER II

CENTRALIZED TRAFFIC CONTROL

C.T.C. Aids Train Movement on Union Pacific

William "Bill" Jeffers and the Union Pacific. Those names are synonymous, and will live forever in American Railroad history. They stand for progress, for foresight, for courage.

When the final chapter of World War II has been written and the green lights glimmer for a clear track ahead, Bill Jeffers and the Union Pacific can proudly point to their page in the record book where it is written that the U.P. exerted every effort toward the efficient and safe transportation of troops and war materials, along with old John Q. Public and his family.

And right there at the top of the page it will be set forth that Centralized Traffic Control was one of the stout cogs that helped keep the wheels rolling. A 171-mile installation in the wild vastness of the Mohave Desert between Las Vegas, Nevada, and Yermo, California, is providing the most efficient and effective method of train dispatching ever developed.

Here is an excellent example of how Centralized Traffic Control affords the extra track capacity needed to handle unprecedented increases in war traffic. Immediately after Pearl Harbor, the Union Pacific's Salt Lake City–Los Angeles line, of which the C.T.C. territory is a part, became an especially strategic transportation artery.

Factors contributing to its importance were the great steel mill Henry Kaiser built near San Bernardino, California, another that sprang up at Provo, Utah, and the world's greatest basic magnesium plant just outside of Las Vegas, Nevada. The latter was located at this point to take advantage of the enormous amount

9

of power generated at Boulder Dam. This dam in itself has added significantly to the importance of the line.

Let us consider a few tonnage figures before we start poking into the vitals of this thing called Centralized Traffic Control. The tonnage handled between Las Vegas and Yermo during the first quarter of 1942 was 35.5 per cent greater than in the same period of 1941, and 60.5 per cent greater than the first three months of 1940.

Now we're thinking in big numbers, so hold your hat. Stated in gross tons the increase represented from the first quarter of 1940 to the same period in 1943 was 149,402,929 gross tons. In other words, the jump was from 246,956,665 gross tons in the first quarter of 1940 to 396,359,594 gross tons in the first quarter of 1943.

This is a lot of tonnage to handle over a single-track line, particularly inasmuch as heavy mountain grades limit the tonnage of each freight train to 2,500 tons for both eastbound and westbound drags. At the time the first C.T.C. studies were made, it required each day an average of 9.33 passenger trains, 19.33 freight trains, 16 helper engines, and 2.34 light engines, or a total of 47 movements to handle the tremendous volume of business.

West of Las Vegas the C.T.C. territory climbs out of the great Las Vegas Valley and tips over into that enormous hinterland, the Mohave Desert. Many people associate any desert with a vast, flat expanse of sand and nothing else, a place where a man who is lost walks in circles and meets himself coming back. True, there is a lot of flat country in the western deserts; there are, also, a lot of mountains—he-mountains with mountain sheep on them; mountains with snow on them in winter. Mountains predominate in the Mohave Desert.

Leaving Las Vegas on the Union Pacific, the line lifts sharply to the summit of a sprawling mountain range about fourteen miles to the westward, and subsequently follows the contours of this range. Curves are necessarily sharp, some having a six-degree curvature, but prevailing grades are held to a maximum of one per cent for the eighty miles to Cima, California, which is the highest point on the Las Vegas–Yermo subdivision.

Beyond Cima, the line descends sharply for eighteen miles to Kelso at a continuous gradient of 2.2 per cent. Because of this steep grade it is necessary to use as many as three helper engines on all eastbound trains between Kelso and Cima. Before the installation of Centralized Traffic Control an especially serious bottleneck existed in this section because of the difficulties arising in handling light helper engines against such dense traffic.

West of Kelso the line descends at a gradient not exceeding one per cent to Cork, California, which is approximately twenty-eight miles west of Kelso. The remaining forty-four miles of the territory is a continuously ascending westward grade of one per cent or less. Here the track skirts the weird, sandy reaches of the Devil's Playground, crosses the Mohave Sink, and comes finally to Yermo, on the flats under the gay-colored Calico Mountains.

This, then, is a brief word relief map of the Union Pacific's Centralized Traffic Control district.

The Union Pacific, the pioneer, the road that drove the golden spike at Promontory, Utah, in mid-spring of 1869, has established another milestone in the bright history of railroading by completing the *longest* stretch of Centralized Traffic Control in the world to be controlled from one location.

During 1942 traffic in the Las Vegas–Yermo territory had closely approached the saturation point. Delays were frequent, congestion had assumed alarming proportions, and, as a result, equipment could not be utilized efficiently. For this reason construction work on the C.T.C. project was rushed to the greatest possible extent. Portions of the territory over which the greatest delays were occurring were hurried to completion first. As the various portions were placed in service, the congestion began to ease, and by the time the entire installation was operating congestion had disappeared entirely.

Not only have delays ceased, but trains can now actually make up an almost unbelievable amount of time while they are in C.T.C. territory. Freight trains can save approximately a minute a mile. Fast passenger trains, when late, can make up twenty minutes over the entire C.T.C. district.

Let us go back now and see what makes this C.T.C. thing tick.

With Centralized Traffic Control, the train dispatcher can virtually do everything but shake hands with the engineer and conductor. One little machine does it—one little machine crammed with gadgets born of American ingenuity. Oh, yes; there are some wires strung out along the line, but they were there anyway.

A quarter of a century ago the man attempting to dream up a scheme whereby the engineer of a heavy-tonnage freight on single track might be directed to slip his train into a passing track a few scant seconds ahead of a speeding limited coming against him, without the use of train order tissues, would have promptly been thrown in the pokey, being regarded as far too dangerous a character to be on the loose.

"Smoke orders," they would have termed such a meet, and somebody would have sure been hauled onto the carpet.

Yet today these same paint-scorching meets are merely a part of the scheme of things on many of the Nation's most vital rail lines, and they are accomplished with an unsurpassed degree of safety.

Long ago, operating officers visualized as the ultimate in signaling a centralized system of train dispatching whereby one man would have under his hand complete control of the switches and signals over extended distances of track. He would, they foresaw, authorize the movement of trains by signal indications rather than by written train orders on concise, up-to-the-minute knowledge of train progress, which would be furnished by indications on a track model on the wall before him.

Such a system, using direct wire circuits, was installed. However, to control the vast and intricate functions over long distances required enormous quantities of line wire, which prohibited the economical and feasible application of such a method.

But the Union Switch and Signal Company soon proved that there is more than one way to get over a mountain, and it came up with what was called the "Time Code System." It reduced to two the number of line wires required to provide centralized control of traffic over extensive territories. And Centralized Traffic Control was on its way.

The earlier C.T.C. systems were relatively short, but there followed a trend toward longer installations. By the end of 1937,

the silver Denver Zephyrs of the Burlington were flashing across
an entire subdivision of 105 miles, guided and protected by Centralized Traffic Control all the way.

Under the written train order method of operation, the dispatcher must rely upon train reports (OSes) from the various
telegraph operators along the line for information concerning the
location of trains under his jurisdiction. Since some operators
may allow considerable time to elapse after a train passes or
leaves a station before they send their "OS," and since there is
always a variance in the time the different operators require to
report a train, the dispatcher does not have a true picture of the
train's progress. He must therefore arrange for meeting points
according to the rather incomplete and inaccurate information
he has available. In addition, he must make allowances for the
time consumed in issuing, transmitting, and delivering written
train orders.

Under the best conditions, the written train order method of
operation is inefficient compared to the C.T.C. Where traffic
is heavy, the delays occurring in the issuance, transmission, and
delivery of your "19" or "31" order can alone create serious bottlenecks. Add to this delay those caused by the necessity of
stopping trains, throwing switches, starting heavy drags again,
and a busy main line can soon make a mess of schedules.

With Centralized Traffic Control, information concerning the
progress of a train is transmitted to the control office automatically as the train passes through a certain designated track section. This information is conveyed to the dispatcher by means
of small but brilliant lights, which are inserted in a track model
replica of the controlled territory at points representing the "OS"
sections. These "OS" sections are usually located at the ends of
passing tracks, or at any other point where such information is
desirable. Since it is practicable to have many more "OS" points
than would be possible under the written train order method of
operation, the dispatcher is afforded more comprehensive knowledge of train progress at all times.

With the information furnished by the lights on the track
model, the dispatcher is enabled to arrange meeting points on
the most efficient possible basis. When a meeting point is de-

13

cided upon, the dispatcher merely flips a miniature switch lever and signal lever on the control machine; then presses a code-starting button. Immediately things begin to happen, five, ten, twenty, or one hundred or more miles away.

The switch at the desired end of the selected passing track moves to the reverse position and the signal displays the proper indication for a movement into the siding. As soon as the train designated for the passing track is in the clear, this information is transmitted to the dispatcher. He immediately restores the switch lever to its normal position, moves the signal lever to clear the signal for the train that is to proceed on the main line, and again presses the code-starting button. Upon completion of the code, the switch returns to the normal position, the signal clears, and the train on the main line is on its way.

The switch at the opposite end of the passing track is reversed by the dispatcher now, and the train "in the hole" is directed to re-enter the main track by signal indication.

Tremendous savings in train time result from the fact that the switches at the ends of passing tracks in C.T.C. territory are controlled by the dispatcher, thus eliminating the necessity of stopping trains while trainmen throw the switches by hand. Studies of actual installations disclose that power switches save a tonnage freight about six to eight minutes when entering a passing track and some eight minutes when departing.

A tonnage freight can be advanced from one station and into the passing track at the next station in approximately ten minutes less time than is required where switches are operated by hand. A train can pull out of one passing track, proceed to the next station and get in the clear approximately fifteen to eighteen minutes quicker than if it was required to stop at both stations so that switches could be operated by a trainman.

Proper meeting points in Centralized Traffic Control territory can be selected so accurately, and the switches and signals controlled so swiftly that a high percentage of the meets are accomplished without stopping either train. Trains can be advanced one or two or more stations farther than would be possible if their movements were authorized by written train orders.

The benefits of C.T.C. are especially evident during peak

14

traffic hours. Since the dispatcher knows the exact location of all trains in the territory at all times, and since he is not delayed transmitting train orders, he can accept additional trains into the district whenever they are made up and ready to go.

Serious traffic congestion, under the written train order method, may result from such unforeseen incidents as a journal running hot, a draw-bar pulling out, or a locomotive stalling on a grade. For example, a capable dispatcher may have established a meeting point; he knows the crews, the tonnage of the trains, the characteristics of the engines. Everything is moving smoothly. But after the meeting point is selected, a storm hits the Mohave, let us say—a wind storm. It is a cross wind, and blows the sand the engineer is applying to the rail into the next county. The locomotive is on a heavy grade and the big drivers are fighting for traction. Without sand, the engine "slips badly"—the drivers spin. It becomes necessary to "double the hill"—cut the train in half and move each section to the summit separately.

Perhaps a number of passing tracks intervene between this grade and the established meeting point. The opposing train is "in the hole" miles away. There is nothing to do but wait, and precious time is lost. Both trains now are running late.

That is what happens when unforeseen delays occur to one of the trains involved in a meet under the written train order method of operation. This is single track, you understand, and other hurrying trains are bound to be affected, for traffic is dense. Since the dispatcher is unable to communicate promptly with the crew of the train in difficulty, he cannot immediately change the order in such a manner as to advance the other train beyond the meeting point already established.

Now let us see what happens when a similar situation arises in Centralized Traffic Control territory. C.T.C. cannot, of course, prevent hot boxes, broken draw-bars, or sand storms, but it can minimize the effects of such occurrences.

Here we have this freight drag doubling the hill. The lights on the track model in front of him convey to the dispatcher the information that this train is delayed. It is not necessary now for him to hold the opposing train at that previously selected meeting point. Instead, the dispatcher immediately directs it to proceed under signal indications.

This train, the *Challenger*, say, continues to advance during the time the freight is doubling the hill, with the result that the delay to the *Challenger* has been minimized; perhaps not even delayed at all. The freight clears in the siding at the top of the grade; the meet is consummated and both trains proceed.

The advantage of Centralized Traffic Control adds up to greater over-all train speeds and vastly increased capacity of existing trackage, with consequent intensified utilization of existing cars and locomotives.

Since the outbreak of the war, serious restrictions have been placed upon the purchase of new rail, cars, and locomotives. For this reason, the railroads have turned to C.T.C. for at least a partial solution to their problems.

Centralized Traffic Control has proved to be just what the doctor ordered, and the slightly groggy railroad patient gets a new lease on life.

C.T.C. can be installed in an exceptionally short time, and, considering the results obtained, with a justifiable expenditure of critical materials. In territory where Centralized Traffic Control has been put in operation, it has postponed indefinitely the need for additional trackage; in some cases it has actually made it possible to eliminate extra tracks. In several instances where C.T.C. has been installed on single track between sections of double track, it has been found that trains can be operated more efficiently in the single-track than the double-track territory equipped with only straight automatic signaling.

The advantages of Centralized Traffic Control are not, however, limited to single track. Where traffic is dense on multiple-track lines it has been demonstrated that greatly improved operation results by signaling each track for reverse running and authorized train movements by C.T.C.

In view of the tremendous amount of work accomplished by a C.T.C. control machine, the reader might assume that it is a massive affair. Actually it is surprisingly small, as for instance all the levers on the machine controlling the 171-mile Union Pacific

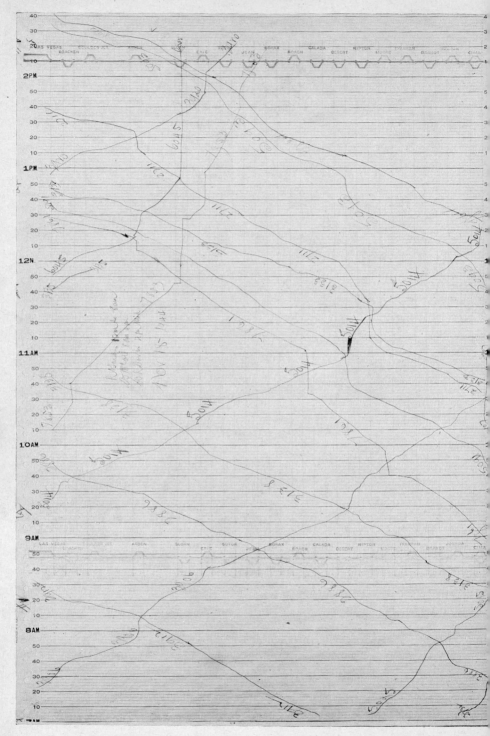

Graph from C.T.C. machine at Las Vegas, Nev., showing run of westbound Extra #5014 on which author was riding from Las Vegas to Yermo, Calif., Nov. 18,

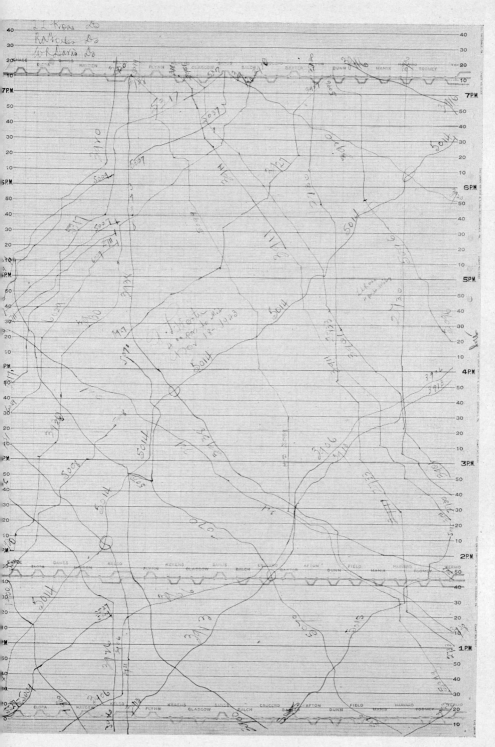

1943. Each line with number represents train or light engine. Where these lines cross, a meet. *Courtesy of T. L. Foster, U.P. Dspr., Los Angeles Div.*

installation are within easy reach of the dispatcher from a sitting position.

The switches and signals at the ends of thirty-three passing tracks are controlled by the dispatchers at the C.T.C. machine at Las Vegas. In addition, movements to and from the passing tracks at less frequently used sidings are made on signal indications, although the switches are hand thrown.

The C.T.C. machine at Las Vegas consists of a five-foot center section, with two two-and-one-half-foot wing sections at either end, arranged in semi-octangular fashion. Although under the load of present wartime traffic two men are employed on each trick to operate the control panel, under normal conditions it is considered that one man will be sufficient.

With its maze of brilliantly colored lights and rows of tiny levers and push buttons, the Centralized Traffic Control machine may appear complicated to the casual observer. But to a dispatcher who for years has been working under the time-consuming and complex method of issuing written train orders, it represents a phenomenally simplified means of directing train movements.

The track model, control levers, and code-starting buttons are arranged in a vertical panel on the front of the cabinet. The track model, which is located at the top of the panel, is a miniature representation of the actual track and signal layout within the controlled territory. Small red lights inserted in the lines of the track model indicate to the dispatcher the progress of each train. Beneath each point on the track model designating a switch is located a switch lever, and under the switch lever is a signal lever. Lights are inserted in plates behind each lever to indicate the position of the controlled function. Usually a red light indicates a switch in the reverse position, and an amber light shows that the switch is in normal position. When a signal is at stop this fact is indicated by a red light. When it is clear a green lamp is lighted. If a particular location is furnished with a maintainer's call signal, a toggle switch is provided for its control below the switch and signal levers. A code-starting button is placed under each group of switch and signal levers. Other levers and push buttons can also be furnished for mounting on

17

the control panel according to the individual preferences of the railroads.

A horizontal surface, placed directly under the control panel, forms a desk for making out reports. An automatic train graph, protected by plate glass, is made an integral part of the desk. The train-graph mechanism continuously operates a parallel lined chart, which is printed for direct reading of time. This chart passes over a set of inked pens at the rate of three inches an hour. An individual pen is provided to make a recording on the graph paper each time a train occupies a corresponding "OS" section within the territory. By connecting the recordings made by the graph pens, the dispatcher makes a complete train-graph chart of each train that passes through the C.T.C. territory. The completed graph shows the exact time each train passes the different "OS" sections, and, also, where and at what time the various meets are made.

Now we come to the "coding" apparatus, which is contained within the control cabinet. This apparatus is rather complex and will not be discussed at great length. Substantially, it provides a means of sending out a control code to operate the various functions in the field. Likewise, the office coding apparatus receives an indication code from the field which illuminates the indication lamps and informs the dispatcher of the movement and positions of the various controlled functions.

Here, briefly, is how the coding system works.

Normally, the dispatcher retains the signal levers in the center position, which controls all signals to the stop position. The switch levers are placed in the normal position to line the switches for main line movements. Lever lights indicate which signals have been controlled and also the position of the switches.

Now, suppose the dispatcher wishes to direct a train to go into a passing track. He places the desired switch lever in the reverse position, turns the corresponding signal lever to the position controlling the signal governing movements into the passing track and then presses the code-starting button. The latter manipulation immediately sets a sixteen-step control code into operation. The code is composed of a series of long and short

18

impulses, individual character of the code being established by the sequence in which the short and long impulses are arranged.

The first impulse, which is always long, is used to detect that the code line is not already in use, and also locks out the line so that a second coding operation will not be started and interfere with the one already initiated. The next seven impulses, three long and four short, select the station where the switch and signal are to be controlled. This is accomplished by the sequence in which the impulses are transmitted. The following seven impulses, which may be long or short, depending upon the character of the code, are used to control the switch to the desired position and provide the proper indication at the signal. The sixteenth or final impulse, which is long, resets the apparatus to the normal condition.

After the control code is finished and the functions have completed their movement, coding apparatus in the field, which is similar to that in the office, automatically transmits an indication code to indicate to the dispatcher that the functions have responded. The first impulse, always short, checks and locks the code line in the same manner and for the same purpose as was accomplished during the control code. Likewise, the next seven impulses, three long and four short, select the station in the same manner and the following seven impulses are used to indicate that the functions have responded correctly to the control code. As with the control code, these seven impulses may be long or short, depending upon the character of the code. The final impulse restores the apparatus to the normal position. Upon completion of the indication code, the lights on the levers indicate whether or not the functions have responded correctly.

In connection with the C.T.C. code line, it is interesting to note that the same pair of wires can also be utilized for telephone and telegraph circuits. Almost any type, number, or combination of circuits can be superimposed on the code line without interference with each other. In general, if an existing telephone or telegraph line is mechanically strong, it is not necessary to construct a new C.T.C. code line. On the other hand, if such a line does not exist, a new one can be constructed during the installation of the C.T.C., and other desired circuits can be superimposed on the same line later.

It should be emphasized that the code system serves only as a means of communication between the office and the field and also between the field and the office. Actually, a C.T.C. system retains all the features of automatic signaling plus full-circuit interlocking protection at switches.

If a dispatcher should attempt to clear a signal for one train to leave a station while another train is in the block, the automatic field circuits would cause the signal to continue to display a stop indication. However, if a train should advance to the next block the signal would automatically display the proper approach indication for the train leaving the station. A switch cannot be reversed for a movement into a passing track unless opposing signals are at stop and the signal governing the movement into the passing track is displaying the proper restrictive indication for such a movement.

Safety of train operation in C.T.C. territory is further increased because the authorization of train movements by signal indication eliminates the possibility of an error occurring in the issuance, transmission, delivery, or execution of written train orders.

An especially large amount of intricate, precision-built instruments, interconnected by complex electrical circuits, are required for a C.T.C. system such as the Union Pacific installation. The instruments and other equipment required at the ends of passing tracks are contained in metal instrument houses, amply ventilated to assure a free circulation of air. Inasmuch as temperatures in the Mohave frequently reach 120 degrees, sufficient ventilation is of paramount importance to the men whose duties require them to inspect and maintain the apparatus.

A separate compartment containing a telephone is furnished in each house to provide a means of communication between the dispatcher and train and maintenance men.

In order to speed construction work on the Union Pacific, the instrument houses were wired complete at the Union Switch and Signal Company factory, where all the signal apparatus was designed and manufactured. The houses were shipped to the railroad ready to be set on the foundations, whereupon connections to the line wires and rails were made by the railroad construction forces.

The signals at the ends of passing tracks are the type known as searchlight signals. Such signals afford three long-range indications—red, yellow, and green, using only one lamp bulb and signal unit. This is accomplished by a mechanism that places a red, yellow, or green roundel in such a position that a concentrated light beam is reflected upon the roundel by an elliptical reflector. After passing through the roundel, the light is spread upon a lens, which in turn concentrates the light into a beam possessing the color of the roundel. This beam provides an intense, unmistakable day or night indication, even under adverse weather conditions.

The signals used between the various stations are the color-light type. The color-light signal employs a separate unit and optical system for each indication. On the Union Pacific the units are arranged in a vertical fashion.

In order to conserve battery, all signals are normally lighted off an alternating-current line, which parallels the tracks. In the event of a power failure, a relay automatically transfers the source of energy to a "standby battery." Further battery economics are afforded by "approach lighting" the signals. This means that normally the signals are dark, but automatically light upon the approach of a train.

The automatic signal circuits are designed on what is known as the A.P.B. (Absolute Permissive Block) principle. This means that, for the utmost safety, when a train leaves one town all signals governing opposing movements are set at the most restrictive indication all the way to the next town. However, the signals behind a train that govern following movements go to the approach and clear positions as the train progresses through the blocks, in order to afford the greatest possible track capacity.

An important and interesting feature of the installation is that in spite of its length and magnitude, only two code-line wires are·required. Until recently, the number of stations that could normally be controlled by one pair of line wires was limited. However, by means of a Union Switch and Signal Company development known as Coded Carrier Control, the flexibility and capacity of the two-wire C.T.C. system were increased to such an extent that now installations of any desired length or station capacity can be controlled over only two code-line wires.

Here, nontechnically, is how Coded Carrier Control works, as applied to the Union Pacific C.T.C. system. The territory is divided into three approximately equal sections. The first section, extending from Las Vegas (site of the control machine) to Calada, is fundamentally the conventional thirty-five-station Union C.T.C. system, and is operated on normal direct-current impulses. The second section, extending between Calada and Flynn, and the third section, between Flynn and Yermo, can quite well be called separate C.T.C. systems. Each section is controlled by separate high-frequency alternating current impulses, known as carrier currents.

These carrier currents, along with the conventional d. c. circuits, are superimposed on the same pair of line wires. However, by means of filters, the apparatus of each section is allowed to respond only to the correct current for that particular section. In this manner, all sections can be controlled simultaneously from only one control machine, with no increase in coding time. In addition, a voice communication circuit is also superimposed on the pair of C.T.C. line wires, filter equipment making it practical to carry on telephone conversation at the same time that C.T.C. codes are on the line.

The use of carrier frequencies for the handling of the two remote sections of the C.T.C. installations and the derivation of a telephone communication circuit from the one pair of line wires resulted in a large saving in critical materials, which would have been required if these facilities had been obtained by the use of additional line wires. Consistent with the general policy of conserving critical materials, the conductors of this C.T.C. line are Copperweld forty per cent conductivity. These conductors contain approximately forty per cent copper and sixty per cent steel.

In conjunction with the Centralized Traffic Control work, the majority of the passing tracks were extended a sufficient distance to accommodate 120-car trains. This not only makes it possible to handle longer trains, but the extended passing tracks increase the possibility of accomplishing nonstop meets. In this, as well as other C.T.C. installations, a considerable percentage of the meets are made on a nonstop basis.

The over-all result is that in spite of the unprecedented volume of traffic moving over single track across the mountains and valleys of the Mohave Desert it is kept moving smoothly, swiftly, and without unnecessary delays.

As of March, 1944, the Union Pacific is moving about 1,800 cars daily between Las Vegas and Yermo. The "helper" mileage on this district reaches the rather startling total of 3,600 miles daily. All freight trains are "helped" between Las Vegas and Cima, eighty-one miles, also between Kelso and Cima, eighteen miles.

Before the installation of Centralized Traffic Control, it was necessary to "patch" from four to ten trains daily between Las Vegas and Yermo. In 1942, traffic in this territory had just about reached the saturation point. Now the Union Pacific is handling a traffic increase of better than twenty-five per cent over that of the period prior to the C.T.C. installation. And trains are making the 170-mile run in seven and eight hours.

Centralized Traffic Control stands out as a most important contribution to the war effort by the Union Pacific, as well as the many other railroads of the country, which are today employing this wizard of the main line to keep the supply trains moving.

Yes; C.T.C. and the American Railroads are helping to "pass the ammunition."

CHAPTER III

THE SOUTHERN PACIFIC SOUNDS . BATTLE STATIONS

A Railroad at War

There is nothing on earth that so possesses the power to fire men's blood, to bring their nerves to singing tautness, as the call to battle stations. Men turn brittle, tense. Lips tight, eyes sharp, they spring to their posts, awaiting orders to open fire.

The enemy has been sighted; soon the first salvo will slam out, and crashing guns will tear the world apart. Now the endless days of training and preparation will bear fruit. Without this training and weary drill, the greatest dreadnaught afloat would be rendered totally incapable of action.

No battleship, no bomber, no regiment could hope to perform successfully without tedious, painstaking preparation.

No American railroad could have met the crisis that exploded on our doorstep on December 7, 1941, if it had not been ready. And no railroad in the United States was more fully prepared to answer the call to battle stations on that fateful Sunday morning than the Southern Pacific.

The people of America can well be proud of their Army, their Navy, their Air Force, their Merchant Marine. They can be proud, too, of American Railroads.

Here we will attempt to draw a cross-section of the war job performed by the Southern Pacific, whose principal lines are located in extremely strategic areas.

The Southern Pacific has felt the full force of the national defense and war program, particularly on its far-west lines, as have few other railroads. Many factors were involved, among them a vast increase in revenue passenger-miles, which were over one

24

Union Pacific #4012, world's largest locomotive, and only 4-8-8-4 Type ever built, running 40 miles an hour with a westward extra of 3440 tons on the Eighth Subdivision of the Wyoming Division west of Green River, Wyoming. These locomotives built by the American Locomotive Co. have turned in a remarkable performance. Photo by Otto C. Perry.

Union Pacific #21, the Pacific Limited, with Engine 829, latest U.P. 4-8-4 Type, at Archer, Wyoming on the Fourth Subdivision of the Nebraska Division. Photo by Preston George.

Heavy steel invasion boats destined for the Navy ready to roll to the coast behind Erie 3387, 2-8-4 Type Class S-4. Picture was taken at Meadville, Pa. Courtesy Erie Railroad.

Troops leaving main train on arrival at a Texas camp. Kitchen car in right foreground. Note the excellent Pullman equipment with which the railroads have supplied troops in World War II. Courtesy U. S. Army.

U. P. 5306, 2-10-2 Type, crossing the Snake River east of Huntington, Oregon on the Fourth Subdivision of the Idaho Division with a westward extra; 3215 tons, 74 cars. Photo by R. H. Kindig, U. S. Army.

The retainers are up and inspection is over. U. P. Extra 3938 West with oil-burning 4-6-6-4 Type leaving Summit, California, about to descend the 3% grade in Cajon Pass. Photo by H. W. Pontin Railroad Photographs.

hundred per cent greater in 1942 than in 1929, resulting largely from the increased industrialization of the West Coast, where war plants mushroomed up with magic rapidity.

The traffic load in 1941, as measured in net ton-miles of freight moved, increased thirty-seven per cent over 1940. It was more than forty-seven per cent above 1929, and was the greatest in the history of the Southern Pacific. Yet, up to the actual declaration of war, the railroad handled this increase without undue delays, an indication that the S.P. had been moving ahead all through the depression years.

Came then the declaration of war, and the burden imposed immediately thereafter was staggering. It was like a slugging right to the jaw by a vicious adversary, but the Southern Pacific did not falter. Railroad men are tough, and long ago the Iron Horse proved that it is a brute for punishment.

Railroad officials, trainmen, trackmen, operators—every man jack of them took a hitch at his belt, spat on his hands, and cried, in effect, "We can lick the Nip who threw the brick!"

Depression days left the railroads lean and hard and tough. Too soft living spoils the best of men, as well as railroads. The lean years taught America that we can take it—and come back swinging.

In common with every other railroad in the country, the Southern Pacific suffered under the heel of hard times. However, its executives foresaw the possible increase in traffic and were determined not to be caught asleep at the switch. No good railroad man ever is.

Between 1929 and 1940, the S.P. dug deep and came up with $170,000,000, which was spent for improvements on its Pacific lines alone. In the five years ending with and including 1940, the Southern Pacific spent $38,121,202 on additions and betterments, and $50,315,635 for equipment—a combined gross expenditure of $88,436,837 for improving its plant.

Between $49,000,000 and $51,000,000 went into rolling stock alone in 1941 and 1942. In addition to this, the S.P., jointly with the Union Pacific, entered into a program of $10,500,000 expenditures for new cars, for the rebuilding and repairing of cars for their subsidiary, the Pacific Fruit Express. This in 1942-

43, which brought the total money spent for Pacific Fruit Express equipment since 1936 to $56,500,000.

These figures will be analyzed in detail later, but they serve to show that huge sums were expended to insure that adequate facilities and rolling stock be available. No one in his wildest imagination could have foreseen the terrifying flood of traffic that was to descend on the Southern Pacific. But, without these vast expenditures, the transportation of war materials and men on the West Coast would have become involved in a well-nigh hopeless morass.

Almost overnight, troop movements and other Army traffic began to pile up, soon reaching hitherto unheard of proportions, but the Southern Pacific was able to meet and absorb this greatest of all rushes, and in a manner entirely satisfactory to military authorities.

Under the terrific load, civilian freight and passenger traffic, naturally, was subjected to some delays, but the intrinsic soundness of the property and of the operating methods employed was demonstrated, as the railroad met its problems, and despite the increased traffic load and other wartime difficulties. A measure of this increase is found in the fact that, in two months in 1942, the Southern Pacific Transportation System's net railway operating income was the largest for any railroad in the country.

Let us, for a moment, examine the figures.

FREIGHT AND PASSENGER TRAFFIC INCREASES
S.P.—Pacific Lines   Gross Ton Miles (Thousands) *

	Freight	Passenger	Total	Revenue Passenger Miles #
Year 1929	37,989,651	10,925,734	48,915,385	1,414,684,311
Year 1939	37,603,623	10,664,870	48,268,493	1,421,374,409
Year 1940	42,217,511	10,680,280	52,897,791	1,328,150,750
Year 1941	54,384,708	12,138,282	66,522,990	1,746,057,784
Ten Months Period 1929	32,337,364	9,105,843	41,443,207	1,208,908,784
" " " 1939	31,164,256	8,950,890	40,115,146	1,220,012,950
" " " 1940	34,426,513	8,873,768	43,300,281	1,110,037,377
" " " 1941	44,752,065	9,875,451	54,627,516	1,409,823,799
" " " 1942	57,281,560	12,600,799	69,882,359	2,675,441,850

* Cars and contents, excluding weight of locomotive and tenders.
# Excludes passengers carried in electric service.

26

WHERE THE TRAFFIC CAME FROM

Almost every development of national economic importance in the last few years has served to increase traffic on the Southern Pacific. The national defense program brought an immense number of airplane and other war-production factories to its territory. This area, too, bristles with Army camps, airfields, Navy land and air stations, and other kindred war enterprises. The Southern Pacific serves more of these than any other railroad in the country.

Naturally, the advent of actual war material increased the already heavy traffic moving to and from these establishments, both as to men and materials. This not only is true with transcontinental traffic, but also with traffic moving between the Pacific Northwest and Southern California. The abandonment of intercoastal shipping via the Panama Canal brought a marked increase in the road's long-haul traffic, much of it lumber and other bulk freight that for many years had been carried by water.

The cumulative effect of all of these developments is indicated in the character of the traffic revenue from products of mines, which, for example, increased more than forty-four per cent. Next in order of increases were manufactured products, forest products, and many miscellaneous items.

On the other hand, agricultural products, normally one of the largest items in Southern Pacific traffic, increased less than fifteen per cent. The general trend of loaded traffic had been predominantly eastbound throughout Southern Pacific history. Today westbound tonnage is greater. This in itself necessitated further changes in operating methods, as the S.P. became more of a delivering than an originating carrier.

These changes have brought many problems. Greatly increased utilization of cars and locomotives became imperative. Track capacity had to be increased largely by the construction of additional facilities, including Centralized Traffic Control and other signaling. The manpower needs soared to heights never before reached, and the conditions that exist in the Pacific Coast labor market have made this situation extremely acute.

TRAFFIC ROUTES ON THE PACIFIC LINES

The Southern Pacific is essentially a single-track railway, but it is in the fortunate position of having alternate routes between many points that afford the equivalent of double-track operation. All such opportunities were used to the utmost to meet the war emergency.

It is interesting to examine this steel network—the life lines of a great railroad, spinning its web across mountain and desert.

From El Paso west, the S.P. has a direct line to Tucson, Arizona, via Deming, New Mexico, and Lordsburg, a distance of 312 miles. An alternate route is available via the former El Paso & Southwestern, through Douglas, Arizona, to Tucson, 340 miles. Between Tucson and Picacho, 46 miles, only a single track is available. However, between Picacho and Wellton, two routes are again available—one of 167 miles, via Maricopa, and the other of 211 miles, via Phoenix.

West from Wellton, the line is double track to Dome, 18 miles; then single track to just east of Yuma, 16 miles; and double track to Ariz Junction, 11 miles. From this point to Niland, California, the principal main line, via Glamis, 59 miles, is supplemented by a second route through Mexicali, Mexico, 96 miles. From Niland to Los Angeles, 185 miles, the line is single track, except for about five miles of double track near Los Angeles.

However, during the war emergency, the S.P. has made arrangements with its subsidiary, the Pacific Electric, to handle about one hundred cars of freight a day in each direction between Colton, California, and Los Angeles, 57 miles.

Two routes are again available between Los Angeles and San Francisco, the Coast Line, via San Luis Obispo, 470 miles, and the valley line, via Fresno, 483 miles.

Between San Francisco and Portland, Oregon, a variety of routes have been pressed into service, as this is one of the heaviest traffic lines. Between Oakland, California, and Davis, 74 miles, the line is double track. From Davis to Tehama, a single-track line runs via Woodland, 111 miles, and another route is available via Sacramento and Roseville. The latter is 25 miles longer, but is double track between Davis and Roseville, 31 miles.

Between Tehama and Black Butte, the line is single track, but between Black Butte and Eugene, Oregon, the Siskiyou line, 303 miles, via Ashland, and the Cascade line, 278 miles, via Klamath Falls, are available. The Siskiyou line was the main line until the Cascade line was built some years ago. It then became a secondary line, because of the curvature and heavy grades, some of which were as high as 3.3 per cent. Today, however, heavy through freights are slogging over it, relieving the pressure on the Cascade line.

A third route is also being used during the emergency. This is the Alturas line between Klamath Falls, Oregon, and Fernley, Nevada, thence the main line between Fernley and Oakland. This route is much longer, since it is normally used only for freight traffic between the Pacific Northwest and eastern points.

The Central Pacific line of the Southern Pacific between Oakland, California, and Ogden, Utah, 780 miles, does not afford alternate routes, but, of the 780 miles, 581 miles are double or paired track, a fact which has been of great benefit in getting trains over this busy overland route. This double track is of particular benefit across the Sierra Nevada range, where the normal difficulties of mountain operation are complicated by unusually heavy snows during the winter.

All across this vast network of steel, day and night, we hear the far call of locomotive whistles, the clamoring cavalcade of wheels, the hot, quick pant of exhausts. Mighty trains, rushing men and guns to the battle lines.

The first link between our far-flung forces and Uncle Sam's backyard is a steel rail. The first forward movement on the road to war is made when an iron-fisted coupler grabs a freight car and the man at the throttle takes it away.

The biggest parade in the world is marching today. It is marching in America, in these United States, an endless column of cars. From ocean to ocean they reach; from Canada to Mexico. Cars under the escort of great locomotives—American Railroads' men of war.

GETTING THE MOST FROM CARS

Early in 1941, as a step in its preparedness program, the Southern Pacific ordered 2,849 freight cars, and, in June, 4,000 additional cars, 1,150 of which were open-top cars.

To increase the efficiency of car-handling and to take care of other transportation matters, the office of General Superintendent of Transportation was placed on a twenty-four-hour per day basis, with a responsible official on duty at all times. This required the appointment of four assistants to the superintendent, as well as an increase in office personnel.

In June, 1941, to intensify the checking of car movements, to minimize delays and generally insure maximum utilization of equipment, six district car service agents were appointed, with headquarters at San Francisco, Oakland, Sacramento, Bakersfield, and Los Angeles, California, and Eugene, Oregon.

During the later part of 1942 new positions of superintendent of freight car service and passenger car service were established, thus assuring the proper supervision over the distribution of freight and passenger car equipment so essential to the care of the tremendous increase in both lines that developed, particularly since December, 1941.

Daily checks are made of all cars on hand for repair or cleaning. This includes an examination of cars and equipment on industry and house tracks, where the car initials, number, kind, capacity, home route, loaded or empty, date received, days detained loading and unloading, and the date the car became empty are all recorded.

These reports receive a daily check in the office of the division superintendent, and action is taken to secure prompt movement or release of equipment. To increase the car supply, special devices for loading automobiles were removed from about one thousand boxcars, thus permitting use in general service.

The loading of merchandise cars is carefully watched to insure compliance with O.D.T. Order No. 1. Where the minimum tonnage cannot be secured, the traffic is diverted to the S.P. highway subsidiary, the Pacific Motor Trucking Company, or to competing transportation agencies. By these methods, the Southern

Pacific has shown reductions in merchandise loading of more than seven thousand cars a month.

The results of efficient car handling are illustrated in the table, in which it will be noted that freight car miles and freight car days are not showing increases anywhere nearly commensurate with the increase in traffic, while the average miles per car per day are approaching sixty and are twenty more than they were in 1929.

The Southern Pacific uses oil as fuel in its locomotives except on one division, and to put every possible tank car into use, commercial oil movement has released all private-line tank cars formerly used to handle fuel oil. In addition, upon request from Washington, the S.P. has turned over twenty of its own 8,000-gallon tank cars to the fish-oil industry.

The number of tank cars under load with company fuel is under constant supervision to determine whether the number may be reduced. The oil companies further aid by loading on a six- or seven-day basis instead of a four- or five-days basis, as formerly.

Car repair practices on the Pacific Lines have, for the duration, been changed, and hundreds of cars are now repaired and put back in service that would in other times have been junked, it being uneconomical to repair them.

The only cars now retired and dismantled are those that have been severely damaged in wrecks, or those that require extensive rebuilding of underframes or structural parts. Not only are all possible cars repaired, but the percentage of bad-order cars is now down to an average of 2.75 per cent, as compared with 5.34 per cent as late as January 1, 1941, which at that time was considered an excellent record. Cars unfit for general service are carefully examined and, if found suitable for the purpose, are used for rough loading where only a switching movement or short haul is involved.

The slow, uncertain movement of cars on branch lines has been eliminated as much as possible. Having in the Pacific Motor Trucking Company an agency that can supply substitute transportation on a much more efficient basis in many instances, the Pacific Lines began a program of branch-line abandonment in 1931.

The railroad pattern is shaped around the lowly freight car. How well or how badly transportation officials deal with this Ishmael of the steel empire is quickly reflected in figures compiled, with cold, hard-rock statistics. Here they are, and the Southern Pacific can lay the cards on the table with a feeling of justifiable pride.

CAR HANDLING STATISTICS

	Freight Car Miles	Freight Car Days	Freight Car Miles Per Car Per Day
Year 1929	983,015,110	25,049,924	39.2
Year 1939	934,747,537	20,848,085	44.8
Year 1940	1,038,083,931	20,492,296	50.7
Year 1941	1,308,555,738	22,767,861	57.5
10 Months Period 1929	835,933,619	20,943,307	39.9
" " " 1939	776,063,809	17,389,586	44.6
" " " 1940	846,708,067	17,049,236	49.7
" " " 1941	1,084,249,841	18,528,307	58.5
" " " 1942	1,320,100,584	22,521,537	58.6

CO-OPERATION WITH MILITARY FORCES

The Southern Pacific has maintained a "co-ordinator's office" since the war began for the purpose of co-operating with the Army in the handling of military traffic.

This office is in charge of an assistant general freight agent. In addition, the Southern Pacific has assigned freight representatives permanently to military offices at various points in the San Francisco Bay area. Similar arrangements are in effect with the Navy, particularly in San Diego.

The Army has set up traffic-regulating stations at Odgen, Albuquerque, Spokane, and El Paso. Traffic moving to Pacific Coast ports is controlled at these points. For the purpose of releasing cars from use as railway storage facilities at ports, tariffs have been drafted to permit the railroad to place the freight awaiting boats in public warehouses without penalizing the shippers for demurrage or storage charges.

Southern Pacific Extra 3811 West, 2-8-8-4 Type Class AC-9, leaving Tucumcari, N. M. with 101 cars on the Rio Grande Division. Photo by R. H. Kindig, U.S. Army.

Solid train of westbound troop sleepers, 1200 of which were built by the Pullman Standard Car Company, climbing the high Sierras on the Sacramento Division behind a Class AC engine 4-8-8-2 Type. Courtesy Southern Pacific R.R.

Southern Pacific #824, eastbound fruit block double-headed with two 4-10-2 Type Class SP-3 running over the Los Angeles Division between Colton, California and Yuma, Arizona. Photo by H. W. Pontin, Railroad Photographs.

How necessary this co-operation is can be realized by pointing out that every day the railroads of the country deliver to military camps, naval stations, shipyards, ports of embarkation, enough freight cars to make a train 150 miles long. And that is but a small part of the freight movement.

YARD OPERATIONS MOST IMPORTANT

Make-up yards play an important role in the prompt movement of freight. Long trains roll in. They are broken down, shuffled, and reassembled, and are again sent on their way. Before the war, the Southern Pacific's two largest yards were the Taylor Yard at Los Angeles and the yard at Roseville, California. Facilities at these yards have been enlarged to accommodate the increased war traffic.

The yard at Fresno, California, has been rehabilitated and put back into operation after being out of service for some years. Apart from its local functions, this yard now takes care of much preclassification, thus relieving other yards.

In 1942, facilities were increased at West Oakland, including 40,000 feet of additional tracks and sixteen new tracks, with a capacity of 670 cars. In the train yard there are four repair tracks, accommodating ninety-two cars, two tank car cleaning tracks, a track for washing gondolas, two spur tracks, and an interchange track. From the standpoint of trackage, this is now the largest yard on the system, comprising 390 miles of tracks.

Additional yard tracks and facilities have also been built at Gerber, Dunsmuir, Brooklyn, San Jose, Roseville, Bayshore, Mojave, Los Angeles, Taylor, and Clement Junction, California; at Klamath Falls and Eugene, Oregon, and at Tucson and Yuma, Arizona. All of these are flat yards, except Taylor Yard, which is a hump yard.

The additional tracks in the Bay area yards were constructed largely to assist in the handling of export freight. The government has contractors building holding yards on railway property here, under an arrangement whereby the Southern Pacific leases the property and assists in the designing and engineering.

Yards continued operations during blackouts. The switch-lights were equipped with metal hoods. Yard engine lights were equipped with hoods in the same manner as main-line locomotives, and their fireboxes were shrouded. During blackout periods, floodlights were extinguished, and hand lanterns were used, being extinguished except when actually giving signals.

All precautions were taken, and yet the work of making-up cars went on, with fighting transportation squarely behind the fighting men at the front.

COMMUNICATION SYSTEM AIDS OPERATIONS

The Southern Pacific owns and operates transcontinental telegraph and telephone circuits that spread their network of wires across the West. Greatly increased traffic has put this system to a severe test, and more than three hundred thousand telephone calls have been handled in a single day.

Since the war emergency began, nineteen new positions have been added to switchboards on the Pacific Lines; 700 new telephone stations have been installed, and telephone carrier channels have been set up in increased wire capacity between:

Portland and Eugene, Oregon;
Dunsmuir, California, and Klamath Falls, Oregon;
Klamath Falls and Reno, Nevada;
San Francisco and Salinas, California;
Tucson and Phoenix, Arizona.

In April, 1943, three more switchboards were added to the general office installation at San Francisco, making a total of sixteen boards to handle the 2,000 stations in the Bay area. More than fifty new operators have been employed, bringing the total to 200 operators in charge of the thirty exchanges on the Southern Pacific.

GETTING ENOUGH LOCOMOTIVES

Despite huge orders for new locomotives, the problem of getting sufficient power to handle the trains and do the yard work has remained a persistent headache.

34

In 1929 the Pacific Lines owned 1,771 locomotives, but by October, 1941, this had been reduced to 1,556. From August, 1939, until the United States' entry into the war, the Southern Pacific had received or was awaiting delivery of 110 steam locomotives and 72 Diesel-electric switch engines.

In March, 1942, another large order, involving an expenditure of $12,000,000, was placed. This comprised thirty steam locomotives of the Articulated-Consolidation type, ten streamlined, "Daylight" general-service type steam locomotives, and thirty Diesel-electric switchers. This addition to the already large fleet of Diesel-electric switch engines will permit the release of still more Consolidation and Mikado locomotives for road service, where, the Lord knows, they are urgently needed.

Meanwhile, on March 1, 1941, the Southern Pacific launched a large repair program, designed to bring every last piece of serviceable motive power back into use as soon as possible. Because of material shortages, it soon became apparent that the new locomotives on order might not be delivered promptly; so, to fill the gap, every repairable piece of existing equipment was started on the road to restoration.

Old girls that had been rusting on rip tracks and in the railroad boneyards were rushed to the shops. Long-cold boilers came to life; hot steam coursed through the veins of many an old iron horse. Their husky-voiced exhausts shouted again; their whistles screamed on the main line, demanding recognition.

The work week of repair shops went from a five-day to a six-day basis. The number of men employed in the mechanical department jumped from 12,089 to 19,173. Grimed men repaired and rebuilt equally grimed engines.

In the meantime, the hunt was on—the hunt for old power, anything that could turn a wheel. Locomotives were returned from the Southern Pacific of Mexico, some of them forty years old. The Northwestern Pacific came up with six engines. Yards and sidings and enginehouses all over the system were combed. From the byways and the hedges they came—big engines, little engines. A motley crew, but now answering the call to arms. Many of the men who had built them were under the sod, and, no doubt, now squirmed gleefully in their graves.

Three locomotives were returned to service after years in the work of lowly stationary boilers. Imagine their joy at sprouting running gear and again clanking down the iron road. Their iron-fisted hands went out to greet trains of soldiers, trains of guns, trains of war material.

Many of these old sisters had been ruthlessly stripped, and were minus parts, but soon hardy mechanics had restored them and they pranced away to war. Some engines had to be converted from coal to oil, fitted with modern devices. This was expensive and, in normal times, would have been considered uneconomic. But with the Sons of Heaven stalking the Pacific and Hitler's hordes tearing the world apart, it was no time to think of dollars and cents.

An old man cannot do the work of a young man; an old, out-moded engine cannot haul the tonnage of the new engines, but it can go places and pull cars. And every little bit was another nail in the coffin of the enemies of America. Many an old loco-motive helped a big brother over the hump, saving another big fellow for another train.

Shop facilities, of course, were enlarged. A number of new 126-foot turntables were installed. At smaller shops, new loco-motive hoists were placed in operation, relieving the strain on the big shops. New water-softening plants were installed, reser-voirs were enlarged, coagulating basins and filters installed.

New buildings sprang up at West Oakland, Roseville, Los Angeles, Dunsmuir, Eugene, Tucumcari, and Tucson. The Southern Pacific built huge plate-bending rolls for shipyards in its shops; some the largest ever built. In addition, the shops manufactured gear parts, machined castings, and made parts for ships anchors.

This was war, and the Southern Pacific and the other railroads of the nation lost no time in putting their shoulders to the wheel.

KEEPING UP THE TRACK

From 1932 up to 1941, the Southern Pacific Transportation System spent $146,000,000 for additions and betterments to its equipment and fixed properties. As late as October, 1940, however, the S.P. had hardly felt the effects of the increased traffic resulting from the defense industries, but, in the closing months of that year, traffic began increasing so rapidly that the ton-miles of freight carried in 1940 were the greatest in its history up to that time.

Foreseeing a continuance and probably further increase in this traffic, the Southern Pacific immediately allocated increased appropriations for improvements. The expenditures for selected types of improvements in the fixed plants were increased by $5,320,000, or 165 per cent, in 1941 as compared with 1940. Expenditures in 1942 would have continued at the same rate if the shortages of materials and manpower had not intervened.

In 1940 and 1941, the S.P. System laid 657 miles of new and heavier rail, replacing 90-pound with 113-pound and 132-pound rails on vital sections. In 1942, on Pacific Lines alone, the program called for laying 336.2 miles of 113-pound and 93.7 miles of 132-pound rail. The larger part of this program was carried out. Rail purchases for 1943 were set at 433 track miles, involving 89,992 net tons, of which 329 miles were to be 113-pound and 104 miles 132-pound rail.

ADDITION AND BETTERMENT EXPENSES

	1942	1941	1940
Bridges, trestles, and culverts	$1,162,000	$1,165,000	$1,124,000
Signals	433,000	421,000	232,000
Centralized Traffic Control	1,721,000	1,284,000	
Renewal of rail, ties, and tie plates	1,922,000	1,225,000	1,179,000
Tunnel improvements	181,000	238,000	328,000
Ballasting	233,000	242,000	128,000
Extending sidings, additional track yards	2,230,000	3,960,000	234,000
Total	$5,982,000	$8,545,000	$3,225,000

In addition to normal maintenance problems, the S.P., because of the mountainous nature of the territory it traverses, encounters heavy grades on all of its main lines. The operation of trains up and down steep grades requires unusually high standards of track maintenance. To increase the capacity of the railway as well as its track standards, the S.P. lengthened passing sidings in 1941 to the number of ninety-two, and fifty in 1942.

Expenditures for the construction of new bridges have been heavy. To remove a single-track gap in a double-track line between Tracy, California, and Stockton, construction of a new, double-track bridge, 475 feet long, including a 106-foot 6-inch truss lift span, was undertaken. This replaces the single-track bridge over the San Joaquin River near Lathrop, California. Many other bridges and viaducts are being strengthened or replaced to eliminate interference with heavy traffic.

A major construction project involved a line change of thirty miles between Redding, California, and Delta. The new line was constructed by the Government in exchange for the Southern Pacific right-of-way traversing what will be the bottom of the great Shasta Reservoir. This track, placed in operation in March, 1942, passes over eight steel bridges and through twelve tunnels. The largest trestle is over half a mile long and stands 500 feet above the canyon bottom.

Other construction projects include line changes between Vincent, California, and Paris, and between Wave and Punta.

Always it has been a battle to increase track capacity. And that brings into the picture that magic wand known as C.T.C., Centralized Traffic Control. This puts the train dispatcher in direct control of block signals and switches in the entire district, and, on single iron, provides for seventy-five per cent of double-track capacity.

It releases operators for other duties, does away with train orders, and generally cracks bottlenecks wide open. The S.P. installed C.T.C. systems between Delta, California, and Black Butte, fifty miles; between Santa Margarita and San Luis Obispo; between Bena and Tehachapi. In addition to C.T.C., the signal department has made many signal changes as a result of revised track layouts.

There is a continuous program of spring switch installation, and about $30,000 annually is being spent for slide-detector fences in territory where earth and rock slides are common. Numerous bridges have been provided with increased fire protection; remote-control interlocking plants have been built.

An important activity of the maintenance and signaling department has been to assist the Army and Navy where possible. The engineering department has made surveys of new rail lines in arsenals; has supplied cost estimates and plans for track layouts within such plants, and gone all out in every way in an effort to lessen the burden of Uncle Sam.

HANDLING SOLDIERS AND SAILORS

Approximately 350 troop trains per month are being handled on the Pacific Lines as this is written, involving 5,500 cars. In addition, 2,000 more carloads of troops are being moved monthly on regular trains.

Besides these movements, the Southern Pacific was called upon to handle 125 trainloads of Japanese from Pacific Coast to interior relocation centers. It, further, is called upon daily to handle hospital trains, Coast Guard, C.C.C. trains, and alien specials.

To aid in the troop movement, the S.P. established a special military bureau in April, 1941. At first this bureau worked the normal eight-hour shift, but it has been expanded to a twenty-four-hour-a-day basis. The bureau works directly with the Western Defense Command and the Fourth Army at the Presidio in San Francisco, with all naval bases in the Bay area, with the Marine Corps, and with C.C.C. officers. It has direct contact with the Western Military Bureau in Chicago.

On receipt of advice as to a movement of a troop train, the bureau gives the railway's transportation department the necessary information so that the required equipment can be made available and the schedules arranged. Thereafter, it serves as an information and service center, advising the representatives of the armed forces as to the starting time, giving passing reports en route and the arrival at destination.

The Southern Pacific eliminated twenty-seven passenger trains in 1942, including two of the highly profitable Coast Daylights; thus saving 163,154 passenger train miles monthly. Yet the handling of large numbers of troops, as well as a vastly increased civilian traffic, has presented complex problems.

The S.P. abolished excursion fares and eliminated most of the "luxury" cars from its trains, making more room for revenue equipment. Even so, practically all trains are crowded, and an acute shortage of dining car space developed. The Southern Pacific has conducted an advertising campaign, requesting passengers not to ride during rush periods unless it is absolutely essential.

To meet the dining car problem, brought about by the necessity of feeding 200 to 300 troops on regular trains before other passengers were served, the S.P. began selling box lunches in coaches and Pullman cars in December, 1942. This proved effective in relieving some of the dining car congestion.

Ever since Pearl Harbor, the Southern Pacific, along with the other railroads of the country, has been proving that where there is a will there is a way. But often it takes a lot of will, and mostly the way is stony. Yet, after all, the little hardships we must endure are but a small return for the privilege of living in God's Country.

MANPOWER PROBLEM GROWS SERIOUS

Manpower has proved one of the biggest problems the railroads have had to face. The Southern Pacific, on January 1, 1943, was confronted with a shortage of nearly 10,000 employees. In 1939, 42,000 persons were employed on the Pacific Lines. This number was increased to more than 60,000.

Ten thousand employees of the S. P. entered the armed forces. Thousands of others have been attracted into war production industries in California.

The Southern Pacific was severely handicapped, as the road needed men in every department. These shortages are indicated on page 41.

Thousands of dollars were spent in advertising for help. The railway set up its own employment agency, with representatives in large eastern cities. In May, 1942, foreseeing the shortage of men for section and extra gang work, the Southern Pacific requested permission to import 5,000 Mexican workers under bond. This request was refused, and the S.P was told that sufficient native common labor was available in the East.

Accordingly, the S.P. solicited every possible Government employment agency. Of 2,896 men referred to them, 2,783 actually boarded trains, but 722 men disappeared between the point of origin and the West Coast, and 267 refused to go to work upon arrival. Another 406 were rejected because of serious physical defects, or else worked less than three days before disappearing.

The request for importation of Mexican labor was renewed. In April and May, 1943, some three thousand Mexicans were brought up and put in service.

MANPOWER SHORTAGE — PACIFIC LINES
January 1, 1943

	No. of Men Needed
Transportation	1,081
Maintenance of way	5,207
Stores	268
Maintenance of equipment	2,031
Others	1,234
Total shortage	9,821

Maintenance of locomotives and cars required a large increase in the number of shop craftsmen. As early as March 1, 1941, the mechanical department began a campaign to secure such workers. The upper age limit was raised from forty-five to fifty-five. More than one thousand of the some five thousand men who signed up in eighteen months were over forty-five. Two hundred new foremen were appointed. All repair shops were put on a six-day basis. On September 28, 1942, all "dead-work" forces in the locomotive back shops went on a ten-hour-day schedule, with vacations in the locomotive and car departments canceled, although, of course, the railroad pays for such vacations.

Helpers and apprentices were rapidly advanced. The minimum age limit was reduced to sixteen on May 1, 1942, since which time nearly one thousand boys of the sixteen-eighteen age group have been employed, with some fifty-five per cent still in service.

About five hundred women have been employed in the mechanical department. They are serving as steam-hammer operators, rivet heaters, turntable operators, blacksmith helpers, locomotive wipers, stores helpers, crew callers, tractor drivers, and a wide variety of other operations not normally regarded as women's work.

The so-called "weaker sex" proved more than adequate, and America can well tip its hat to these ladies of the iron road. We see Mrs. Ida Edwards filling a locomotive lubricator, and comely Blanche Tuttle supervising an all-woman track gang near Watsonville, California, spreading ballast. The husbands of many of these valiant women railroaders are in service. When this war is done, the railroads could well post an honor roll of women in greasy overalls who have done men's work.

Two free telegraph schools have been established by the Pacific Lines at Oakland, California, and El Paso, Texas. More than one hundred graduates are now employed as operators. Freight and passenger traffic departments established schools for the training of men.

In spite of foresight and preparation in attempting to meet the labor problem, the Southern Pacific, as of mid-1944, needs 10,000 added employees to bring operations to the highest degree of efficiency.

A COMPETENT PUBLIC RELATIONS JOB

In the course of moving troops and war supplies on schedule, ordinary commercial freight has had to take a back seat. The Southern Pacific has spared no effort to do its primary job well —that of supplying the necessary transportation to aid in victory. It has continued its more normal functions to the best of its ability. However, freight schedules have been lengthened and many passenger trains annulled for the duration.

The treasured on-time performance record of the S.P. passenger trains has been permitted to lapse; the percentage, once high in the nineties, is now closer to sixty and sometimes lower.

While the average railway passenger or shipper is fully conversant with war conditions as a whole, he is not always particularly understanding as concerns the Iron Horse, and sometimes feels, perhaps, that "the old gray mare ain't what she used to be."

Just to keep John Q. Public acquainted with what the Southern Pacific is doing, the road has conducted a broad campaign of publicity regarding its transportation difficulties. A real effort has been made to remain gracious, to reply promptly and courteously to inquiries. In fact, such interrogations are anticipated, in that cards are passed out, explaining the problems of the railroad. And off-line agencies have supplied shippers with information.

The vastly increased industrial development of Southern California has been recognized, and an expanded traffic service department created to assist these shippers. This department is supplied with extensive facilities for handling telephone inquiries. Because of the growth of the vegetable industry and the increased activities of Army camps near Salinas, California, a new traffic service headquarters was established there.

So the Southern Pacific works to serve this new industrial West. This is a land of trail blazers, pioneered by covered wagons. Here the first S.P. tracks were laid in 1863.

The Southern Pacific has grown up with the West, and is a part of its hopes and its traditions. Since the days of '49 an empire has been carved—an industrial empire. Today over fifty per cent of America's shipbuilding industry is on the West Coast. Aircraft factories here turn out half of the nation's planes. Aluminum plants have sprung up; great magnesium plants; steel mills. Texas is roaring with industry—Texas, the giant, land of cattle, oil, and agriculture. New Mexico and Arizona are pouring out essential copper, potash, zinc; livestock.

California and its booming fruit trains, charging over the mighty Sierra Nevadas—"The Hill." Clipper Gap and Gold Run —the way of the Forty-Niners, echoing to the chant of great Articulated-Consolidations.

War trains. Troops on the move. So the Southern Pacific serves the West, as it will continue to serve after the war is won and happy days are here again.

For all of this, A. T. Mercier, President of the Southern Pacific, likes to give credit to the men and women out on the line— soldiers in the Battle of Transportation, answering the call to Battle Stations.

43

CHAPTER IV

SANTA FE LOCOMOTIVES

Long-Distance Champions

A little over seventy-five years ago, a steel rail was laid on the first unit of the Santa Fe System Lines. That was in 1868. The line extended from Topeka to Carbondale, Kansas, a distance of seventeen miles. Today the great Santa Fe covers 13,000 roaring miles of main-line track.

Seventy-five years! In normal times that would have called for a diamond jubilee. But with the world rocking under the guns of war, there was no time for celebrating; so the Santa Fe merely took a hitch at its iron pants and knuckled down to keeping the Victory Trains rolling.

Santa Fe, in Spanish, means Holy Faith. Faith performs miracles—faith and two-fisted go-gettedness. Faith moves mountains; so do Santa Fe locomotives—mountains of freight and passengers —and moves them fast.

In the dear departed days, happily gone beyond recall, a locomotive, having covered one division of some one hundred to one hundred and fifty miles, called it a day, and went to the roundhouse for service and adjustments.

But not any more. A whacking big locomotive couples onto a train and stays with it for a thousand miles, for seventeen hundred miles. We find steam engines running through from Chicago to La Junta, Colorado, and from La Junta to Los Angeles; steam locomotives running from Kansas City to Los Angeles, 1,765 miles, on passenger runs. We see freight engines covering 877 miles between Kansas City and Belen, New Mexico; 637 miles between Kansas City and Clovis, New Mexico.

Freight and passenger engines today thunder over hundreds of

44

miles of plains, deserts, and mountains, under every possible operating condition, and with temperatures ranging from zero to 110 degrees in the shade, and no shade.

"Utilization" is the name they give it—a ten-dollar word. The utilization of locomotives, a phase of railroad operation that has been studied consistently over a period of years. It has grown in major importance, and now is vital in the handling of the war transportation.

Realizing the importance of improving utilization of locomotives, the Association of American Railroads, in 1924, established a joint committee on Utilization of Locomotives, consisting of three Mechanical Officers and three Chief Operating Officers.

This committee directed a study of practices followed in utilizing locomotives on thirteen railroads, and reports of the committee became available in the proceedings of the A.A.R. Mechanical Section. These committee reports covered the recommendations and outstanding practices followed by the thirteen railroads. Many of these practices are today in effect on various railroads.

However, further study of the recommendations may suggest means of added improvements over present-day operation. Many of the recommendations, thus advanced, have been adopted by various railroads, enabling them to improve their performance.

The responsibility of getting maximum utilization out of locomotives is a joint responsibility of the Mechanical and Operating Departments, and has been so recognized by railroads, as well as by the A.A.R., in establishing the personnel of their committee to study utilization of locomotives.

Locomotives are in the hands of the Operating Departments, except for the time they are undergoing repairs and servicing at intermediate terminals. In some instances the yard layout location with reference to the roundhouse is such that the locomotive cannot be serviced and returned to the train in the time that is required to switch a freight train. In this case, it is often necessary to relay the locomotives to the next train following, rather than run them through on the same train.

The Operating Department must watch the accumulation of power at turn-around terminals, keeping the amount of engines at such terminals to the minimum required to protect the business being handled. Notification of any idle engine hours beyond the necessary requirements should be at the maintenance terminal in order that major repairs can be made during such layover. This, in many cases, will result in keeping the locomotive in service rather than having to be held out of service for such repairs.

In switch service the character of work performed by the individual switch tricks governs, to a great extent, whether a locomotive can or cannot be regularly used on a two- or three-trick basis without being returned to the roundhouse. This necessitates study on the part of the Operating Department, in order to group all of the switch tricks possible for two- or three-trick continuous operation.

The general practice in effect forty years ago, as regarded utilization of locomotives, was that each road locomotive was assigned to an individual engineer. This confined the utilization of this locomotive to the mileage made by the crew, which in freight service averaged approximately three thousand miles per month, and in passenger service approximately four thousand miles per month.

About thirty years ago a program to pool locomotives was started, working them on a first in–first out basis, which allowed the engine to go back into service ahead of the rest period and layover time of the crew. This program was confined largely to through passenger and freight service. It resulted in a great improvement in the mileage made per locomotive per month, and the iron horse really began to earn its oats.

In the period of 1918 to 1920 the practice was inaugurated of extending locomotive runs over more than one engine-crew district, giving the locomotive servicing attention at the intermediate point, and either running it through the terminal on the same train, or relaying it to the following train. The usual practice was to give the engine such repairs at the turn-around terminal as were necessary to get it back to the maintenance terminal. Heavy running repairs were handled at the latter point, which was usually on one end of the run.

After a few years, locomotive runs were extended over two to three or four engine-crew districts, and by 1922 runs over four engine-crew districts in passenger service and three engine-crew districts in freight service were not uncommon. This handling, in the years to follow, was built up to a point where steam locomotives in passenger service were operated continuously from 1,000 to 1,800 miles, and locomotives in freight service from 500 to 800 miles.

Today very few through freight or passenger locomotives are operated over but one engine-crew district, and in practically all through freight and passenger service the locomotives are operated on an extended program, which is worked out to give maximum utilization consistent with the service to be handled and the location of the terminals where heavy maintenance is performed.

A complete list of extended locomotive runs being operated on the Santa Fe System, showing location, length of run, type of power, number of engine crews, and other information will be included later in this chapter. Here will be found complete information on all freight and passenger extended locomotive runs being operated on the system at this time.

The extended locomotive run has necessitated a high standard of maintenance. In order to get the maximum utilization out of locomotives in these assignments it is necessary that the maintenance work be centralized at one point, which should be at the end of the extended locomotive run. Extended locomotive run engines must be maintained in such a manner that they will make the round trip with a minimum of repairs.

Each locomotive in extended-run assignments is assigned to a maintenance terminal, and the Master Mechanic in charge at this terminal is responsible for the maintenance work and the condition of the locomotive. The terminals through which the locomotive passes on extended runs are responsible for proper servicing attention, and such minor repairs as are needed to get the engine back to its home terminal.

In addition to the regular running repair engine program, the Santa Fe follows the practice of making certain inspections and repairs at the time of monthly inspection. These are in addition to the items required by the Interstate Commerce Commission, and which have materially resulted in reducing out-of-service days for such repairs. These items are as follows:

1. Examine, grind in boiler and line checks, clean opening in boiler.
2. Grind, clean and repack: water glass and gauge cocks and drain valves.
3. Remove caps from tank hose strainer box. Examine strainer and threads.
4. Examine tank valves and strainer and see that valves are properly seated to stem.
5. Examine and clean cylinder and channel cocks.
6. Examine and test electric headlight: dynamo and wiring.
7. Wash out feed-water heater.
8. Check grate shaker post and bar with template.
9. Test out mechanical lubricator to engine truck.
10. Test out mechanical lubricator to cylinders and valves.

A great deal of study as concerns both classified and running repairs on locomotives has resulted in expediting this work, and the Santa Fe has succeeded in their program of turning locomotives out of the shop in thirty days for the average Class Three repairs. The time required to handle Class Four repairs is approximately twenty days, and for Class Five repairs the time is about twelve days.

In order to get rapid turning of power at maintenance terminals, it is necessary to have a sufficient force on the second and third shifts in the roundhouse to be able to repair and turn the power arriving on these shifts with the same regularity of turning time as that on the first shift.

The Santa Fe insists that locomotives be inspected just as soon as possible after they reach the maintenance terminal at the end of the run. In fifty per cent of the cases the locomotive is inspected within one hour after its arrival at the turn-around terminal. Rarely does an interval of two hours elapse before this inspection is made. As a result, the roundhouse foreman can first service and repair the locomotives that have the minimum work to be performed, holding engines that require heavier work for attention later. Thus he can always furnish power when required.

The usual terminal layout established for locomotives on short runs involved an inbound and outbound track to the engine

Engine 3767, 4-8-4 Type Santa Fe 3765 Class, descending the east slope of Raton Pass near Jansen, Col., with Fischer's Peak in the background, hauling #20, the Chief. Photo by Otto C. Perry.

Santa Fe Ranger #5, crack Chicago-Texas train, hauled by Engine 3450, first of the Santa Fe 4-6-4 Type, coming out of the Cimarron River Valley north of Guthrie, Okla. on the First District of the Oklahoma Division. The engine has come from Kansas City and will run through to Galveston without change. Photo by Preston George.

First of the Santa Fe 4-8-4 Type, built in 1927: 3757, 3751 Class, climbing the 2.2% grade up Cajon Pass with #20, the Chief, with 13 cars on the First District of the Los Angeles Division. These engines now run through to Kansas City with trains 1 and 2, 23 and 24. Courtesy Santa Fe Railroad.

Chesapeake & Ohio #6, the eastbound FFV Limited, with Engine 306, 4-6-4 Type Class L-2, at Clyffeside, Kentucky, on the Kanawha Subdivision of the Huntington Division. Courtesy C. & O. Railroad

house, with fuel, water, sand, and fire-cleaning facilities so located that it was necessary to stop at three or four different locations in order to supply the engines. The time required was approximately thirty minutes. This time and the time required to move the locomotive from the train to the roundhouse and back and make the air test was often greater than the time required to switch the train, as has been pointed out.

In order to relieve this condition, made necessary by running locomotives through terminals, an arrangement of facilities in many cases has been provided where the engines are supplied with fuel, water, and sand, and given fire-cleaning attention at one point. Here pits are provided for the handling of underneath inspection and replenishing of driving-box grease if required. The result has been to reduce roundhouse delay for inspection to about ten minutes. During this time, the outbound engineer is oiling around and looking over the locomotive.

In switch service each terminal assignment is analyzed and such switch tricks as possible are grouped so that the locomotive will work three consecutive tricks before being turned into the roundhouse for repairs and servicing attention. Further analysis has resulted in the grouping of all tricks possible so that the engines will work two consecutive tricks. Such tricks as cannot be so grouped are worked by turning the locomotive into the roundhouse after each trick, and, after giving it necessary attention, it is placed on another following switch trick.

That maximum utilization may be obtained it is necessary to reduce to a minimum the time of handling roundhouse maintenance; also reduce intermediate terminal servicing as well as turnaround terminal time. It is, of course, equally important that the time of handling classified repairs be reduced to a minimum.

For many years, the usual practice in the handling of classified repairs was to work the back shops and general repair shops one shift of eight hours per day, six days per week. This program has been modified at all Santa Fe general repair shops; also in many of the shops where Class Four or Class Five repairs are made. Now there is a second shift, with the shop working sixteen hours instead of eight, resulting in a substantial decrease in out-of-service days for locomotives receiving classified repairs.

49

This has resulted in engines being available a greater percentage of the time, and the out-of-service days have been reduced approximately forty per cent.

The work of the second shift is confined largely to the tight spots in the particular shop involved, such as stripping-gang work, boiler work, machine work, and floor work. These men on the second shift are used to expedite the particular character of work that is holding back the output of the shop, and their activities are changed to meet the particular conditions existing.

The percentage of power out of service on the Santa Fe for general repairs, consisting of Class Three repairs and heavier, ranges from three to four per cent. Locomotives out of service for Class Four and Five repairs is about the same.

The time steam freight engines are in service, time undergoing repairs, and time waiting for train after repairs are completed show, for a twenty-four-hour period, an average of approximately twelve hours working, eight hours undergoing repairs, and four hours waiting for assignment. On passenger locomotives the hours are about the same. For switch engines the hours working are about sixteen per day.

A recognized unit for measuring utilization of locomotives is the miles made per active locomotive per day or month, which takes into consideration all active locomotives, but does not include those that are stored serviceable. In present operations of most railroads, no through freight or passenger power is so stored. As a result it is generally possible to use as a yardstick the average miles made by all locomotives in the extended-run assignment, whether they are working or in for repairs.

On the basis of average miles per active locomotive per day, the Santa Fe, for the month of July, 1942, averaged a total of 318 miles for all engines in passenger service; 167 for those in freight service; 94 for those in switch service.

At the present time on the Santa Fe, approximately ninety-five per cent of all through freight and passenger locomotives is operated on extended-run schedules. In July of that year the principle classes of through freight steam locomotives averaged 6,166 miles per locomotive for the 418 engines assigned. The highest mileage on the system in this service averaged 9,015 miles per locomotive.

In steam passenger service the average was 9,928 miles per locomotive for the 129 engines assigned, and the highest mileage made by any individual run averaged 15,382 miles. This in July.

These figures are quoted on the basis of locomotives assigned, regardless of whether they were in the shop for classified repairs, in the roundhouse for running repairs, or actually in service.

During the month of July, the maximum mileage made by any individual steam freight locomotive was 10,397 miles. The maximum made by any individual steam passenger locomotive over the same period was 20,290 miles.

The Santa Fe Railroad, along with other western roads, is confronted with the problem of using water for locomotives that is, of course, available in the territory. This water is considerably higher in sulphates and carbonate salts, which produce scale, and also in alkali, than water in other parts of the United States.

Twenty years ago it was the practice to wash boilers after about five hundred miles of service, and most of the water was treated with lime and soda-ash at tanks along the right-of-way. The treatment of water has been improved, with the result that today locomotives are being operated thirty days between washout periods. Locomotive boilers are now operated at a higher rate of evaporation per square foot of heating surface than formerly, with a reduced amount of foaming and priming.

Another major factor contributing to improved utilization of locomotives results from an advance in methods of lubrication of all engine parts. A higher quality of engine oil, valve oil, and grease has been developed to meet requirements of high-speed service now demanded. Mechanical lubrication of valves and cylinders, also engine trucks, shoes and wedges, guides and trailers, has contributed to reducing hot bearings. This has reduced maintenance formerly required in roundhouses for such operations as renewing cylinder packing and valve rings, rebabbitting crossheads, changing engine-truck and trailer wheels, hot driving boxes, and pins.

Roller-bearing driving boxes, engine-truck trailer and tank boxes have further reduced maintenance work. Two 4-8-4 type passenger locomotives equipped with roller-bearing rods have, at this writing, been in Santa Fe service for about three years. Performance indicates that less maintenance time is required with this type of bearings.

On the Santa Fe, Diesel locomotives are being used in freight, passenger, and switcher service to the extent of seven per cent of the total gross ton-miles for the system in freight service; thirteen per cent of total car-miles in passenger service, and seventeen per cent of the total switch-engine miles.

At the time of writing, the average miles of Diesel freight locomotives assigned amounted to 11,056 miles; Diesel passenger locomotives 17,117 miles, and Diesel switch engines 4,125 miles.

It is the practice to give preference to the use of Diesel locomotives, where both steam and Diesel engines are assigned, in order to get the maximum utilization out of the Diesel locomotives, which results in some loss of mileage to steam locomotives.

Utilization of locomotives, as measured by total miles per locomotive per month, or by work hours per month, is at the present time the greatest that has ever been secured. The study being given improved utilization is greater now than ever before.

This, in part, is due to critical material not being available to secure readily new steam or Diesel locomotives; also to the fact that a large part of the locomotive builders' facilities are being used on defense work. This has made it necessary for the railroads to handle the staggering increase of business offered with the power which they now have.

Thus we see that this overworked "ten-dollar" word, "utilization," is a vital factor in the force and drive of locomotive power in wartime.

There are 32,000,000,000 parts in all cars and locomotives now in service—32,000,000,000 parts that have to work together and hold together to keep America's wartime traffic rolling.

The problems of American Railroads worked out in peacetime are now handily applied to railroads that have gone to war. Theirs is the necessity of doing the best it is humanly possible to do with what they have and can get. And they are valiantly marching down the iron warpath. Smoke signals lift against the sky—the smoke of the thundering exhausts of thousands of straining engines, blending with the smoke of guns on our far-flung battle fronts.

Every locomotive whistle, screaming on mountain or plain, is a war cry, shouting defiance at the enemies of the United Nations.

SANTA FE
EXTENDED LOCOMOTIVE RUNS
Passenger Service

From	To	Miles	Number Engine Crews	Trains Operated Daily	Train Numbers
Chicago	Los Angeles	2,226.6	14	4#	17-18; 21-22
Chicago	La Junta	991.7	5	4	7-8; 19-20
Chicago	Kansas City	651.4	3	2	3-4
Chicago	Kansas City	451.1	2	6	1-2; 5-6; 23-24
Chicago	Oklahoma City	850.3	5	2	11-12
Kansas City	La Junta	540.6	3	2	9-10
Kansas City	Tulsa	256.1	2	2	47-50
		256.1	2	2	211-212
Kansas City	Galveston	972.9	6	2	5-6
(Via T & No & Houston District)					
Kansas City	Oklahoma City	399.2	3	2	27-28
Arkansas City	Lindsay	242.4	2	2x	51-305; 306-52
Newton	Cleburne	432.2	3	2	15-16
Cleburne	Galveston	340.4	2	2	15-16
(Via T & No & Houston District)					
Ft. Worth	San Angelo	240.2	2	2	77-78
Wichita	San Angelo	515.5	3	2	45-46
Amarillo	Sweetwater	243.1	2	2	93-95; 94-96
Clovis	Temple	467.0	3	2	91-76; 75-92
Kansas City	Los Angeles	1,788.7	12	4	1-2; 23-24
Kansas City	Los Angeles	1,765.0	12	2	3-4
La Junta	Los Angeles	1,234.0	9	4	7-8; 19-20
Phoenix	Cadiz	498.6	4	1	117-118
(Round Trip)					
Bakersfield	Oakland	312.8	2	4	1-2; 23-24
		312.8	2	4	60-61; 62-63

Semi-Weekly.   x Daily Except Sunday.

EXTENDED LOCOMOTIVE RUNS
Passenger Service

Type of Locomotive	Fuel	Date Effective	Points Where Crews Change and Mileage		
			From	To	Mileage
Diesel	Oil	5-10-36	Chicago	Ft. Madison	234.6
			Ft. Madison	Kansas City	216.5
			Kansas City	Newton	185.1
			Newton	Dodge City	153.1
			Dodge City	La Junta	202.4
			La Junta	Raton	104.6
			Raton	Las Vegas	110.0
			Las Vegas	Albuquerque	131.6
			Albuquerque	Gallup	160.5
			Gallup	Winslow	127.7
			Winslow	Seligman	143.2
			Seligman	Needles	149.4
			Needles	Barstow	166.7
			Barstow	Los Angeles	141.2
Hudson & Diesel	Oil	12-5-37	Chicago	Ft. Madison	234.6
			Ft. Madison	Kansas City	216.5
			Kansas City	Newton	185.1
			Newton	Dodge City	153.1
			Dodge City	La Junta	202.4
Pacific & Hudson	Oil	4-4-42	Chicago	Ft. Madison	234.6
			Ft. Madison	Kansas City	216.5
			Kansas City	Newton	200.3
Pacific & Diesel	Oil	10-1-31	Chicago	Ft. Madison	234.6
			Ft. Madison	Kansas City	216.5
Diesel	Oil	12-10-39	Chicago	Ft. Madison	234.6
			Ft. Madison	Kansas City	216.5
			Kansas City	Emporia	127.3
			Emporia	Arkansas City	151.3
			Arkansas City	Oklahoma City	120.6
Pacific & Hudson	Oil	10-27-40	Kansas City	Newton	185.1
			Newton	Dodge City	153.1
			Dodge City	La Junta	202.6
Pacific	Oil	5-1-41	Kansas City	Chanute	126.2
Diesel	Oil	12-10-39	Chanute	Tulsa	129.9
Hudson	Oil	4-23-33	Kansas City	Newton	200.3

54

Type of Locomotive	Fuel	Date Effective	Points Where Crews Change and Mileage		
			From	To	Mileage
Hudson	Oil	4-23-33	Newton	Arkansas City	78.3
			Arkansas City	Purcell	153.9
			Purcell	Cleburne	200.0
			Cleburne	Bellville	211.1
			Bellville	Galveston	129.3
Pacific	Oil	5-7-39	Kansas City	Newton	200.3
			Newton	Arkansas City	78.3
			Arkansas City	Oklahoma City	120.6
Gas-Electric	Gasoline	10-23-39	Arkansas City	Shawnee	166.2
			Shawnee	Lindsay	76.2
Hudson	Oil	5-20-34	Newton	Arkansas City	78.3
			Arkansas City	Purcell	153.9
			Purcell	Cleburne	200.0
Pacific	Oil	11-27-25	Cleburne	Bellville	211.1
			Bellville	Galveston	129.3
Atlantic	Oil	3-1-37	Ft. Worth	Brownwood	142.2
			Brownwood	San Angelo	98.0
Gas-Electric	Gasoline	4-1-36	Wichita	Fairview	129.1
			Fairview	Altus	131.3
			Altus	San Angelo	250.1
Atlantic & Pacific	Oil	8-10-30	Amarillo	Slaton	136.9
			Slaton	Sweetwater	106.2
Pacific	Oil	1-10-37	Clovis	Sweetwater	220.3
			Sweetwater	Brownwood	114.5
			Brownwood	Temple	132.2
4-8-4	Oil	5-23-42	Kansas City	Newton	192.7
			Newton	Wellington	61.3
			Wellington	Waynoka	106.6
			Waynoka	Amarillo	206.0
			Amarillo	Clovis	103.7
			Clovis	Belen	239.8
			Belen	Gallup	144.2
			Gallup	Winslow	127.7
			Winslow	Seligman	143.2
			Seligman	Needles	149.4
			Needles	Barstow	166.7
			Barstow	Los Angeles	147.4
			Kansas City	Newton	185.1

55

Type of Locomotive	Fuel	Date Effective	Points Where Crews Change and Mileage		
			From	To	Mileage
4-8-4	Oil	4-4-42	Newton	Dodge City	153.1
			Dodge City	La Junta	202.6
			La Junta	Raton	104.6
			Raton	Las Vegas	110.0
			Las Vegas	Albuquerque	131.6
			Albuquerque	Gallup	160.5
			Gallup	Winslow	127.7
			Winslow	Seligman	143.2
			Seligman	Needles	149.4
			Needles	Barstow	166.7
			Barstow	Los Angeles	141.2
4-8-4	Oil	12-7-37	La Junta	Raton	104.6
			Raton	Las Vegas	110.0
			Las Vegas	Albuquerque	131.6
			Albuquerque	Gallup	160.5
			Gallup	Winslow	127.7
			Winslow	Seligman	143.2
			Seligman	Needles	149.4
			Needles	Barstow	166.7
			Barstow	Los Angeles	141.2
Pacific	Oil	6-12-38	Phoenix	Parker	164.6
			Parker	Cadiz	84.7
			Cadiz	Parker	84.7
			Parker	Phoenix	164.6
Pacific	Oil	1-1-38	Bakersfield	Fresno	110.4
Diesel	Oil	7-1-38	Fresno	Oakland	202.4

EXTENDED LOCOMOTIVE RUNS
Freight Service

From	To	Miles	Number Engine Crews	Type of Locomotive
Chicago	Ft. Madison	228.6	2	Mikado & Mountain
Ft. Madison	Kansas City	220.7	2	Mikado & Mountain
Kansas City	Newton	182.5	2	Mikado
Kansas City	Wellington	221.1	2	Mikado
Kansas City (Via Newton)	Wellington	242.8	3	Mikado
Kansas City	Belen	877.2	8	Diesel & 4-8-4
Kansas City	Clovis	637.0	7	4-8-4
Kansas City	Arkansas City	225.5	2	Mikado
Emporia (Via Newton)	Purcell	305.8	3	Mikado
Kansas City	Cleburne	579.4	5	Mikado
Cleburne	Bellville	211.1	2	Santa Fe
Cleburne	Galveston	315.1	3	Mikado
Temple	Sweetwater	244.2	2	Santa Fe
Newton	La Junta	353.9	2	Mikado & Mountain
La Junta	Albuquerque	347.7	3	Santa Fe
La Junta	Denver	182.3	2	Santa Fe
La Junta	Amarillo	258.1	2	Mikado
Wichita	San Angelo	507.5	4	Consolidation & Decapod
San Angelo	Alpine	226.9	2	Consolidation & Decapod
Wellington	Clovis	416.3	4	Mikado & 2-8-4
Wellington	Belen	655.0	6	2-10-4 & 2-8-4
Amarillo	Sweetwater	239.0	2	Mikado
Clovis	Sweetwater	217.5	2	Mikado
Clovis	Belen	239.8	2	Santa Fe & 2-10-4
Belen	Winslow	271.9	2	Mikado & 2-10-2
Winslow	Barstow	459.3	3	Santa Fe & Diesel
Barstow	Wickenburg	292.0	2	Mikado
Bakersfield	Richmond	301.9	3	Pacific & Mikado

EXTENDED LOCOMOTIVE RUNS
Freight Service

Fuel	Date Effective	From	To	Mileage
Coal	7-5-21	Chicago	Chillicothe	124.1
		Chillicothe	Ft. Madison	104.5
Coal	7-5-21	Ft. Madison	Marceline	112.7
		Marceline	Kansas City	108.0
Oil	6-22-26	Kansas City	Emporia	107.9
		Emporia	Newton	74.6
Oil	6-22-26	Kansas City	Emporia	107.9
		Emporia	Wellington	113.2
Oil	6-22-26	Kansas City	Emporia	107.9
		Emporia	Newton	74.6
		Newton	Wellington	60.3
Oil	10-6-41	Kansas City	Emporia	107.9
		Emporia	Wellington	113.2
		Wellington	Waynoka	106.6
Oil	11-15-43	Waynoka	Canadian	108.1
		Canadian	Amarillo	99.2
		Amarillo	Clovis	102.4
		Clovis	Vaughn	130.8
		Vaughn	Belen	109.0
Oil	6-22-26	Kansas City	Emporia	107.9
		Emporia	Arkansas City	117.6
Oil	4-28-28	Emporia	Newton	74.6
		Newton	Arkansas City	77.3
		Arkansas City	Purcell	153.9
Oil	3-27-41	Kansas City	Emporia	107.9
		Emporia	Arkansas City	117.6
		Arkansas City	Purcell	153.9
		Purcell	Gainesville	106.1
		Gainesville	Cleburne	93.9
Oil	6-18-21	Cleburne	Temple	99.5
		Temple	Bellville	111.6
Oil	11-20-34	Cleburne	Temple	99.5
		Temple	Bellville	111.6
		Bellville	Galveston	104.0
Oil	3-1-25	Temple	Brownwood	132.2
		Brownwood	Sweetwater	112.0

Fuel	Date Effective	Points Where Crews Change and Mileage		
		From	To	Mileage
Oil	9-1-27	Newton	Dodge City	151.5
		Dodge City	La Junta	202.4
Coal	11-1-27	La Junta	Raton	104.6
		Raton	Las Vegas	110.0
		Las Vegas	Albuquerque	133.1
Coal	10-8-30	La Junta	Pueblo	64.7
		Pueblo	Denver	117.6
Oil	7-1-40	La Junta	Boise City	134.2
		Boise City	Amarillo	123.9
Oil	1-1-40	Wichita	Fairview	126.1
		Fairview	Altus	121.3
		Altus	Hamlin	138.5
		Hamlin	San Angelo	111.6
Oil	8-1-29	San Angelo	Ft. Stockton	164.3
		Ft. Stockton	Alpine	62.6
Oil	9-7-26	Wellington	Waynoka	106.6
		Waynoka	Canadian	108.1
Oil	10-15-39	Canadian	Amarillo	99.2
		Amarillo	Clovis	102.4
Oil	1-1-31	Amarillo	Slaton	135.6
		Slaton	Sweetwater	103.4
Oil	No Record	Clovis	Slaton	114.1
		Slaton	Sweetwater	103.4
Oil	1920	Clovis	Vaughn	130.8
		Vaughn	Belen	109.0
Coal & Oil	5-1-21	Belen	Gallup	144.2
		Gallup	Winslow	127.2
Oil	3-1-40	Winslow	Seligman	143.2
		Seligman	Needles	149.4
		Needles	Barstow	166.7
Oil	6-2-40	Barstow	Parker	181.5
		Parker	Wickenburg	110.5
Oil	1-15-33	Bakersfield	Calwa	107.5
		Calwa	Riverbank	101.1
		Riverbank	Richmond	93.3

59

CHAPTER V

CHESAPEAKE AND OHIO RAILWAY

Coal – Motive Power – Industry

A great transportation artery of steel, winding through the valleys of the New River and the Kanawha. A steel rail, banding the mighty Alleghenies, threading through and across the beautiful Blue Ridge Mountains. Steel spinning its stout fiber over the backbone of the Appalachian Range. Steel to the Great Lakes. Steel to the Atlantic seaboard.

This is the Chesapeake and Ohio—a name carved by iron men and iron horses. The Chesapeake and Ohio is a vital link in America's rail transport, and what the C.&O. has done for Victory, we shall attempt to review in these pages.

Perhaps nothing can so sharply bring a railroad into focus as the power and the glory of a locomotive working steam, and so we present you with a picture of a Lima-built 2-6-6-6, or "Allegheny" type, engine, the first of this wheel arrangement to be built anywhere. The locomotive is a symphony in itself—a symphony of iron and steel, built in America for America.

Let us ride this engine down the rails of the Chesapeake and Ohio, the locomotive with a *6-wheel* trailing truck.

Before we do anything else, it might be worth while to pause for a brief look at this 2-6-6-6 Articulated, which hauls freight trains over the Allegheny Mountains. Its Chesapeake and Ohio classification is H-8, the 1600 series. It has a tractive effort of 110,200 pounds. The total weight of engine is 724,500 pounds; the total weight of engine and tender, 1,162,100 pounds. The drivers are 67-inch; the tender capacity is 25 tons of coal and 25,000 gallons of water.

More complete specifications will be found in subsequent tables. Here we are merely giving a little preview of just about the last word in Chesapeake and Ohio freight motive power. The 2-6-6-6 Allegheny was built by the Lima Locomotive Works, Incorporated, of Lima, Ohio. And they have done a grand job. You can't beat the builders of American locomotives. Lima, Baldwin, American, Electro-Motive. They gave us the engines to win the battle of transport, the locomotives that helped smash the Axis powers, not only at home but abroad, as well.

The outstanding achievement of the Chesapeake and Ohio during the first calendar year of the war following Pearl Harbor was the combined one of meeting unusual demands in transportation when definite restrictions were applied to securing additional equipment, materials, and labor for normal repairs, for manning and servicing locomotives, cars, track, necessary in performing the task.

The Chesapeake and Ohio serves a vast coal-mining district, frequently referred to as the "Coal Bin" of America. Coal, "black diamonds," as vital to the needs of war as the "black gold" called oil.

Coal is the most important economic mineral known to man. And we can well go down on our knees and thank God that we have buried in the underground vaults of the United States an estimated coal supply sufficient to last three thousand years.

Oil, at the rate that it is being used at the present time, and, unless new vast fields are developed, will one day become exhausted. Should that time ever come, America will be able to turn to our enormous reserves of oil shales and—coal. For oil from coal is no misty scientists' dream, but a reality. One fifth of England's gasoline comes from coal. Germany's wartime needs for motor-fuel and lubricant were met to a large extent by synthetic oil and gas wrung from coal.

In the United States, at the Bureau of Mines, gasoline is being produced from coal by direct hydrogenation, and our chemists have only begun. If the time ever comes when oil is no longer available in the quantities necessary to sustain us in motor and. air transport, we will ride our magic carpets through the use of fuel produced from that humble mineral, in the plentiful bins under the sod, called coal.

Endless grimy coal trains roll on the Chesapeake and Ohio. We watch a train pulling into NY Cabin, just outside of Newport News—160 to 180 cars, 13,000 to 15,000 tons, which is hauling tonnage with a vengeance.

Coal from the Greenbrier Field, the New River Field, the Winding Gulf Field. Coal from the Kanawha District, from the Kentucky District, the Hocking District. Coal from the southern fields of West Virginia. Coal from eastern Kentucky. Coal from southeastern Ohio.

Coal for steel mills, coal for locomotives, coal for heating, coal for Nylon, for medicines, chemicals, dyes, plastics. Coal for war!

Before we are done we will be gloriously mantled with Black Diamond dust, but to know the Chesapeake and Ohio better we are going to examine something of its make-up and plant. We are going to remember, too, that if the Chesapeake and Ohio had not anticipated the needs of "Tomorrow," had not taken advantage of modern designs and practices, never in this world could it have handled successfully the amount of traffic made mandatory under war conditions.

The total mileage of the Chesapeake and Ohio is 3,092 miles of steel rail. This comprises 1,708 miles of main line and 1,384 miles of branch lines. Add to this approximately 2,063 miles of other trackage, which includes 1,300 miles of switching lines, 338 miles of way switching tracks, 425 miles of passing tracks, crossovers, and turnouts.

Nine hundred thirty miles of main line are double-tracked. In addition, there are forty-three miles of third and fourth main tracks through territory of heavy traffic density. Something like 1,050 miles of branch-line territory are devoted almost entirely to handling coal. Coal mining is also heavily concentrated on the double-track main line at Meadow Creek and Hawks Nest, West Virginia, for a distance of forty miles.

The larger branch lines are as follows:

Big Sandy Sub-Division, serving the eastern Kentucky field, 266 miles. Logan Sub-Division, serving the Logan field, 168 miles. Coal River Sub-Division, serving the Coal River field, 165 miles. Piney Creek Sub-Division, serving the New River and Winding Gulf fields, 74 miles. Cabin Creek Sub-Division, serving the

62

Kanawha field, 59 miles. The Nicholas, Fayette and Greenbrier Railroad (operated jointly with the New York Central Railroad), serving the Greenbrier field, 104 miles. There are many smaller but important branches in New River, Kanawha, and Hocking Sub-Divisions.

Freight and passenger lines on the Chesapeake and Ohio extend from Norfolk, Old Point Comfort, Newport News, Virginia, and Washington, D. C., to Louisville, Kentucky, Cincinnati and Toledo, Ohio, and Chicago, Illinois, through the States of Virginia, West Virginia, Kentucky, Ohio, Indiana, and a short distance beyond the Indiana-Illinois state line at Chicago.

Intermediate cities served include Richmond, Charlottesville, Staunton, Lynchburg, Clifton Forge, and Covington, Virginia; Hinton, Beckley, Montgomery, Charleston, Logan, Huntington, and Kenova, West Virginia; Ashland, Lexington, Pikeville, Maysville, Newport, and Covington, Kentucky; Columbus, Marion, Logan, Athens, Pomeroy, and Fostoria, Ohio; Richmond, Marion, Muncie, Peru, and Hammond, Indiana; also a large number of smaller but important localities scattered throughout this territory.

Direct interchange connections are maintained with principally all of the trunk-line carriers and many important shortline roads, serving the Southern, Middle-Atlantic, Central, and Western states, totaling 72 railroads and including 216 connecting points.

The Chesapeake and Ohio, through the development of its properties and the purchase of equipment, was numbered among the best prepared to aid in the war effort. This through keeping abreast of the times in the transportation world. It was possible for the Chesapeake and Ohio to meet its responsibilities in connection with the prosecution of the war because of immense outlays of money invested in additions and betterments of the physical property for the furthering of efficient service in handling of traffic.

During the twenty-two years prior to 1943, the total plant investment was increased from $280,000,000 to $615,000,000, or in the amount of $335,000,000. All classes of physical property and facilities were included in this tremendous increase of capital expenditures. The major items were: purchase of existing railway properties; additional cars of modern design; additional locomotives of greater tractive effort, of modern design, and adapted to service acquirements; construction of new main lines; construction of branch lines; the improving of existing branch lines, and the further acquiring of such branch lines to better co-ordinate the service in certain fields.

There was construction and improvement of terminals, yards, sidings. Classification yards were expanded to provide more efficient handling of traffic. Greater main-line speeds were made possible through the increased weight of rail, better ballasting, and the relocation, enlarging, relining and elimination of tunnels. Came newer types of locomotives such as the Allegheny 2-6-6-6. Shopping facilities were improved. Coal and ore facilities of the latest type have proved their value. Wharves and docks were enlarged, modernized; bridges were renewed and strengthened. Second main tracks were built, aiding train movements. Where possible, grades were eased; grade crossings eliminated; lines relocated.

Came safer, more efficient train operation; modern water and coaling stations. Attention was given to stations, office buildings, telephone lines for train dispatching, automatic signals and interlocking; roadway machines, work equipment, shop machinery, and tools.

Many improvements were necessary for the handling of increased business; others were included to promote operating economies.

The Chesapeake and Ohio is most strategically situated, particularly so in wartime, for here its steel rail links the Great Lakes and Newport News, at seaboard, bisecting the greatest coal fields in the Nation. On the line are located many industries essential to the prosecution of war, which rely on the C.&O. as their chief—and in many cases only—means of transportation.

Enormous sums were expended for improvements to line and new equipment in the years following World War I, and then came the arch fiends of all time, Tojo and Hitler, and the Chesapeake and Ohio threw away the purse strings. The American Dollar had been at work before, but now it was working Sundays and holidays, and all around the clock.

64

Chesapeake & Ohio #1602 2-6-6-6 Type Class H-8 with #94 eastbound Manifest train at OX Cabin just west of Allegheny, West Virginia, on the subdivision of that name. This locomotive built by the Lima Locomotive Works has been highly successful. Courtesy C. & O. Railroad.

Designed during World War I, and modernized for World War II, C. & O. #547, 4-8-2 Type Class J-2, running light to the Union Station, Washington, D. C. from the Ivy City enginehouse to haul #1, the George Washington, pride of the C. & O.'s excellent passenger train fleet. Photo by H. W. Pontin Railroad Photographs.

Latest addition to the C. & O.'s great fleet of locomotives. #2704, 2-8-4 Type Class K-4, east-bound with manifest train #92 at Catlettsburg, Ky. on the Kanawha Subdivision of the Huntington Division. Courtesy C. & O. Railroad.

A veteran of World War I sees service in World War II. This locomotive, one of three built in 1911, is famous for being the first 4-8-2 type placed in operation on any road. C. & O. Class J-1. Courtesy C. & O. R.R.

View of the New York Central's Mt. Carmel, Illinois yard with a loaded oil train heading north
en route east while a train of empties waits to
pull out for Norris City behind an H-7E 2-8-2
type. The engine in the foreground is an 0-8-0
type Class U-1E. Courtesy New York Central
R.R.

Eastbound Santa Fe mixed main near Solvay, Kansas on the First District of the Western Division double-headed with two 1800 Class 2-6-2 Type locomotives that were brought out of storage and are turning in a commendable performance in troop train service. Courtesy Santa Fe Railroad.

Wartime expenditures jumped $23,000,000 a year. The acquisition of new equipment included 74 passenger cars, 11,100 freight cars, and 59 steam locomotives. This brought the equipment owned by the C.&O. at the close of the year of 1943 to 435 passenger cars, 70,163 freight cars, with an average capacity of fifty-three tons, and 860 locomotives. Of the latter, 110 were assigned to passenger service, 523 to freight service, 218 to switching, and 9 to work service.

We will discuss the more modern passenger and freight locomotive power a little later, for certainly it is worth a page in the records.

Back down the years, the slogging freight train made heavy going. It took a long time to get anywhere, and its crew was often tied up by the sixteen-hour law before it reached its terminal. Trucks began to gather around the festive board. The depression hit the freight train a lick, and things in general down the iron road were pretty awful.

And then, all at once, railroad officials began to sit up in the buggy. They went to the whip, and when the old iron horse came into the stretch she had her ears back and was really stepping. Yes; the gentlemen in the front office rolled up their sleeves and laid on the gad. The result was ultimately pleasing to all concerned. Take the Chesapeake and Ohio as an example. The speed of freight trains increased 65 per cent. The size of freight train loads increased 78 per cent. Gross ton-miles handled per train-hour increased 191 per cent. The tractive effort of locomotives increased 40 per cent.

Momentous events were shaping in the world, grim events. The railroads, possibly, were not aware of those storm clouds gathering; nevertheless, wittingly or otherwise, they were building up their plants to meet the hard-swinging wallop of war. And then Mars was riding the rails, and the Chesapeake and Ohio and all of the rest were toughened to make a fight of it that was beautiful to behold.

Let us take a glance at the increase of traffic on the C.&O., which indicates in cold figures what kind of two-fisted fighter the railroad turned out to be.

Comparing the war period (1943) with the peacetime period

(January 1, 1936 to December 31, 1939), the average increase in business handled may be measured by the following percentages:

	Increase (Per Cent)
Coal handled	42
Other commodities handled	86
Freight train miles	34
Freight car miles	34
Passenger train miles	44
Passenger car miles	93

MODERN FREIGHT AND PASSENGER POWER

To handle the enormous increase in traffic it was necessary to have motive power to command—brawny, big-muscled engines, clamoring giants that could bite hard and fast at the steel rail.

The development of large, modern freight and passenger power on the Chesapeake and Ohio Railway began around 1930, and at a time when the Nation was staggering from the collapse of 1929. People were beginning to cry about the "good old days," and lamenting the fact that the country was going to the dogs.

Fortunately for America, there are, even in the darkest days, men and institutions with vision, courage, and foresight. The Chesapeake and Ohio had no crystal ball with which to plumb the future, but it had two-fisted fighting men at the throttle— men who knew that no battle is won by limply standing by the roadside and moaning.

One day, they knew, traffic was bound to increase, and, at the same time, realizing the necessity of economy throughout the depression, it was deemed advisable to design and acquire locomotives capable of handling maximum tonnage with a minimum of operating expense.

The C.&O. had taken over the Hocking Valley Railroad, and had constructed its own line from Russell, Kentucky, to Columbus, Ohio. Russell is a name to keep in mind, for Russell is important on the Chesapeake and Ohio.

Prior to this time, the major main-line traffic was handled by what may now be called semimodern power, in that the clearances and weight restrictions were such that it was not possible to obtain 100 per cent boilers, nor was it possible to design locomotives of sufficient power to handle train loads or sufficient tonnage to produce the maximum possible overall operating efficiency.

These so-called semimodern locomotives were built in 1924-26 and were designated as H-7, K-3, and F-19 classes. The H-7 and K-3 classes were 2-8-8-2 and 2-8-2 types, respectively, and were in freight service. The F-19 class was a 4-6-2 type and in use in passenger service. While today these locomotive classes could be improved from the standpoint of design, they are by no means obsolete.

Having decided on a program of expansion as concerned the acquisition of more modern motive power, clearances and track conditions were investigated, and it was found that they were such as to permit axle loads of around seventy-five thousand pounds, together with increases in heights and widths. Accordingly, a new locomotive was built and put into service.

This was the T-1 class, a 2-10-4 type locomotive, with a high-cylinder horsepower, supplied by a one hundred per cent boiler. There was a wide firebox, with ample grate area to provide a comparatively low rate of combustion, and Type E superheaters, which materially increased the expansive value of steam.

Dynamometer tests were run, and they came up to expectations, insofar as efficiency was concerned, and, by having large-capacity tenders, the engines could be run through Columbus into Toledo, with a minimum turning time at that point.

In fact, these engines were so successful that clearances and track conditions were surveyed between Clifton Forge and Charlottesville, Virginia, across the Blue Ridge Mountains, and between Handley and Clifton Forge, across the Alleghenies, to find out whether it would be possible to take advantage of the same improvements, if and when new power was required for these territories.

With passenger business looking up in 1935, it was found necessary to build new passenger equipment for operation over the Blue Ridge Mountains. The Class J-3, 4-8-4 type, locomotive was designed, using the same ratios and improvements as had been incorporated in the T-1 engine. The hustling, all-around 4-8-4 locomotive amply measured up to expectations.

In 1941, when traffic conditions made it necessary to acquire new freight power over the Alleghenies, and to acquire new passenger engines for operations between Hinton, West Virginia, and Cincinnati, Ohio, as well as between Hinton and Toledo, the H-8 class, the Allegheny 2-6-6-6 type, was born. Also the L-2, 4-6-4 type. The latter the famous Hudson.

These engines, in addition to the modern ratios, were equipped with locomotive beds in order to cut down frame maintenance. Needle-valve gear pins, providing better steam distribution throughout a longer period, were installed, and they were further equipped with roller bearings to decrease roundhouse maintenance and to facilitate quicker turning and correspondingly greater availability.

Availability and *utilization*. Two of the biggest words in the railroad lexicon.

A number of locomotives of the Class J-3-A, 4-8-4 type, were also built to supplement passenger-train service over the mountains between Charlottesville and Hinton, West Virginia.

Plainly it stands out that if the Chesapeake and Ohio had not at an early day anticipated its needs, and had not taken advantage of modern designs and practices, it could not have handled successfully the staggering traffic that was created by wartime conditions.

The following tables tell the story, as they show the comparison of locomotives built between 1924 and 1929 and those built since 1929.

TYPE OF SERVICE		*FREIGHT SERVICE*		
Railroad Classification	*K-3*	*H-7*	*T-1*	*H-8*
Type of Locomotive	2-8-2	2-8-8-2	2-10-4	2-6-6-6
Date Built	1924	1924	1930	1941
Weight on Drivers	271,000 lbs.	493,070 lbs.	373,000 lbs.	471,000 lbs.
Total Wt. of Locomotive	355,000 lbs.	567,500 lbs.	566,000 lbs.	724,500 lbs.
Total Wt. of Tender	217,600 lbs.	210,200 lbs.	415,000 lbs.	437,600 lbs.
Cyl. Diam. & Stroke	28" x 32"	23" x 32" & 23" x 32"	29" x 34"	22½" x 33" & 22½" x 33"

68

TYPE OF SERVICE	FREIGHT SERVICE			
Railroad Classification	K-3	H-7	T-1	H-8
Diam. of Driv. Wheels	63"	57"	69"	67"
Steam Pressure	200 lbs.	215 lbs.	265 lbs.	260 lbs.
Tractive Force Engine	67,700 lbs.	108,550 lbs.	93,350 lbs.	110,200 lbs.
Tractive Force Booster	None	None	15,275 lbs.	None
Tractive Force Total	67,700 lbs.	108,550 lbs.	108,625 lbs.	110,200 lbs.
Cylinder Horse Power	2,824	4,092	4,014	4,734
% Boiler H.P. to Cyl. H.P.	98.4	98.0	110.9	97.5
Grate Area	80.8 sq. ft.	112.2 sq. ft.	121.0 sq. ft.	135.0 sq. ft.
Total Heating Surface	4,461 sq. ft.	6,580 sq. ft.	6,623 sq. ft.	7,240 sq. ft.
Superheater Surface	1,173 sq. ft.	1,849 sq. ft.	3,030 sq. ft.	3,186 sq. ft.
Tender Style	Vanderbilt	Vanderbilt	Rectangular	Rectangular
Tender Water Capacity	*12,000 gal.	*12,000 gal.	23,500 gal.	25,000 gal.
Tender Coal Capacity	*15 tons	*15 tons	30 tons	25 tons

* Now carry 21,000 gals. of water, 25 tons of coal.

TYPE OF SERVICE	PASSENGER SERVICE		
Railroad Classification	F-19	J-3, J-3A	L-2
Type of Locomotive	4-6-2	4-8-4	4-6-4
Date Built	1926	1935-41	1941
Weight on Drivers	200,000 lbs.	278,300 lbs.	217,500 lbs.
Total Wt. of Locomotive	331,500 lbs.	477,000 lbs.	439,500 lbs.
Total Wt. of Tender	245,900 lbs.	381,700 lbs.	393,000 lbs.
Cyl. Diam. & Stroke	27" x 28"	27½" x 30"	25" x 30"
Diam. of Driv. Wheels	74"	74"	78"
Steam Pressure	200 lbs.	255 lbs.	255 lbs.
Tractive Force Engine	46,900 lbs.	66,450 lbs.	52,000 lbs.
Tractive Force Booster	None	14,355 lbs.	12,600 lbs.
Tractive Force Total	46,900 lbs.	80,805 lbs.	64,600 lbs.
Cylinder Horse Power	2,624	3,468	2,866
% Boiler H.P. to Cyl. H.P.	94.3	101.1	100.0
Grate Area	80.7 sq. ft.	100.0 sq. ft.	90.0 sq. ft.
Total Heating Surface	4,237 sq. ft.	5,538 sq. ft.	4,186 sq. ft.
Superheater Surface	1,213 sq. ft.	2,342 sq. ft.	1,810 sq. ft.
Tender Style	Vanderbilt	Rectangular	Rectangular
Tender Water Capacity	12,000 gal.	22,000 gal.	21,000 gal.
Tender Coal Capacity	15 tons	25 tons	30 tons

LOCOMOTIVES PURCHASED IN 1941, 1942, AND 1943

Railroad Classification	C-16A	H-8	J-3A	L-2
Series	240-244	1600-1619	605-606	300-307
Date Built	1942	1941-42	1942	1941-42
Builder	LLW	LLW	LLW	BLW
Type	8-Wh. Swit.	Mallet	Greenbrier	Hudson
Whyte Symbol	0-8-0	2-6-6-6	4-8-4	4-6-4
Service Built For	Switch	Freight	Passenger	Passenger
Tractive Effort—Lbs.	57,200	110,200	68,300 (A)	52,000 (B)
Diam. of Drivers	52"	67"	72"	78"
Wt. on Drivers	244,000 lbs.	471,000 lbs.	290,000 lbs.	217,500 lbs.
Tot. Wt. of Engine	244,000 lbs.	724,500 lbs.	503,500 lbs.	439,500 lbs.
Wt. of Tender	158,400 lbs.	437,600 lbs.	388,020 lbs.	393,000 lbs.
Tot. Wt. Eng. and Tender	402,400 lbs.	1,162,100 lbs.	891,520 lbs.	832,500 lbs.
Capacity Tender				
Water—Gals.	8,000	25,000	22,000	21,000
Coal—Tons	12	25	25	30

Railroad Classification	C-16A	H-8	K-4
Series	245-254	1620-1644	2700-2739
Date Built	1943-44	1943-44	1943-44
Builder	LLW	LLW	ALW
Type	8-Wh. Swit.	Mallet	Kanawha
Whyte Symbol	0-8-0	2-6-6-6	2-8-4
Service Built For	Switch	Freight	Freight
Tractive Effort—Lbs.	57,200	110,200	69,350 (C)
Diam. of Drivers	52"	67"	69"
Wt. on Drivers	244,000 lbs.	471,000 lbs.	292,000 lbs.
Tot. Wt. of Engine	244,000 lbs.	724,500 lbs.	461,000 lbs.
Wt. of Tender	158,400 lbs.	437,600 lbs.	393,000 lbs.
Tot. Wt. Eng. and Tender	402,400 lbs.	1,162,100 lbs.	854,000 lbs.
Capacity Tender			
Water—Gals.	8,000	25,000	21,000
Coal—Tons	12	25	30

	(A)	(B)	(C)
Tractive Effort without Booster (Lbs.)	68,300	52,000	69,350
Tractive Effort with Booster (Lbs.)	82,655	64,600	83,750
Tractive Effort of Booster (Lbs.)	14,355	12,600	14,400

June 1, 1944

INDUSTRIAL ACTIVITIES

The Chesapeake and Ohio Railway is surrounded by untold wealth. Factories, docks, and mines are closely linked by a steel rail. The giant arteries of the railroad carry finished products and raw materials in quantities that beggar description. The human mind cannot conceive the traffic tonnage that is handled by a road such as the C.&O. in wartime, let alone grasp the astronomical figures representing the total freight and passenger traffic moving in these United States during the days of a Titanic struggle such as World War II.

In 1943 the Chesapeake and Ohio handled approximately 77,700,000 tons of bituminous coal, of which 62,600,000 tons originated on the line, and 23,700,000 tons of merchandise freight, for a total of 101,400,000 tons.

Traffic density on the C.&O. in prewar years was among the highest in the country; it was substantially greater in 1942. Under normal conditions, practically all of the coal carried by the Chesapeake and Ohio for ultimate delivery to northern and New England markets was handled through Newport News, where it was dumped over the coal piers into coastwise vessels. The submarine menace of 1942 and war-shipping demands made it necessary to route this coal north by rail through gateways already congested with war traffic.

These routes involved heavier grades, requiring shorter trains and a greater number of locomotives. Such conditions naturally increased the operating problems. However, the Chesapeake and Ohio, because it had maintained its roadways and equipment in top condition during the depression years, was prepared to meet the war emergencies in a manner that did the road credit.

Aside from coal, the territory served by the C.&O. produces oil, natural gas, flint, plastic clays, shales, timber, limestone, and many more raw materials. Finished products include almost every article under the sun, most of them vital to the needs of war.

At Norfolk, Virginia, are located warehouse terminals of fifteen to twenty large distributing firms, and in addition there are huge cold-storage facilities. The port of Norfolk, expanded to meet war conditions, became a veritable beehive of activity, with Government-operated Municipal Piers, Navy Operating Base, the Army Base at Sewell's Point, and the Navy Yard at Portsmouth. The C.&O. serves many industries through the Norfolk and Portsmouth Belt Line.

Newport News is the chief Atlantic port of the Chesapeake and Ohio Railway. Here adequate docks and facilities have been developed. There are many Army and Navy camps and warehouses, most of which are under Government supervision and operation.

Westward from seaboard, there are large chemical industries at Charleston, West Virginia, and from here come many of the synthetic materials that are products of coal, salt, limestone. Here is located a Government-operated armor heat-treating plant. Plate weighing as much as 125 tons is transported from the Pittsburgh District to the Charleston plant for treating and finishing.

Chemicals come from Huntington, and from Covington, West Virginia, by-products of the pulp and paper industry. A huge iron furnace is located at Ashland, Kentucky, with a capacity of 1,000 tons of pig iron a day. Foundry products, castings, structural steel come from Richmond, Virginia; cast iron and cast-iron pipe come from Lynchburg, Virginia; pig iron and pipe come from Jackson, Ohio; iron and steel castings from Columbus and Marion, Ohio; machine tools from Cincinnati; high-speed tools, automatic drills, tapping machines from Richmond, Indiana, and the nationally known glass Mason jars from Muncie, Indiana.

All up and down the Chesapeake and Ohio are foundries and machine shops; plants producing by-products of gas and coal. Old-World Cathedral Glass is produced at Milton, West Virginia. Lamp chimneys come from Culloden and Scott, West Virginia, and from Lancaster, Ohio, come tumblers, jars, bottles, novelty glassware. Goshen, Virginia, produces silica sand for this glass industry, as does Thayer, West Virginia. In wartime glass products conserve iron and steel for the needs of the battle machines.

72

Textiles, rayons, rugs, carpets, garment industries at Glasgow, Goshen, Augusta Springs, Craigsville, Charlottesville. Sawmills; forest products add to the bustling industrial development along the C.&O. From the timber regions of Virginia, West Virginia, and Kentucky come large supplies of wood for the pulp and paper industry at Covington, Buena Vista, Coleman, Lynchburg, and Richmond, Virginia; for the tannic acid plants at Ashland, Kentucky; Durbin and Marlinton, West Virginia; Buena Vista and Iron Gate, Virginia.

From the Olive Hill district in Kentucky come high-grade flint clays used in the manufacture of firebrick. Tobacco, cement, slate originate in the territory along the C.&O. Nickel ore, mined and smelted in Canada, follows the path of the steel rail to Huntington, West Virginia, where it is rolled into various forms, including mono metal.

It is impossible to begin to list all of the industries served by the Chesapeake and Ohio Railway between the Great Lakes and the Atlantic seaboard—industries that include the limestone quarries at Staunton, Eagle Mountain, Rocky Point, Virginia; Renick and Fort Springs, West Virginia; Olive Hill, Kentucky, and Carey, Ohio; the cement plants at Fordwick, Virginia, and Kenova, West Virginia; the slate quarries near Bremo, Virginia —for they are almost interminable. But vast as they are there are freight cars to serve them—freight cars that build into trains, hauled by husky-voiced locomotives like the Allegheny 2-6-6-6.

No minute of the day or night when countless thousands of iron feet are not tramping the rail on the C.&O.—a ceaseless marching army of supply, hauling in one war year over one hundred million tons of freight.

CHAPTER VI

OIL AND THE DIESEL LOCOMOTIVE

"Black Gold" – Tank Cars – Diesel Development

His name was Drake. He was a railroad conductor. Funny, Ed Drake, swinging a highball on the New Haven. This was in 1849. The gold rush was on. Gold in California!

Ten years later, Ed Drake started the biggest rush in the world —the "black gold" rush of 1859. Ed Drake set the world afire. Because of Ed Drake, a fire was kindled under the crown-sheet of the first oil-burning locomotive; Diesel engines were born. Drake, the man who made possible the bombing of London, Tokyo, Berlin.

Drake, the man who drilled a hole in the ground at Titusville, Pennsylvania, and, on the twenty-seventh of August, 1859, brought in the first oil well in the world. Edwin L. Drake. "Colonel" Drake, who started a billion-dollar industry, and died in poverty in 1880.

Other men had dug in the ground for oil—six thousand years ago, they say. It is reported that the ancient Egyptians used a kind of petroleum to embalm their dead. The Chinese, we are told, drilled for oil before Christ was born. But it was Ed Drake who started 2,000 barrels of commercial oil to the refineries. Wagons hauled it—wagons and barges. The first bulk shipments moved down the Allegheny River to Pittsburgh in flatboats. At Pittsburgh the oil was barreled and reshipped to seaboard.

In 1864 the first tank car made its appearance—a boxcar into which three wooden tubs were built. In 1867 a platform car with two wooden tanks anchored to it appeared. In 1869, John

74

D. Rockefeller was laying the foundation for the Standard Oil Company.

Petroleum—the oil for Aladdin's Lamp. The Big Parade was on. The automobile; the submarine; the airplane; the oil-burning locomotive—the Diesel-electric streamliner. Santa Fe Diesel-electric freight hauler No. 100, sliding out of the yards in Shopton, Iowa, in February, 1941.

December 7, 1941!

Twenty thousand tank cars were standing idle in sidings and railroad yards in the United States. And then, suddenly, oil was the life blood of the Nation. Almost before we knew it, Nazi submarines were slashing at our jugular vein, which was our tanker transport on the coastwise shipping lanes.

Immediately those idle tank cars were conditioned and started rolling. By mid-1943, the railroads were hauling over 900,000 barrels of oil to the Atlantic seaboard a day.

Prior to the outbreak of the war, an average of 1,500,000 barrels per day of petroleum and its products was consumed in the Atlantic seaboard states. Something like a tanker an hour was leaving Gulf ports. A small trickle of 5,000 barrels a day went by rail, which accounted for those 20,000-odd idle tank cars.

Then the picture changed. The tiger of the sea was loose in the Atlantic. The U-boat was preying on the tanker fleet. Men were dying in flaming oil. Precious tanker cargoes were being gutted. And almost overnight the task of transporting the staggering tonnage previously moving down the sea lanes was dumped into the lap of the railroad.

There immediately began a hunt for tank cars—a hunt as desperate as was the search for locomotives. Those 20,000 idle tank cars were conditioned and rushed back into service. Synthetic rubber tanks were installed in boxcars; gondolas were converted into petroleum carriers; oil drums were loaded aboard trains.

Oil and gasoline for our Allies, for our tanks and trucks and airplanes. Oil for industry; oil for heating homes. The greatest black gold rush of all time.

In the first big push, tank cars moved in ordinary freight trains, making it necessary to send them to classification yards in the North to be broken down and made up into new trains. Then oil began to move in solid oil trains of ninety and one hundred cars, and they were highballed from one railroad to another. Fifty railroads and sixty-six routes were involved. Yards were enlarged, new steel laid, and bridges built. Oil had to move— and fast.

There were 154,000 tank cars burning up the rails. The movement grew. Petroleum flowed to the eastern seaboard until there came the day when the railroads reached an all-time peak of 933,966 barrels delivered in twenty-four hours. Of this 912,919 barrels were hauled by tank cars and 21,047 barrels in drums loaded into boxcars.

To illustrate this accomplishment, the cars of one company —the Union Tank Car Company—for the six months' period ending June 30, 1943, moved approximately 56,000,000 barrels of petroleum and its products into the eastern area, and most of it from distant points.

So the lowly tank car came to be the vital cog in America's battle of oil transport. It was the stopgap between the dark threat of disaster and ultimate victory.

The "Big Inch"—a twenty-four-inch pipe line, the world's largest—was being pushed through over plains and mountains. It reached out from Longview, Texas, to Norris City, Illinois. Later, it was completed to the East—to Philadelphia and New York refineries. Fourteen hundred miles—across eight states, beneath twenty rivers and over the Appalachian Mountains. Three hundred thousand barrels of oil per day pass through the Big Inch—a crawling black mass, traveling at an average speed of 100 miles in twenty-four hours. Tank cars make about 220 miles a day, but the Big Inch lightened their load, allowing many of these rail carriers to take time out for needed repairs.

Too much credit cannot be given the railroads of the Nation for the magnificent part they played in that early tank-train movement, for oil was "Hot Cargo." Through the establishment of scheduled trains and the "channeling" of cars, loaded and empty, via roads capable of handling them with the greatest efficiency, oil was highballed through. Oil for the battle fleets, oil for planes, oil for tanks—oil for Victory.

The railroads, the private owners of tank cars, the oil companies, the Office of Defense Transportation, the Office of Petroleum Administration for War, the War Production Board—all joined hands to promote successfully the movement of petroleum and its products by tank car.

The transfer of short-haul tank cars to long-haul service completely dislocated the normal trend of things, and required quick changes by the mechanical departments in order that proper repair facilities might be maintained.

The oil industry in general performed remarkable achievements in installing vast facilities in the form of racks, pumps, pipe lines at loading and unloading points, making possible a quick turnaround of tank-car equipment. This involved securing large quantities of material, which was accomplished through the co-operation of the War Production Board.

The tank cars themselves had to be improved and readied for the faster service required of them. This involved the application of steel wheels and the installation of snubbers, a device inserted in the springs of the trucks to prevent oscillation of the cars, as well as many other details necessary to maintain these tank cars at the highest possible state of efficiency.

But oil was on the move. Oil, riding the path of the steel rail. The oil trains, thundering through, were every day hammering home nails in the coffins of Tojo and Hitler. The Southern Pacific, the Santa Fe, the Burlington; the Rock Island, the Missouri Pacific, the Texas & Pacific, the Southern, the Erie; the Pennsylvania, the New York Central, the Illinois Central—these and other American railroads were rushing the long trains of solid tank cars through. Big engines with iron hearts were wheeling them.

The pen is mightier than the sword. Oil in war is mightier than either. Oil and the steel rail.

THE DIESEL LOCOMOTIVE

One of the miracles born of oil was the Diesel-electric locomotive.

The Diesel principal dates back to 1897, when Dr. Rudolf Diesel, of Germany, completed the first workable Diesel engine.

The first American Diesel was built in St. Louis in 1898, and slowly passed through many stages before reaching its present state of perfection. Of the some 120 streamlined trains in operation in 1942, about three-fourths were drawn by Diesel-electric locomotives. The present Diesel is proving its worth in main-line freight service.

There are two principal roots of the modern Diesel main-line locomotive. One goes back to the desire of engineers—both in the railroad and automotive fields—to apply the economies of the internal-combustion engine to rail transportation, following in the wake of the birth of motor truck and bus. The other springs from World War I, and was created through necessity.

The earliest worth-while application of the internal-combustion engine to the task of propelling a standard railroad car came in 1905 when the first rail motorcar was built by the Union Pacific.

This led to the founding of the McKeen Motor Car industry. In this same early babyhood of the internal-combustion engine, the General Electric Company was working at Schenectady on a gasoline motorcar with electric drive for the Delaware and Hudson Railway Company. Work was started on this car late in 1904. Records indicate that it was brought out on February 1, 1906, thus giving McKeen the honor of being the first motorcar to ride the steel rail.

Between 1906 and America's entry into World War I, the McKeen company put 155 motorcars on the rails. During the same general period, General Electric built some 90 cars, which went into service on branch lines. These gasoline-electric cars went loping down the track with a husky *plunkety-plunk*, and when they whistled it sounded as though they had a cold.

When World War I came along, McKeen and General Electric quit building these cars.

About that time the idea that the internal-combustion engine could be applied to a knotty and unusual transportation problem took root in the fertile brain of a Mr. H. L. Hamilton, now a vice-president of General Motors.

Ed Drake was a railroad man; so was H. L. Hamilton. Funny, what a steel rail does to a man. Mr. Hamilton had been a fireman, an engineer, and then a minor railroad official. Finally he turned to the automotive field, the pastures of which seemed a bit greener about that time. Eventually he became manager of a prominent motor-truck manufacturer's Denver office.

One day the home office tossed a little problem his way—a problem that was to result in the development of the Diesel-electric locomotive.

As in World War II, critical material shortages developed back there in 1917. For instance, a certain alloy was desperately needed in the manufacture of war products. It was discovered that steel rails purchased in Great Britain during an earlier period were high in content of this alloy.

Miles of these rails lay on old logging roads, mining roads, and other abandonments. For the most part, this track was in rough and inaccessible country. A contractor in Minnesota, employed to tear up fifteen miles of an old lumbering road, made a survey. Roadbed and bridges were in poor shape. The track might sustain the weight of a flatcar and a few rails, but not much more. Getting to a railhead with a truck was out of the question, and a truck alone wouldn't do the job anyway.

The contractor puzzled over the matter. A motor truck with flanged wheels to ride the rails, pushing a flatcar in ahead of it might do the trick. He appealed to a truck manufacturer in Cleveland, and was referred to Mr. Hamilton.

Mr. Hamilton looked the situation over. He said that no truck transmission of that time would stand up, but, in view of the urgency, the contractor's scheme was worth trying. The job was undertaken. As Mr. Hamilton had predicted, the transmission soon played out. Frequent replacements, however, kept the equipment going until the last rail had been salvaged.

For a long time, Mr. Hamilton had been toying with the idea of rail motorcar transport. He was familiar with the McKeen and General Electric developments. His experience with the motor truck on that old logging road revived the half-formed patterns of things. The result was that he quit his job, and, out of savings, hired a staff of assistants.

And so there was created the first gasoline-engined rail car of the present great Electro-Motive Company.

The car developed by H. L. Hamilton worked. And there, in its swaddling clothes, stood the forerunner of the mighty, present-day Diesel-electric locomotive.

Today they ride the rails all over America—on the Santa Fe's Arizona Divide, on the high steel of the Denver and Rio Grande Western, there on the roof of the continent in the Colorado Rockies, on the Mechanicsville run on the Boston & Maine, on the rails of the Atlantic Coast line, the Seaboard, Western Pacific, the Baltimore and Ohio, New Haven, Rock Island, Milwaukee, Southern, Union Pacific, Southern Pacific, Chicago & North Western, Illinois Central, Great Northern, Burlington, Northern Pacific, New York Central, Kansas City Southern, Florida East Coast, Missouri Pacific, and Louisville and Nashville.

Hamilton's first car sold. A second was built, and H. L. Hamilton was on his way. Between 1923 and 1930, Electro-Motive put more than five hundred of these cars on the rails, most of which are still in operation on branch lines.

Mr. Hamilton and his associates in Electro-Motive amassed a wealth of valuable information concerning the problem of applying the power of the gasoline engine to the steel rail through electric transmission. They learned, too, about car construction.

Meanwhile, a third important phase of the development of the Diesel locomotive had been in incubation. Charles F. Kettering, vice-president of General Motors in charge of research, and his associates had been working since 1928 on the development of a Diesel engine—an engine that would be free of the high disadvantages of excessive weight and size, which had held down the application of the Diesel's higher thermal efficiencies to many applications since the invention of this engine by Rudolf Diesel in 1896.

General Motors' engineers joined forces with the engineers of the Winton Company at Cleveland. Winton was one of America's leading Diesel-engine builders, and at that time supplied gasoline engines for the Electro-Motive rail cars. This liaison was welded into a complete union in 1930 when General Motors purchased both Winton and Electro-Motive for the purpose of equipping the corporation with broader facilities with which to develop and prove Diesel engines.

The streamliner City of San Francisco, whose wartime make-up consists of 17 deluxe coaches and Pullman cars hauled by a 3-unit 6000 horsepower Diesel on the Wyoming Division. This train runs over the C. & N. W. from Chicago to Omaha, the U.P. from Omaha to Ogden and the S.P. from Ogden to Oakland, and operates every third day. Courtesy Union Pacific R.R.

Getting the empty oil cars west is almost as big a job as bringing the loaded ones east. Here is a train of empties leaving Selkirk yard for Norris City. Engine #3005, 4-8-2 Type Class L-3A. Note the 43-ton tender, largest for coal capacity in the U.S. On account of the water pans it is not necessary to carry more than 15,600 gallons of water for these engines. Courtesy New York Central.

Santa Fe #21, the El Capitan, famous streamlined coach train and only extra fare deluxe all-coach train in the U.S., running twice weekly from Chicago to Los Angeles; descending the west slope of Raton Pass. Photo by Otto C. Perry

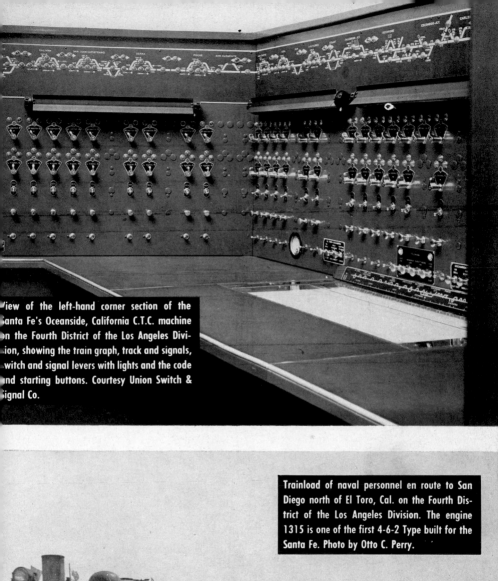

View of the left-hand corner section of the Santa Fe's Oceanside, California C.T.C. machine on the Fourth District of the Los Angeles Division, showing the train graph, track and signals, switch and signal levers with lights and the code and starting buttons. Courtesy Union Switch & Signal Co.

Trainload of naval personnel en route to San Diego north of El Toro, Cal. on the Fourth District of the Los Angeles Division. The engine 1315 is one of the first 4-6-2 Type built for the Santa Fe. Photo by Otto C. Perry.

Fresh from the Baldwin Locomotive Works #2920, one of the 30 latest 4-8-4 Type on the Santa Fe, drifting by the Emporia, Kansas station, western terminus of the Eastern Division, with #39, the Oklahoma-Texas fast freight, on a rainy afternoon with 4100 tons and 101 cars. Courtesy Merrill Kennedy.

#20, the Santa Fe Chief, climbing the west slope of Raton Pass with 15 cars. The helper is 1797, 2-8-8-2 Type former N. & W. Class Y-3. These engines were bought from that road for use in helping service on Raton Pass during the war effort. The road engine is 3777. Photo by Preston George.

There was no intent to build a Diesel locomotive at that time. Rather, the thought was that there might be use for Diesels in rail motorcars, as well as in the marine field in which Winton occupied a high place.

General Motors placed its first Diesel of the new design on display as a partial source of power for the Chevrolet assembly line in the General Motors' building at the Chicago Century of Progress Exposition in 1933. Kettering and his associates had successfully applied the two-cycle principle to a high-speed engine—that is, high speed compared with the previous, lumbering Diesels. The result was a reduction to about one-fifth the weight and one-fourth the size of the best previous Diesel in the high-horsepower ranges.

Here, at last, was the internal-combustion power plant that would make possible the dream of a streamlined train—the train that progressive railroad men long had visioned.

Soon there appeared the Union Pacific's M-10001, as sparkling as a new dipper, and the Burlington Zephyrs. Other railroads, notably the Santa Fe and Baltimore and Ohio, put pressure on Electro-Motive to make the new power available in separate locomotives. The result was that in 1935 the Santa Fe *Super Chief* and the Baltimore and Ohio *Royal Blue* were powered with the first real road locomotives.

And the Diesel parade was on.

DIESEL ADVANTAGES

From the standpoint of railroad-operating departments, the advantages of Diesel locomotives that have become apparent through more than ten years of service follow:

Faster scheduled operation.
Fifty per cent decrease in operating costs.
Fifty per cent decrease in maintenance costs.
Higher availability.
Greater flexibility.
Freedom from costly supporting services such as ash-dumping and removal, water treatment and storage, boiler-washing, and the like.

Less wear on track due to elimination of hammer blow inherent in steam locomotive.

Important contraction of back-shopping facilities due to far longer periods between major overhauls and the fact that the Diesel is a collection of small, standardized, prefitted parts.

Uniform operation in all variations of weather, climate, and terrain.

To examine these advantages more in detail:

The decrease in operating costs by roughly fifty per cent accumulates largely from: saving in fuel, due both to the inherent thermal efficiency of the Diesel engine and in the transportation and handling of fuel.

Generally speaking, one tank car of fuel oil does the same work in a Diesel locomotive that twelve cars of coal do in a steam locomotive. The saving in supporting services also is important. Diesel engines require no frequent watering service, and, due to their ability to run long distances without refueling—generally 650 miles for a passenger locomotive and 500 miles for a freight locomotive—require far less frequent fueling facilities.

The decrease in maintenance costs is largely due to the inherent design of the Diesel locomotive for ease of service. The locomotives are designed so that they are made up of relatively small, easily handled, quickly replaced parts, as contrasted with such pieces of a steam locomotive as boilers, drivers, driving wheels, et cetera. Parts are standardized so that no elaborate fitting operations are required in replacements. For example, a piston can be removed from the 600-horsepower engine in a GM switcher and be put into one of the 1,350-horsepower engines of a GM freight locomotive without fitting operations. As a result of the ease of service and the fact that they can be accomplished so rapidly, most repairs are actually "running repairs," performed between scheduled runs.

The fact that such repairs are accomplished as running repairs is one of the principal contributions to the high availability of Diesels.

Greater flexibility of Diesel locomotives is purely a matter of their inherent design. A 7,000-horsepower Articulated remains a 7,000-horsepower engine regardless of the load it has to pull. Since all main-line locomotives built, for instance, by General

Motors are in units that can be quickly coupled or uncoupled by the train crew, the locomotive horsepower can be "tailored" to the job to be done. As an example, a 5,400-horsepower freight locomotive, within fifteen minutes, can become two 2,700-horsepower locomotives, or one 4,050-horsepower locomotive with a spare unit resting.

The faster schedules which Diesel maintains, both in freight and passenger service, accrue from the following:

Faster acceleration, higher speed up grades—and down grades, in the case of the freight locomotive with electric holding brakes —ability to take curves at about ten miles per hour faster than steam locomotives due to Diesel's low center of gravity, minimum of service stops, elimination of locomotive changes.

As a matter of fact, the top speed of a Diesel locomotive probably is not as great as that recorded by some steam locomotives on demonstration runs—the top speed of a Diesel passenger locomotive being regarded as about 117 miles per hour. The Diesel advantage of ten hours under the fastest steam schedules between Chicago and the Pacific Coast is due to time saved by the before mentioned advantages, not excessive speed.

GENERAL MOTORS' DIESELS

All classes of regular railroad service are covered by General Motors' Diesel locomotives. General Motors has 1,200 locomotive units in service on 75 American railroads.

Some of the passenger units have been in continuous service on fast schedules since 1934. Certain passenger locomotives have accumulated more than two million miles in service. They have made outstanding records for availability and periods between motor overhaul. There has been no class of service, to date, on GM Diesel locomotives that could be called "back-shopping," in the sense of the term as used in steam practice.

Among notable availability records are two 4,000-horsepower locomotives that the Chicago & North Western kept in continuous service, without missing a trip, for 733 days. Seven days a week each of these locomotives hauled the fast "400" one way and brought the 16- to 18-car Standard Pullman North Western

Limited back at night. This on the route between Chicago and St. Paul–Minneapolis. This meant an assignment of over eight hundred miles a day for each locomotive.

The national average all-time availability record for the 1,200 units in service is ninety-five per cent, compared with the traditional all-time record of thirty-three per cent for all classes of steam locomotives, and about sixty per cent for the most modern steam locomotives.

One of the outstanding contributions of the railroads and the locomotive builders in World War II will go down in the record books as—the mighty Diesel locomotive.

CHAPTER VII

WARTIME SANTA FE

Working for Victory – Argentine Yard – C.T.C.

The Santa Fe today is playing its part in the new "Winning of the West." None of the color and little of the romance and spirit of adventure have been lost. Picture a world of towering red mesas, of Navajos in gaudy dress, of hogans, of squaws squatting before their primitive hand looms, of stalwart Navajo men tending their flocks of sheep. Vision against this age-old setting a vivid-hued, streamlined Diesel-powered train, the *Super Chief*, flashing down the rails. The *Chief*, roaring through behind a big 4-8-4 locomotive of the 3776-class.

This is the great Arizona frontier. Here swift ultramodern limiteds meet in Navajo land a civilization of the deep past. Here traveled the explorer priests as early as 1540, and they found a people and a culture already established—towns of the Moqui, of the red man.

Garcia Lopez de Cardenas, discoverer of the Grand Canyon, joined with Francisco Vasquez de Coronado and together they blazed the white man's trail across the West—the Trail of the Santa Fe.

Farsighted men looking ahead, faces west—the steel rail threading the new frontier. Engines of the Santa Fe shouting in this red wilderness. Trains wheeling on toward the blue Pacific. States joined—Illinois, Iowa, Missouri, Kansas, Oklahoma, Texas, Colorado, New Mexico, Arizona, California. The Atchinson, Topeka and Santa Fe.

Big things are happening today in Santa Fe land. The soundness of vision of yesterday's railroad builders is now playing a

85

big part in the winning of the greatest war this world has ever known.

Heavily burdened freight cars are rolling; troop transport is on the move.

The Santa Fe links vast sources of raw material with great mills and factories. All around the clock the Santa Fe serves the shipyards and plane plants of California, the agriculture and mining districts of Arizona; moves essential potash, zinc, steers, sheep from New Mexico; wheat from Kansas; oil from Oklahoma—to mention but a few of the states and industries.

The Santa Fe and the other railroads of America are performing, to quote a high-ranking Government official, "the most stupendously efficient task ever performed by any human organization."

Let us look at a few sidelights, small things, in a way, but vital, performed by the Santa Fe.

It is the morning of December 11, 1941. The country is still rocking under the shock of the cowardly attack on Pearl Harbor. Thirty-six carloads of structural steel have arrived at the interchange yards in Chicago—steel billed to dockside on the Pacific Coast. A cargo vessel is waiting.

In the normal course of events, the trainload of steel would have arrived on the West Coast the eighth morning after leaving Chicago. The rails were cleared. A train containing those cars of vital steel highballed out. Ninety-six hours later cranes were loading that steel into the hold of the waiting ship. The running time had been halved—2,500 miles at an average speed of pretty close to twenty-six miles an hour.

The run was made without change of engine or caboose. Crew changes often required as little as three minutes.

This was not an isolated instance of moving war freight fast across the long miles between Chicago and the Coast. It has been done whenever the need arose, and is made possible only through the co-operation of every mother's son along the line —railroad men of the Santa Fe.

The human body requires oxygen, or it would cease to function. The same applies to a shipyard. Oxygen for welding, oxygen for ships, building on the feverish ways of war.

86

On the Pacific Coast, a storekeeper reported to the production manager of a big yard that only a two days' supply of this highly important liquid gas remained. A frantic call went out; every possible available source was canvassed, but no one had any of these heavy steel tanks of oxygen to spare.

The cry went out to the Santa Fe. A check was made of the manifests of trains en route west. Here and there, on the line and in the yards, between Chicago and Amarillo, Texas, were carloads of the needed chemical. The wires went hot. At Amarillo, Texas, at Topeka, Kansas, and other points, switch engines snatched these cars from yards and trains. Road engines rushed them westward. The cars converged at last in the San Joaquin Valley in California. A locomotive and caboose were waiting. The oxygen tanks rolled into the shipyard, where less than a six-hour supply remained. The Santa Fe had delivered. The Santa Fe was fighting a war.

Little things. For want of a horseshoe nail a battle was lost.

A war plant was close to the stopping point for want of a certain kind of special washers. A carload of these washers was en route in a Santa Fe merchandise car. The car was opened at Kansas City. Three cases went through by air express; three more moved west by Railway Express. The first arrived the next day; the second one day later. The wheels of the war plant were kept turning.

A big airplane factory needed sheet aluminum. A trainload was on the way. Santa Fe men on the job in Chicago. They transferred seven crates, 35,000 pounds, to an express car. Three days later that sheet aluminum was being shaped into fighting ships of the air.

The Gods of War do not wait. If you have only a musket, it is with a musket you fight. Newer and better weapons are as an unloaded gun until they and the ammunition for them are delivered into the hands of the men on the battle fronts.

In America, the first forward movement of the tools of war begins on a steel rail. The black funeral pyre was still lifting its mourning veils of smoke over Pearl Harbor when the railroads of these United States began wheeling war supplies to dock-

87

side. Big modern engines bowed to the burden thrust on their steel shoulders—engines representing the last word in motive power.

Competitive transportation created these locomotives during the depression era. Free enterprise!

In Europe the screaming atom called Hitler buried free enterprise beneath the black sod of Nazism. The bloody midget and his slaves built war machines and military highways. German railroads deteriorated. In America railway transportation came to stand as the Nation's greatest bulwark.

To vizualize something of the scope of a railroad plant like the Santa Fe, one has only to examine the tables of Locomotive Runs in a preceding chapter. Many toiling hands are required to push a train across those long miles—a small army of men and women, thousands of cars, hundreds of roaring engines.

It is a tribute to railroad management that the carriers accomplished tremendous development of plant efficiency between 1918 and December 7, 1941.

The Santa Fe System Lines operate over twenty thousand miles of main-line, yard, and side track. There has been no increase in trackage since 1928. In fact, there are now a few less miles than in 1931. The Santa Fe owns 1,764 locomotives. This is fewer than it owned in 1910—435 less than it owned in 1918, the peak transportation year of the first World War. It has about 11,000 more freight cars than in 1918, but 10,000 less than in 1931—the present total being just over 80,000. It has about 200 fewer cars in passenger service than in 1918.

The Santa Fe, in 1918, originated on its lines 28,771,448 tons of revenue freight, and carried on its system 36,195,014 tons. In 1943 the Santa Fe originated 37,601.000 tons and carried 57,711,000 tons.

In 1943, the second full year of the war, the Santa Fe carried 10,399,212 passengers. This is somewhat below the peak of World War I. But now let us break this down into passenger-miles to obtain the true picture. In 1918 the average passenger traveled 121 miles. In 1943 the average passenger traveled 560 miles. Thus we discover that the average passenger-mile was 5,827,179,000 in 1943, against 1,676,144,000 in 1918.

In 1918, the Santa Fe's 2,122 locomotives had an average tractive effort of 35,568 pounds. The 1,764 locomotives now in service average 54,997 pounds, for a total of 97,015,500 pounds of pulling power, compared with 75,475,296 pounds in 1918.

Most of the Santa Fe locomotives are standard steam types. However, the first Diesel-electric locomotives were pioneered on the Santa Fe in 1936. The road has seventy-five of these big Diesels in freight and passenger service at the present time, with more on order.

In February, 1941, Santa Fe Diesel-electric No. 100 pulled out of the Argentine yards in Kansas City with sixty loaded freight cars—3,150 tons—bound for the Pacific Coast. The 5,400 thundering horses of the No. 100 wheeled its train across the 1,782 miles of plains, mountains, and high deserts to Los Angeles, California, in fifty-three hours, for the first long-haul run of fast freight anywhere with this type of motive power.

The pattern of a new era in railroading has been set, and mighty, indeed, is the part Diesel-electric locomotives are playing in today's war effort.

A little later we will have an opportunity to examine closely the performance of these sleek 5,400-horsepower giants under the severe conditions imposed by the mountains of the Arizona Divide.

Returning to the Santa Fe steam locomotives: In 1918 about 200 miles was the maximum locomotive run. Today 400 to 500 miles are not unusual in freight service. Again we examine the tables of extended runs in a previous chapter, to find thirty of those all-purpose 4-8-4 locomotives going through from Kansas City to Clovis, New Mexico—637 slugging miles with freight.

In passenger service, a high-wheeling 4-8-4, 3776-class locomotive zips down the rails from Kansas City to Los Angeles without change, 1,788 miles! Later on we will have more to say about these 3776-class engines of the Santa Fe, the sweethearts of the road.

Freight cars on the Santa Fe today have an average capacity of 45.38 tons, against 35.53 tons in 1918. The average speed of a freight car twenty-five years ago was 12.19 miles an hour. Today the average is 18.34 miles an hour, and this despite crowded wartime traffic. This includes time spent in loading and unloading at terminals. These figures speak for themselves.

During the hard-bitten depression years, with traffic at low ebb and net earnings practically nil, the Santa Fe, with wisdom and foresight, planned for the future. Remembering the breakdown of 1918, the road resolved that this would never happen again. In this forward-looking movement, the Santa Fe and other railways of the country, together with the locomotive builders, set their sights high. The result has been achievement of the highest order, and something to frame—a gold-lettered page for the record book.

Men and women of the Santa Fe have contributed enormously to the success of the war job on this great railroad of the West —from the humble Navajo or Mexican section hand to the executive on the high carpet.

Sixty-three thousand workers keeping the war trains rolling— many daily performing tasks beyond the call of duty. Many a glamour girl in greasy overalls, with a smudge on her cheek and grime on her hands, stepping in to do the work of a man gone to war. American womanhood on the Santa Fe. To them we tip our hat.

There are some 12,500 more employees on the Santa Fe today than in 1940, but still 10,000 less than in 1918. There are thousands on the road who have taken on new and unfamiliar jobs, but they have adapted themselves in true Yankee tradition, exactly as the men and women of the early wagon trains adapted themselves to meet the conditions of the new, strange West they had set out to conquer.

The 713th Railway Operating Battalion of the Transportation Corps is manned almost entirely by Santa Fe men, with a former superintendent, Lieutenant Colonel C. D. Notgrass in command. Already thirty gold stars occupy a place in the service flag of the System—Santa Fe men who won't come back when the war is won.

Eighty-seven per cent of the Santa Fe forces are subscribing an average of seven per cent of their wages in war stamps and bonds. Individual subscriptions run as high as fifty per cent, and it is reported that there is at least one employee who is putting his entire pay check into war bonds each fortnight. A million dollars a month on the Santa Fe, invested in Victory.

When the load on the Santa Fe's communications system began to bear down, changes were necessary in order to fit the System to take care of an additional 150 per cent burden.

The Santa Fe set up a new Mining Department to prospect and explore the line's far-flung territory in an effort to uncover deposits of vital metals. Material salvage—rubber, iron, steel, and countless other materials—has added another challenge to the working forces. Reclaiming and substitution move on at battle pace.

ARGENTINE YARD

Argentine Yard, in Greater Kansas City, is the largest terminal on the Santa Fe System. Argentine, Wyandotte County, Kansas—a dot on the map, but a mighty, roaring center of war activity.

Argentine Yard is far too big, too vastly important to review fully in the limited space at our command. We can do little more than high-light its important functions in connection with the movement of mail, passengers, and men and materials of war.

During the holiday seasons the volume of mail and passenger business has been staggering, and it was necessary to employ any civilian, soldier, or truck available. Men worked from a few hours to around the clock. The Santa Fe inaugurated a daily special sixteen-car mail train made up of high-speed boxcars, moving to various points west, including Clovis, New Mexico, and south to Oklahoma City, Oklahoma, thus relieving considerable delay and conserving passenger equipment. The task assumed Herculean proportions, but the Santa Fe came through.

In December, 1941, already burdened with this holiday flood, the Santa Fe was confronted with the urgent necessity of troop movements. The coach yard at Argentine consists of twenty tracks. During previous periods of peak passenger travel, the yard had been taxed to what was thought to be its utmost capacity, but in this war doing the "impossible" has become commonplace.

In addition to the regular heavy traffic passing through it, Argentine Yard serviced as high as ten additional troop movements nightly, to make no mention of troop trains received and dispatched in the daylight hours.

The yards at Argentine, Kansas, are approximately ten miles in length. In days gone by, the car-handling average was three thousand daily, with some seven or eight hundred for interchange with twelve other railroads. There were fifty-five yard tricks then and fifteen yardmasters.

Came World War II, and seven thousand crowding, jostling cars descended on Argentine Yard daily, with fifteen to sixteen hundred for interchange. Now there were seventy-five yard tricks, two general yardmasters, and nineteen yardmasters.

Seven thousand cars a day! There were times in the past fifteen years when yardmen thought they were doing a neat bit of railroading in herding seven thousand shuffling cars a month.

At Argentine Yard, the manpower problem, as elsewhere, has proved to be the greatest difficulty. In normal times any increase in traffic simply meant increasing the yard tricks, but under the scourging whip of war, with its flood of trains and cars, the man and engine power available had to knuckle down and keep the wheels rolling.

Due to the volume of business received west of Chicago and that which originates and interchanges at Argentine Yard, it was necessary to classify and assemble solid trains for California and other points, thus avoiding switching and delays at intermediate terminals.

The interchange work at Argentine Yard is performed by yard crews, similar to road crews. There are classification yards for all connecting line cars. These transfers are made up, waycar coupled on, air brakes tested, and delivered to the specified track in the connecting line yard. Frequently this necessitates using the tracks of other lines, the facilities of which are inadequate. As a result, the indefinite returning time of these crews does not permit the assistant yardmaster to figure the handling of power five minutes in advance.

Trains of men, tanks, guns; trains of fruit; trains of airplane parts; trains of foodstuffs. Through snow, sleet, rain, or fog they come, and day and night they are broken down, switched, classi-

fied, and again sent hurrying on their way by the men of—
Argentine Yard.

C.T.C. ON THE SANTA FE

The volume of traffic that flows over the Santa Fe's Los Angeles–San Diego line is enormous, requiring the operation of one hundred trains a day on portions of the territory, including the movement of helper engines, "running light."

The line is about 118 miles in length, and, except for twenty-four miles of double track, is single iron. Large shipments of citrus fruits originate in this district, necessitating many switching movements. Add to this some twenty-four war industries, among them the largest aircraft plants in the Nation, and the resultant freight and passenger traffic is something to make a railroad man shudder.

Further to gray the hair of Santa Fe officials, the line is beset with many grades and curves, which restrict the speed of trains. Shortly after war was declared, the existing trackage proved entirely inadequate. Double-tracking the line was out of the question, for it would have required precious time and involved the use of critical material.

The crying need for increased track capacity had long since stimulated the use of Centralized Traffic Control all over the country, and the Santa Fe was quick to realize that this modern magician of the rails offered a solution to what threatened to become a serious bottleneck.

Surveys and studies were made, with a view not only to increasing the track capacity but for the intensified utilization of cars and locomotives as well.

The result was the installation of two standard C.T.C. machines, one located at Fullerton, California, twenty-four miles south of Los Angeles; the other at Oceanside, eighty-five miles south of Los Angeles, which placed these machines about midway within the territories they control.

The Fullerton machine controls a thirty-seven-mile stretch of track between El Toro and a point fifteen miles north of Fullerton. It is equipped with twenty-three switch and twenty-three

93

signal levers and the associated indication lights. All switch levers are two-position—normal and reverse. The signals are controlled by three-position levers.

A switch in normal position is indicated by a green light over the normal position of the miniature switch-control lever. A switch in reverse position is indicated by an amber light over the reverse position of the switch-control lever.

When the lever controlling the signals at the end of a passing track is in the center position, the signals are all at *stop*, and this fact is indicated by a red light over the center position of the lever. Moving the lever to the left position clears the northbound signal; moving it to the right clears the southbound signal. The signal that is cleared is so indicated by a green light over the corresponding lever position.

Seventeen toggle switches are located beneath the signal levers for the purpose of controlling electric locks, which are installed at all main-line hand-thrown switches. These locks prevent trainmen from throwing the switch unless permission is obtained from the dispatcher, who sends out a control code to effect an electric *unlock*.

The code-starting push buttons are arranged beneath the toggle switches that control the electric locks. An additional set of toggle switches is provided under the code-starting buttons for the purpose of calling the maintainer in case of trouble.

The standard integral track model is situated directly above the control panel. The normally dark track-occupancy lights, which are inserted in the lines representing the controlled territory, become illuminated red to indicate the presence of a train.

A total of sixty-one lights is provided for the thirty-seven-mile territory controlled by the Fullerton C.T.C. machine, including track-occupancy lights.

The C.T.C. machine at Oceanside controls the territory extending from El Toro, thirty-eight miles north of Oceanside, to San Diego, thirty-eight miles south of Oceanside. Here we find thirty-nine switch and thirty-nine signal levers, together with their associated lights. The progress of trains through controlled territory is indicated by 111 track-occupancy lights.

In order to obtain maximum track capacity on the double-track portions of the line, each track is signaled for train operation in both directions, with the signals controlled by the C.T.C. machine. In other words, each track is operated as a separate single track under full signal protection. Thus, when the preponderance of traffic is southbound, both tracks can be used for southbound trains, or vice versa.

Besides all of their other accomplishments, these two C.T.C. machines talk. A voice-communication system is superimposed on the code line, a calling device that notifies the operator of the machine when a call originates on the line.

BELEN-VAUGHN C.T.C. INSTALLATION

The Chicago to Los Angeles route best known to travelers of the Santa Fe is the line via Kansas City, Missouri, Dodge City, Kansas, La Junta, Colorado, and Albuquerque, New Mexico. Not so well known, but nevertheless of vital importance, is the Panhandle and Pecos Valley route, which branches from the main line at Newton, Kansas, continues westward by way of Wichita and Wellington, Kansas; Waynoka, Oklahoma; and Amarillo, Texas, and so across the famous Texas Panhandle to Dalies a point just west of Belen, New Mexico, where it again joins hands with the Dodge City–La Junta line.

Only four passenger trains a day are operated over the Panhandle and Pecos Valley line, but most of the through freight traffic is handled over this route in order to take advantage of easier grade conditions. In addition, traffic originating at and destined for Galveston, Houston, Fort Worth, and Dallas is handled over this route from Clovis, New Mexico, to Belen. Considering that the line for the most part is single track, the added traffic imposed by the war has caused bottlenecks to exist on certain portions between Clovis and Belen.

Again the Santa Fe turned to Centralized Traffic Control to eliminate the congestion on overburdened portions of this Pecos Division. Hence, it is installing a small two-foot six-inch C.T.C. machine at Clovis, New Mexico, to eliminate the twenty-five-mile westward bottleneck to Melrose, New Mexico. A similar machine will control the eleven-mile overburdened territory extending from Vaughn eastward to Joffre, New Mexico.

The extensive Belen to Vaughn C.T.C. territory, which embraces approximately 109 miles of single track, will be controlled by a fifteen-foot machine situated at Mountainair, New Mexico, with sixty-eight miles of the territory extending east of the machine and forty-one miles west. Switches and signals will be controlled by forty-three switch and forty-three signal levers. Except that it is larger, the machine will be similar to the ones at Oceanside and Fullerton, California.

In general, the grades on the Belen-Vaughn line are undulating and less than one per cent, the exception being twenty-five miles between Mountainair and Becker, where numerous grades as steep as 1.5 per cent are encountered. Curves, for the most part, are easy. The roadbed and track structure are exceptionally well built and carefully maintained, so that high train speeds are possible. The only factor contributing to the bottleneck, therefore, is the tremendous volume of traffic imposed by war conditions.

In planning the C.T.C. installation every consideration was given to providing a facility that would afford the greatest possible increase in track capacity. Both ends of every major passing track used for train meets will be equipped with power switches. Trains, therefore, will not be required to stop while switches are thrown by hand. Train orders, as has been explained in an earlier C.T.C. chapter, will be superseded by signal indications, and delays occurring in the issuance, transmittal, and delivery of train orders will be eliminated. Indication lights on the track model will afford the dispatcher complete, up-to-the-minute information of train progress so that he can establish meeting points on the most efficient possible basis. The movement of trains through the territory will be automatically recorded by a train graph installed on the desk surface of the control machine.

An interesting feature of the Belen-Vaughn installation is that the limits of this line coincide exactly with two consecutive communication carrier repeater stations. The type of communication carrier used provides two channels for telephone and one channel for voice-frequency telegraph. The C.T.C. code line is on the opposite side of the railroad from the communication circuits.

the U.S. Armed Forces really take the military movements over the mountains in wartime. Eastbound main consisting of 15 cars and double-
headed with two 4-8-2 Type Santa Fe 3700
Class being assisted up the west slope of Raton
Pass by #1797, 2-8-8-2 Type. The grade is
3.3%. Photo by Otto C. Perry.

Heat and power for New England. Prior to the war, ocean tanker delivery of oil to the Atlantic seaboard accounted for over 95% of the total reaching this territory. Today deliveries by sea have shrunk to less than 15% with over 85% depending on movement by the railroads. A pair of the original 2-8-4 Type B. & A. Class A-1 double-heading an oil train at Charlton, Massachusetts. Courtesy Lima Locomotive Works.

Scooping water at 60 miles per hour. The east-bound Empire State Express, Train #50, with Engine #5411, Class J-3A, fills tank from the East Palmyra, N.Y. water pan on the Syracuse Division. Courtesy New York Central R.R.

Oil for Great Britain and Russia. New York Central oil train running over the Mohawk Division between Yosts and Fonda behind Engine 2773, Class L-2A 4-8-2 Type, headed for the River Division to Weehawken, N. J., thence overseas. Courtesy New York Central.

The Mercury, New York Central's streamliner between Cleveland, Detroit, and Chicago, leaving Detroit behind a J-3A streamlined 4-6-4. Photo by H. W. Pontin Railroad Photographs.

It will be equipped with filters so that it can be used as a stand-by for the communication carrier circuits. Thus, in the event of a failure of any of these communication circuits between Belen and Vaughn, it will be possible to use the C.T.C. line as a stand-by for this communication service without interfering with the C.T.C. operation.

By accepting Centralized Traffic Control as an effective method of eliminating unnecessary delays that result in congestion, the Santa Fe is providing not only for present conditions but for a highly competitive future.

CHAPTER VIII

THE NEW YORK CENTRAL ENLISTS

Oil Move – The Big Inch – Boston & Albany

The New York Central has written a story in oil that richly deserves to be burned on brass in the railroad hall of fame. Ever since Pearl Harbor, petroleum has provided one of the country's major transportation headaches, its movement entailing serious problems and grave responsibilities, for it is "Hot Cargo" always.

Between February 19 and September 1, 1943, the New York Central hauled 124,193 carloads of oil over a single-track right-of-way deep in a forgotten corner of the state of Illinois. Here, for a time, was one of the hottest stretches of track, concerned with the boiling surge of freight, anywhere in the United States.

The "Big Inch" Pipe Line—the Black Python that crawled sinuously out of Longview, Texas, eventually to lay its head on the doorstep of the sleepy little town of Norris City, immediately swept this community from obscurity into the flaming spotlight of the public eye.

With the coming of this great oil aqueduct, Norris City, Illinois, almost overnight became a roaring boom town, drenched with the black flood disgorged by this great steel snake from the Lone Star State.

Petroleum Co-ordinator Harold Ickes in 1942 was given authority to purchase 534 miles of twenty-four-inch pipe, and when this was laid across the long miles, it reached exactly to Norris City, which was just another "Main Street," drowsing in the sun. Here was a typical American small town, with an occasional coal train trundling past the depot, and one passenger train daily each way. The local station agent was at once operator, ticket seller, baggagemaster, freight clerk, and yardmaster.

And then came the oil boom, and the Norris City station agent found himself directing a bustling depot force consisting of three telegraph operators, one stenographer, nine bill clerks, six yard clerks, and a yardmaster.

Norris City had suddenly become the outgoing rail junction for the oil flowing north through the Big Inch, with as many as 1,211 loaded oil tank cars taking departure in one day, and, of course, an inbound movement of a like number of empties.

Norris City is 170 miles south of Danville, 298 miles south of Chicago, and 90 miles northeast of Cairo at the southernmost tip of the state.

The town is served by the New York Central and a light traffic branch of the Baltimore and Ohio, but, because the latter line would have had to be practically rebuilt to handle its share of the temporary movement, it was decided to use the Central exclusively.

Norris City is situated on what was formerly the Cairo Division of the New York Central (Cleveland, Cincinnati, Chicago & St. Louis), a single-track line extending between Danville and Cairo, a distance of 260 miles. The line was consolidated some years ago with the St. Louis Division, under the jurisdiction of a superintendent whose headquarters are at Mattoon, Illinois.

The former headquarters of the separate Cairo Division, including yards and shops, were located at Mount Carmel, Illinois, forty-four miles north of Norris City. This fact, as we will see, determined the method of operation subsequently employed in the oil movement, Norris City to points east.

The temporary halt of the Big Inch at Norris City threw the entire burden of oil transport at this point onto the shoulders of the New York Central. Eventually, the Big Inch was built through to the eastern seaboard, being placed in operation on this final leg on July 15, 1943. However, since the booster pumping stations along the line were not completed until September 1, the N.Y.C. continued to handle a considerable amount of oil.

In the meantime, a twenty-inch gasoline and products line—the "Little Big Inch"—was constructed as far as Norris City, and the Central also handled its flow. This line, too, was scheduled for the East Coast, but, because of defective pipe, remained unfinished early in 1944.

After the completion of the Big Inch to Norris City, it was tested with water. The water settled in the low portions, and, during the first few weeks after actual pumping of the oil began on February 19, 1943, the line produced about thirty per cent water.

The Big Inch has a theoretical capacity of 300,000 barrels a day. The oil moves at a speed of five miles per hour, which is standard for this line.

On May 19, the line was ruptured and was out of service until May 26. At about that time the Wabash went on a rampage, washing out parts of the railway and its important connections. Continuing high water interrupted train service until June 7. A twenty-inch pipe was installed to detour the break in the Big Inch, which was not repaired until mid-July.

Nevertheless, by a great deal of ingenuity and sweat the Central wheeled through close to 125,000 carloads of oil in less than seven months, a feat that did much to alleviate the shortage on the oil-starved East Coast.

OIL MOVEMENT

The facilities built at Norris City included fifteen storage tanks, with a capacity of 80,000 barrels each. Three loading racks were constructed—two being provided for handling the output of the Big Inch, and the third for the twenty-inch line that delivered gasoline and other petroleum products at this temporary rail–pipe-line junction.

Each loading rack had facilities for the loading of forty-six cars at one time on each side. Oil was loaded at the average rate of fifty cars per hour.

With the big pipe line crawling toward Norris City, the New York Central constructed its own rail terminal facilities, consisting of two yards with six tracks of 300-car capacity each. The railroad, meanwhile, was confronted with the task of setting up the machinery for the oil movement. The road had to fit its operations to existing conditions, which were particularly difficult and exacting by the very nature of things.

There were neither coal nor water stations at Norris City, and the temporary nature of the oil traffic did not justify undue expenditures for their construction. Since yards, engine houses, and complete facilities were available at Mt. Carmel, forty-five miles to the north, it was decided to use this terminal as a base of operations.

The single-track line between Norris City and Mt. Carmel is well built and is laid largely with 105-pound rail, with a few stretches of 90-pound rail. The ruling grade northbound is 0.3 per cent. The passing tracks have a capacity of eighty cars. In normal times, approximately 100,000 cars of coal a year are handled over this line from Harrisburg, Illinois, to Mt. Carmel. In addition, some forty cars of miscellaneous traffic per day each way were handled between Cairo and Evansville.

The coal haul normally is in trains of ninety-five cars, but the addition of the oil movement made it necessary to highball the coal trains over the road on a faster schedule, hence their length was cut to seventy-five cars. The problem of the one passenger train each way was of minor importance.

The oil movement, like all tank-train handling from Texas, was set up on a basis of symbol trains. The oil trains were arranged on a basis of eighty-car drags of empties southbound and seventy-five-car trains of loads northbound. As quickly as the extra five-car lots had been built into seventy-five loads, they were hauled north by an engine and caboose, or light hitch, sent over from Mt. Carmel. Sixty-five engines were assigned to the coal and oil service.

Before the oil rush began, four freight crews were assigned to the south end between Mt. Carmel and Cairo, and nine crews to the north end, Mt. Carmel to Danville. With the introduction of the oil trains, these were increased to eleven assigned crews south and twenty-nine north. This required the transfer of men from other districts and divisions, as well as the hiring of new men. The necessary cabooses were secured from points as far away as the Boston and Albany.

Despite the fact that this heavy movement was handled by a

large number of employees unfamiliar with the road, there were no serious accidents, and the heavy trains roared through with smoothness and precision.

Besides three additional train dispatchers sitting in, there was assigned to the district an assistant trainmaster, a road foreman, and three traveling firemen, all of whom came under the alert eye of a slightly harried but eminently efficient superintendent.

The train movement was accomplished on a turnaround basis. The crew, arriving with a train of empties, turned the engine on the Norris City wye and coupled onto a waiting train of loaded tank cars, received their orders, and highballed out. The southbound empty trains made the trip in about three hours, while the loaded trains thundered northbound in about two hours and forty-five minutes. The run, Mt. Carmel to Norris City and return, required less than eight hours elapsed time.

During the peak oil movement, 10,000 tank cars were assigned to the Norris City pool—10,000 swarming cars, snatching their cargo of black gold at the Norris City terminus of the Big Inch and rushing away, to be caught up by the great, snorting engines of the B.&O., the Pennsy, the Erie, the Lehigh, the Lackawanna, the Boston & Albany, the Boston & Maine—300,000 barrels of vital oil racing down the steel rail in tank cars, from Norris City to seaboard, every twenty-four hours. Ten thousand cars rushing over the New York Central's crowded single-track iron in southern Illinois to the oil-thirsty cities of the East.

The speed of these oil trains, made up of many old tank cars, lacking the more modern design, had to be held down to forty miles an hour, for, without the snubbers built into the newer cars, a vertical motion called "dancing" was set up, which had a tendency to cause break-in-twos.

OPERATIONS AT MT. CARMEL

The Mt. Carmel terminal is double-tracked for four miles and consists of three yards. The North Yard is the shop yard. The Middle Yard, where empty cars are handled, consists of seven tracks and has a capacity of about three hundred cars.

Most of the buildings and equipment at Mt. Carmel were

fairly modern. Light repairs were made at the modern sixteen-stall roundhouse. Four new tracks comprised the only additional facilities required to handle the oil rush.

The Mt. Carmel terminal customarily handles between 1,300 and 1,400 cars a day in and out. With the coming of the oil boom at Norris City, as many as 5,500 cars were handled in one day. The average was between 4,700 and 4,800. Six yard engines on staggered shifts served the yards. The maximum movement was thirty-nine trains, in and out, a day.

The North Yard repair tracks have a capacity of eighty cars. Prior to the oil movement, two men were employed here. To meet the needs of the booming oil trains, this force was increased to forty-two men, of whom thirty were employed in repair and maintenance work. All repairs and inspection were made at Mt. Carmel, there being no facilities for this work at Norris City.

Empty tank cars averaged five per cent bad order, and loaded cars less than four per cent. Wheel defects were by far the most common source of trouble, and about two carloads per day were required for replacements at the height of the oil movement.

The Mt. Carmel yards were supervised by a general yardmaster, four yardmasters, and a relief yardmaster. The clerical force in normal times consists of three yard clerks and a relief man. This was increased to thirteen yard clerks and a relief man. The force of switchmen was doubled.

Empty trains, on the average, were detained at Mt. Carmel about two hours and forty-five minutes; loaded trains averaged less than an hour in this terminal.

Turnaround crews took oil trains to Lawrenceville, north of Mt. Carmel, for the B.&O. connection, and returned with empties. On the main-line movement of the St. Louis Division to Indianapolis, crews changed at Paris, Illinois, the junction point, but the locomotives ran through. Engines also ran through to Danville. So far as possible, the New York Central and its connecting lines exchanged information relative to the movement of oil trains, and synchronized the arrival and departure of the fast-moving oil at junction points.

To destinations such as Pittsburgh, the turnaround of cars averaged six and one-half days; eastern Pennsylvania and some

New Jersey points, eight days, and the most distant points, ten days.

The destinations and routes from Norris City follow:

Destination	Route—N.Y.C. to
Twin Oaks, Pa.	Lawrenceville—B. & O.
Blissville, N. Y.	Black Rock—D.L. & W.
Bayonne, N. J.	Suspension Bridge—L.V.
Bayway, N. J.	Black Rock—D.L.&W.—
	Hampton—C.N.J.
Girard Point, Pa.	Indianapolis—Penn.
Marcus Hook, Pa.	West Newberry—Reading
Everett, Mass.	Mechanicsville—B. & M.
Baltimore, Md.	Lawrenceville—B. & O.
Point Breeze, Pa.	Indianapolis—Penn.
Petty's Island, N. J.	Indianapolis—Penn.
Fall River, Mass.	Marion—Erie—Maybrook—
	N.Y.N.H. & H.
Pittsburgh, Pa.	Indianapolis—Penn.

And so the Hot Cargo that was oil from the Big Inch Pipe Line at Norris City rolled east. On February 19, 1944, Petroleum Administrator Ickes announced that the so-called Big Inch line had delivered from Texas to the East Coast more than 88,000,000 barrels of oil in its first year of operation. As a matter of fact, for seven months in 1943 the New York Central operated up to thirty trains a day both ways on a single track, transporting the

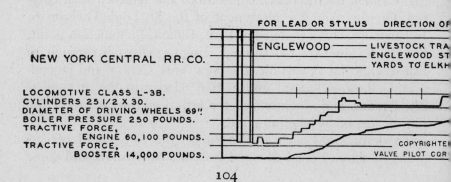

104

oil from the then incompleted Big Inch. When petroleum and its products were desperately needed in the East, the Central and other railroads delivered the goods.

From the records we here list the tank car movement on a typical day—July 8, 1943:

Tank cars loaded previous 24 hours at Norris City	982
Loaded cars billed and on hand for movement at	
5 A.M.	135
Empties placed for loading at Norris City	99
Empties on hand at Norris City not placed	0
Empties en route, Mt. Carmel–Norris City	159
Empties on hand at Mt. Carmel	308
Empties on hand at Lawrenceville	50
Empties en route, Midland to Mt. Carmel	320
Empties on hand at Midland	60
Empties on hand at Lyons	92
Empties on hand at Indianapolis	100
Empties en route, Indianapolis-Midland	72

Long trains of grimy tank cars—fuel for the flaming torch of Liberty. A masterpiece in oils. Once more the Iron Horse and a steel rail had served the Nation in a crisis. A steel rail over which runs the world-famous *Twentieth Century Limited*, premier train of the East.

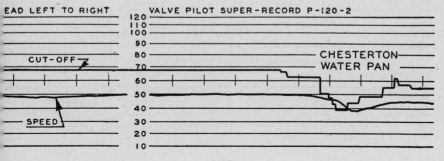

BOSTON AND ALBANY

War places railroads under tremendous strain, revealing their true capabilities and importance to the Nation they serve. This has been, and is, true of the Boston & Albany, a division of the New York Central System.

Because of its location, the Boston & Albany is of strategic importance to New England and the port of Boston. Certainly nothing of the importance of this road as a main artery of traffic in times of peace and war has lessened since it first inaugurated through service in 1841 under the name of the Boston & Worcester and the Western Railroad.

Since 1939, the freight haul on the Boston & Albany has increased 300 per cent, and passenger traffic 50 per cent. The B.&A., safeguarded by automatic signals and automatic train control, with a stone-ballasted roadbed and double-tracked with 105- and 127-pound rail, was quickly adapted to meet the emergencies of war.

Linking the capitals of Massachusetts and New York, the B.&A. vaults the Berkshire Mountains, while its steel rail spins its bright path through the industrial cities of Worcester, Springfield, and Pittsfield. From sea level, the line lifts to an elevation of 1,452 feet at Washington, Mass. Almost half of its main track is on curvature, with one bridge, of ten feet or more, per mile of right-of-way.

The double-tracked main line, 199 miles in length, has 102 miles of tangent and 97 miles of curve, mostly in the rugged,

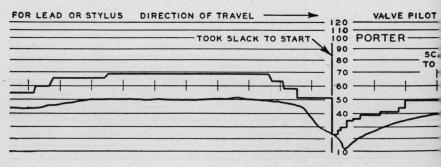

beautiful Berkshires. The heaviest grade eastbound is between North Adams Junction and Hinsdale, Massachusetts, averaging 1.42 per cent, with a maximum of 1.51 per cent; the heaviest westbound grade, over a distance of twenty-four miles between Russell and Washington, averages .95 per cent with a maximum of 1.65 per cent.

To handle heavy commuter traffic, the Boston & Albany has four main-line tracks between Boston and Framingham, a distance of twenty-one miles. It further has seventy miles of triple-track, located primarily where the heavier grades occur. The total trackage of the road, including its fourteen branch lines, is 1,021 miles.

The Boston & Albany maintains seventeen freight interchange points with four foreign roads—namely, the New York, New Haven & Hartford, the Boston & Maine, the Rutland, and the Central Vermont. Normally, the road operates eight eastbound and seven westbound through trains between Boston and Albany and points west. It also maintains through Boston–New York passenger service via Springfield over the N.Y.N.H.&H., New York to Springfield; and the B.&A., Springfield to Boston. South Station, Boston, the eastern terminus of the line, handles one of the largest volumes of commuter traffic in the world over the rails of the B.&A. and the N.Y.N.H.&H.

The Boston & Albany owns 225 locomotives, 3,210 freight cars and 347 passenger cars.

The mighty giants of the freight service haul eighty loaded cars over the Berkshires. Fifty-five locomotives are of the 2-8-4 type,

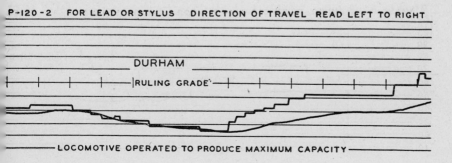

P-120-2   FOR LEAD OR STYLUS   DIRECTION OF TRAVEL READ LEFT TO RIGHT

DURHAM

RULING GRADE

LOCOMOTIVE OPERATED TO PRODUCE MAXIMUM CAPACITY

known as the "Berkshires," and named for the famous Berkshire Hills in western Massachusetts. These are Class A-1s, with a tractive effort of 69,400 pounds, stepped up to 81,400 pounds by boosters.

Other freight engines are 2-8-2 Mikados and 2-8-0 Consolidations, of 48,570 and 45,680 pounds of tractive power respectively. Five Diesel switchers are located in the Boston territory.

Queens of the passenger service are twenty Hudson-type, J-2 locomotives, with a 4-6-4 wheel arrangement, and a tractive effort of 44,800 pounds, increased by booster to 55,320 pounds. They are assisted on the main line by fifteen Pacific-type, K-14s, of the usual 4-6-2 wheel arrangement, and tractive power of 39,420 pounds. Smaller Pacifics are used in local service.

Unusual locomotives used by the B.&A. in suburban service are a double-ender type, which makes a turnaround of the engine unnecessary at the end of its run. Five of these have a wheel arrangement of 4-6-6, with a tractive power of 41,600 pounds and eighteen others, with a 2-6-6 wheel arrangement, and a tractive power of 34,260 pounds.

There are no shops for heavy repairs on the Boston & Albany. All such work on both locomotives and rolling stock has been done, since 1941, at the New York Central shops at West Albany, New York.

Light repairs, however, are made on locomotives at engine terminals, and on passenger coaches at the Exeter Street Yard, Boston, and on freight cars in the yards at West Springfield and Beacon Park, Boston.

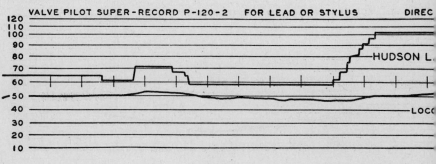

The largest freight yard, located at West Springfield, has a total capacity of 3,270 cars. This is the main classification yard for westbound trains, with a capacity of 1,698 cars. The eastbound yard capacity is 1,417. Here, also is a car-repair yard for 155 cars.

The Beacon Park Yard, on the main line at Allston, and yards on the Grand Junction Branch, terminating in East Boston, serve the industries of Boston and the railroad's own docks and piers. The former has a total capacity of 2,058 cars; the latter, 1,205.

The Terminal at East Boston, now devoted solely to the Nation's war effort, covers an area of 43.32 acres. Located directly on the main ship channel of the port of Boston, it has four large piers and a grain elevator, which is the largest in New England, with a capacity of 1,000,000 bushels.

The tracks of the Terminal are so arranged that it is possible for switch engines to work on each of the piers without interfering with one another. Two piers are also connected with the grain elevator by conveyors.

Selkirk Yard, southwest of Albany, New York, although not a B.&A. yard, is of vast importance to its freight service. All freight leaving the New York Central main line for the Boston & Albany, or coming off that railroad, passes through this yard.

Many eastbound through freights from the Central's main line are previously classified at DeWitt Yard, East Syracuse, and receive at Selkirk only a new train crew and their Berkshire locomotive. Some classification, however, is done here to consolidate trains from the New York Central main line and the West Shore

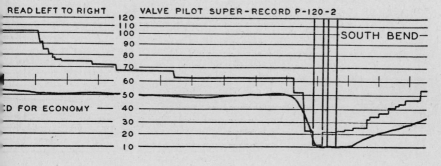

for eastbound movement over the Boston & Albany. This operation is reversed for westbound movement.

The largest passenger car yard on the B.&A. is the Exeter Street Yard in Boston. Here cars are cleaned, serviced, and light repairs made. Here, also, the New York Central Dining Car Service maintains a commissary for its thirteen dining cars moving over the rails of the Boston & Albany. Other passenger car yards are located at Worcester and Springfield, Massachusetts, and Rensselaer, New York.

WAR FREIGHT ON THE B.&A.

Every main category of freight leaped in volume of traffic on the Boston & Albany between 1939 and 1942. The sharpest increases were made in the products of mines and manufactured products.

The principal reason for the increase of volume in mine products was the transfer to rail shipment of former water-borne crude petroleum and coal. The most spectacular increase was the oil movement. In 1939 the Boston & Albany hauled a mere trickle of 527 tons of crude petroleum to New England refineries, the great bulk moving in tankers in coastwise service.

Came then an inundation. Oil! Hitler's undersea wolf pack was on the prowl. American tankers were driven from the sea lanes. We were caught with our guard down. Grimy tank cars, long slumbering in yards and side tracks, were rushed into the

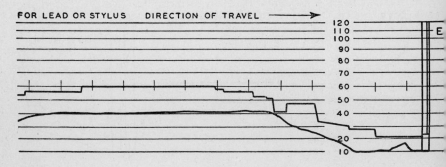

breach. Is it too much to say that the country's railroads and those rusting tank cars staved off disaster?

On the Boston & Albany, that 527-ton haul of oil in 1939 swelled to a roaring black river of 1,529,828 tons in 1942! The railroads, often derided, rose to meet the threat; they warded off the clutching, bloody fingers of the mad beasts of Berlin and Tokyo. How did they do it? By being better prepared than any other agency in America. For ten years they had been fighting a war—a bitter, relentless war created by economic collapse. This condition, which had throttled industry as a whole, simply served to toughen the railroads, to awaken them. With a steel rail as a cudgel, American Railroads beat back the onrushing forces that sought to destroy us.

The Boston & Albany and other railroads of New England, by their outstanding and amazing performance in delivering oil and coal, saved the people of the states they serve indescribable hardship and privation during a severely cold winter.

In the movement of freight on the Boston & Albany, the following increases occurred from 1939 to 1942: Refined oils and gasoline, 154,790 tons to 1,019,844 tons; fuel oils from 123,658 to 1,381,843 tons; iron and steel manufactures, 391,339 to 793,301 tons; canned foods, 63,467 to 135,400 tons; miscellaneous manufactures, 1,007,533 to 1,540,255 tons. The only decline was in the shipment of automobiles, falling from 41,398 to 4,984 tons.

Heavy eastbound shipments consist of coal, oil, iron, and steel. Westbound freight is primarily manufactured goods and less than carload shipments, the greater proportion of which today is materials for war.

A great little road, the Boston & Albany has stoutly placed its shoulder to the wheel of caissons rolling to war.

CHAPTER IX

IRON ORE FOR WAR

Ore Haul of the D.M.&I.R. and G.N.

Red earth from the great open-pit mines of Minnesota is fast writing epitaphs on the tombstones of Hideki Tojo and Adolf Hitler. Shot and shell screaming from mighty guns, that yesterday were ore in the Mesabi Range. Battleships and tanks, born in the upper Great Lakes country, smashing through to Victory.

A kid from Duluth trips the release of the bomb rack in a Fortress, a Liberator, and cries, "Bombs away!" He sits back, tight-lipped. Once more he has delivered a load of concentrated hell on the doorstep of the enemy—packages of devastating destruction, fashioned from the red dust that but a short time before was riding the ore trains of the Duluth, Missabe and Iron Range, the Great Northern, and other railroads of America.

Mother Earth, from her rich bounty, sustains mankind. Ironically, she also spawns the weapons that destroy him.

In the northeastern corner of Minnesota, lying between Lake Superior and the Canadian border, there is a rough triangle that, because of its conformation, is known as the "Arrowhead Country." Here is one of the richest iron ore regions in the world.

The famous Mesabi, Vermilion, Cuyuna, and lesser ranges are pouring into the caldron of war iron ore in an amount that beggars description.

World War I saw 65,000,000 tons of ore rolling from the pits to the docks for a year's output. In 1942 the Duluth, Missabi and Iron Range road alone hauled 45,000,000 tons. Some 92,000,000 tons of high grade moved out of this region altogether in that year behind the roaring engines of the Iron Range line, the Great

Eastbound Chicago-New York meat train on the New York Central with connections from the Rock Island and other western roads approaching Wayneport coaling station, only refueling point for passenger trains between New York and Chicago, located on the Syracuse Division. Engine 2860 is 4-8-2 Type Class L-2C. Courtesy New York Central.

New York Central's world-famous Twentieth Century Limited between Croton and Harmon, New York, at the end of the suburban electrification, hauled by a Class J-3A streamlined 4-6-4 Type. This magnificent train's wartime make-up consists of 17 cars always filled to the last berth by people whose wartime business takes them to or through New York and Chicago, the nation's largest cities. Courtesy of N. Y. C.

Great Northern 3-unit Diesel cut into eastbound manifest train #446 sixteen cars behind road engine 2039, 2-8-8-2 Type Class R-1, to assist up Walton Hill on the 1.6% grade between Blacktail and Summit, Montana on the Second Subdivision of the Kalispell Division. Courtesy Great Northern.

#1, the Great Northern's westbound Empire Builder with Engine 2588 oil-burning 4-8-4, first in this country to be built with 80-inch driving wheels, crossing the Flathead west of Glacier Park, Montana, on the Second Subdivision of the Kalispell Division. Photo by Otto C. Perry.

A 12,000-ton Great Northern ore train behind engine #2024, 2-8-8-0 Type Class N-3, enters the main line at Gunn, Minnesota en route to the company's docks at Allouez (Superior, Wisconsin). Note the Great Northern's excellent train order board signals which are in service over the entire system. Courtesy Great Northern.

Iron ore vessels being loaded at the Great Northern's Allouez docks. The docks are the largest and most modern of their kind in the world and the importance of this entire operation in its aid to the war effort cannot be overemphasized. Courtesy Great Northern.

Great Northern 3-Unit 4050 H.P. Diesel helping the Empire Builder #2 over Walton Hill where the railroad crosses the Continental Divide through the famous Marias Pass, Montana. The road engine is Class S-2, 4-8-4 Type. Courtesy Great Northern.

The east slope of the Alleghenies on the Pittsburgh Division of the Pennsylvania is a busy piece of railroad during wartime. This picture shows a 2-10-0 Type Class I-1 helping the road engine Class M-1 4-8-2 Type with a preference train up the 1.8 grade rounding the famous Horseshoe Curve. Two more I-1's are assisting at the rear end.
Photo by H. W. Pontin Railroad Photographs.

Northern, the Northern Pacific, and the Soo Line. 1943 saw 84,404,852 tons.

But let us turn back the pages for a moment. Ore was discovered in this district in 1872, but it was not until 1883 that the Duluth and Iron Range Railroad began the construction of its sixty-eight miles of line from Tower, in the Vermilion Range, to Agate Bay—now Two Harbors—on the shores of Lake Superior, about twenty-seven miles northeast of Duluth.

In 1892 the great open-pit mines of the Mesabi Range were opened with the building of the Duluth, Missabe and Northern, which brought the ore down to the docks at Duluth and Superior.

In 1930, the Duluth, Missabe and Northern leased the Duluth and Iron Range Railroad, and in 1937 the two properties were joined into the present Duluth, Missabe and Iron Range Railway. This road operates a total of 542 miles, and fully ninety-five per cent of its business is the transportation of ore to the Lake Superior ports. It serves the Mesabi Range as far west as Coleraine. This range includes Hibbing, where is located the great Hull-Rust-Mahoning Mine, the largest open-pit mine in the world. The D.M.&I.R. is the only railroad penetrating into the Vermilion Range, which lies close to the Canadian border.

All of the ore is hauled during the eight months from April to November when traffic is open through the Great Lakes. Road trains average approximately nine thousand tons of ore per trip on the Missabe Division and about six thousand tons on the Iron Range Division where the grades are heavier. The running time southbound varies from two and one-half to four hours over distances ranging from sixty-five to ninety miles. Maximum speed permitted with loaded ore trains is thirty miles per hour.

The ore delivered to the docks at Two Harbors, Duluth, and Superior is loaded into lake steamers and transported through the Soo Canal, thence to South Chicago, Indiana Harbor, and Gary on Lake Michigan, or to Cleveland, Ashtabula, and Conneaut on Lake Erie. From these ports much of the ore moves by rail to the great steel-producing area around Pittsburgh.

The Iron Horse has served well and faithfully the roads comprising the Duluth, Missabe and Iron Range. But one in particular stands out. This is the old *Three Spot*, a 2-6-0 Mogul, built by Baldwin and delivered at Agate Bay in 1883.

The first job assigned the *Three Spot* was that of hauling supplies for the construction of the line into the iron country. Following the completion of the road in 1884, the *Three Spot* was used in freight service. In 1889 it was sold to the Duluth and Northern Minnesota Railway and was set to hauling logs. Thirty-four years later, in 1923, this stouthearted old engine was purchased by the Duluth and Iron Range Thirty Year Veterans' Association. It was restored to its original appearance, and the once-rusty, grimed old engine, now in a bright new dress, went to stand as a permanent exhibit outside the station at Two Harbors.

The tender bears a bronze shield—the gift of the late Samuel M. Vauclain, for many years president of the Baldwin Locomotive Works—on which are inscribed the names of the members of the Veterans' Association.

One can imagine that the old *Three Spot* is pretty happy that she was not sold to Japan to be made into guns for the little yellow men.

Exhibited along with the *Three Spot* are typical wooden ore cars and a caboose of the 1884 period. We would like to see more exhibits like this beside the railroad stations of America. The Thirty Year Veterans certainly did a fine thing.

Close to one hundred Baldwin locomotives have seen service on the lines of the present Duluth, Missabe and Iron Range Railway. This list includes 2-8-0 type Consolidations of the 1905-10 period, ten Mikados built between 1913 and 1923, as well as Pacifics and heavy eight- and ten-wheel switchers.

As early as 1910, the traffic became so heavy that a number of Mallet locomotives, having a 2-8-8-2 wheel arrangement, were purchased from Baldwin. These were followed, in 1916 and 1917, by still heavier Mallets. Several of these old locomotives have been converted to single-expansion engines and are still hauling their quota of iron ore. The early Consolidation- and Mikado-type locomotives are used in yard service around the mines or at the docks.

The increased tonnage necessary to meet the National Defense

Program demanded far more powerful locomotives. As a result, the road placed in service eight Baldwin locomotives that are among the most powerful in the world today.

The new locomotives, Class M-3, are of the single-expansion articulated type, with cylinders 26 x 32 inches, driving wheels 63 inches in diameter, and a working steam pressure of 240 pounds per square inch. They develop a tractive effort of 140,000 pounds. Weight on drivers is 560,257 pounds, and the total weight of engine and tender is 1,131,675 pounds. They have one-piece cast steel locomotive beds with integral cylinders, and all wheels of both engine and tender are fitted with roller bearings. The tender has a capacity of 25,000 gallons of water and 26 tons of coal.

In referring to these engines, P. M. Sullivan, Superintendent of Motive Power and Cars of the Duluth, Missabe and Iron Range Railway, stated:

"These locomotives broke in with practically full tonnage and were released for pool service after three supervised trips. No trouble was encountered during break-in or subsequent trips. No alterations and very few adjustments were necessary. The locomotives steamed perfectly and exceeded the expected fuel performance.

"The 25,000-gallon tender permits through runs from docks to mines, eliminating intermediate water stops, while the coal capacity of 26 tons is generally sufficient for a round trip. The roller bearings, force-feed lubrication and the type of side-rod lubrication make it unnecessary for enginemen to service the locomotives at terminals as required with previous types."

A feature of these ore-hauling behemoths of the D.M.&I.R. that immediately catches the eye is the wheel arrangement on the tenders, which are carried at the front by a four-wheeled truck back of which are five pairs of wheels mounted in pedestals cast integral with the bed. Seven forty-two-inch wheels to a side give the long rectangular tender the appearance of a huge iron centipede.

The arrival of these engines created a great deal of public interest. People went for them like a kid for a red cart. Local papers played them up, and admirers came to stand beside the old

Three Spot to have their pictures taken. Folks gathered at wayside stations and crossroads to watch them go roaring through, pulses quickening, eyes bright.

Bigger locomotives meant more ore hauled from the mines, which foretold greater prosperity for northern Minnesota where iron is gold. These engines, too, meant greater aid in the war effort, which suddenly overshadowed everything else late in that memorable year of 1941.

Having proved themselves over a period of two years, the eight mighty locomotives were augmented in 1943 by ten more, practically identical in design, with a classification of M-4.

These huge engines will handle all the ore on the Iron Range Division from the mines to the docks at Two Harbors. This includes the eighty-mile run from Ely, in the Vermilion Range, and the sixty-five-mile haul from Virginia, in the Mesabi Range. The round-trip run from Ely to Two Harbors requires twelve hours, and the round trip from Virginia about ten hours.

There are numerous adverse grades, the heaviest of which is one of 0.62 per cent.

The ore is hauled in short high ore cars, which hold from fifty to seventy-five tons. The 6,000 gross tons of ore per trip is an increase of about twenty-five per cent over the best tonnage hauled by the converted Mallets. The new power steams freely and has proved its ability to handle this heavy tonnage with worth-while reduction in fuel and water required per thousand gross ton-miles as compared with the locomotives previously used.

In the present war-emergency, these engines are lent to other roads during the winter months when the lake freighters are frozen up.

The great, fiery-tongued blast furnaces at Pittsburgh, Cleveland, and Gary are roaring out their challenge to the world. Steel is in the making—steel for war. Greedily these crucibles of the mills, with their hot yellow breath, are devouring the red earth of the iron ranges of the Arrowhead Country in far-off Minnesota.

The transportation of ore, scooped from the great crimson-gashed mine pits by Titanic steel hands, involves three stages. It moves first by rail from the mines to the Upper Lake docks, thence by boat to the Lower Lake docks, and finally by rail from these lake ports to the steel mills.

Before the ore train leaves the mine, ore samples are taken from a predetermined group of cars and analyzed, for there are many grades and types of this red dust, destined to go into the manufacture of various steel products.

The chemists at the mine work in the laboratory while the train is thundering to dockside. The accuracy of their analysis is uncanny, and the amount of iron, phosphorous, silica, and manganese is held to within a small fraction of one per cent of the mix specified.

When the tests are concluded, the result is telegraphed to the yardmaster at the classification yard at the lake front. Based on the analysis of the ore samples, the groaning gondolas are grouped to make up a boatload of the particular ore specified by the steel mill to which the shipment is consigned. These cars are then moved to the docks.

The Duluth, Missabe and Iron Range Railway owns three docks at Two Harbors. These are 900, 1,000, and 1,300 feet in length respectively. They are approximately seventy-five feet wide, with decks eighty feet above the lake level.

These trestle-like structures are so arranged that the ore boats can be moored along both sides. Strings of loaded ore cars are run up onto this framework and spotted over receiving hoppers. The ore is then dumped into pockets under the tracks. From these bins the ore is fed by gravity through chutes into the holds of the ore boats.

The big lake vessels, which are designed specifically for this service, will hold from 8,000 to 15,000 tons of ore, with larger boats now under construction.

Six boats can be loaded simultaneously from the three docks at Two Harbors, the entire operation, involving the transfer of some 60,000 tons of ore, being accomplished in about four hours. Having dumped their loads, the empties are moved out and more heavy-laden cars replace them.

All around the clock the ore moves, limited only by the boats available. The total shipment through Two Harbors alone in 1942

117

was 11,000,000 tons. In 1943 the D.M.&I.R. handled 40,649,364 tons.

The story of the ore movement here has been devoted almost exclusively to the Iron Range Division of the D.M.&I.R. because of the new Baldwin locomotives in service here. Older engines are moving ore on the Missabe Division from Hibbing to the docks at Duluth, which handled more than half of the total ore tonnage moved from the mines by the Duluth, Missabe and Iron Range Railway.

Once the red earth of Minnesota's mines reaches the great blast furnaces of the steel mills, the trail widens to all of the industrial centers of the United States, and eventually to almost every last corner of the world. Ships, bridging the oceans; locomotives, linking the cities and towns of the Nation; airplane motors, droning in the heavens; bombs and shells, aimed at the crumbling ramparts of Hideki Tojo and Adolf Hitler.

GREAT NORTHERN ORE MOVEMENT

"Give us the boats and you will have the ore!" That is the cry of the railroad men of the sprawling iron range of Minnesota.

Great Northern locomotive No. 2024, the quivering needle of the steam gauge standing at 275 pounds, is cannonading the night with her exhaust. Stretched behind the big articulated engine is a mile-long train of straining ore cars—better than 11,000 tons—moving in on the ore docks at Allouez.

Engine No. 231, of the D.M.&I.R., pulling out of the Mesabi Range with an ore train. Engines of the Northern Pacific and the Soo Line beating out the miles on glimmering steel, reaching away to the lake shore.

The 2018, G.N. Mallet, dragging 175 empty ore cars out of Superior. A deep-laden ore boat disappearing into the blue haze of Lake Superior. Iron ore is on the move—iron ore for war.

"There is no authenticated record of any war plant having closed down for lack of steel."

This published statement of Walter S. Tower, president of the American Iron and Steel Institute, constitutes a fine tribute not only to the country's steel industry, but equally so to American Railroads and the boatmen of the Great Lakes.

The Great Northern transported nearly twenty-five million tons of the Minnesota ore production in 1943, one of the largest ore-hauling assignments in the company's history. Transport of this tremendous tonnage from the sixty-five mines served by the G.N. required an average daily delivery during most of the season of ten trains of some eleven thousand tons of ore each to the company's Allouez docks in Superior, Wisconsin. Eleven boatloads a day, nosing out of Allouez Bay, to start the long trip across broad Lake Superior, through the Soo Canal, down the length of Lake Huron, through the locks at Sault Sainte Marie, across Lake Erie to the ore port of Cleveland. This is the steel industry's vital service of supply.

Twelve hundred miles of land and water between the iron range and the converters and furnaces at Youngstown and Pittsburgh. The navigation season on the Great Lakes did not open in 1943 until well along in April because of the unusually late formations of ice, and then, all during the summer months, the ore boats were hampered by thick and persistent fogs. As one veteran ore boat skipper put it, "No amount of war planning can do anything about the weather on the Great Lakes."

The Great Northern Railway, "Route of the Empire Builder," spins its network of steel from the Great Lakes to the Pacific. Its motive power consists of Diesel, electric, coal, and oil-burning locomotives, each designed for a specific job.

Men and supplies for all the theaters of war move over the rails of the Great Northern. Its thundering freight trains carry armament, steel, explosives, aluminum, magnesium, lumber, plywood, a vast list of foodstuffs, and—iron ore.

In 1940, the Great Northern rebuilt twenty-five old Mallet locomotives of the 2-8-8-0 type, investing nearly $3,500,000 in motive power for the specialized transportation of iron ore. These engines are the N-3 class, and their weight, with tender, is 863,700 pounds. They have a tender capacity of 21,500 gallons of water, and twelve of the twenty-five carry twenty-four tons of coal. They are performing a mighty task in the ore-haul movement.

Kelly Lake, five miles southwest of Hibbing, Minnesota, and the great Mahoning open-pit mine, is one of the largest concentration points in the iron country. This yard, with a track capacity of about 2,000 cars, receives its ore from feeder lines, spinning their web through the range.

Something like 1,800 cars a day were handled at Kelly Lake during the 220-day season of 1943. Empty gondolas move in; loaded ore cars move out. They move them fast at Kelly Lake.

And now we come again to that word "utilization," which has to do with getting the most possible miles out of every locomotive on the line. All roads are hard-pressed for locomotives in wartime, and the Great Northern is no exception.

To insure maximum performance, the Great Northern has a fixed locomotive schedule, and each engine on the ore run makes the more than 215-mile round trip between Allouez and Kelly Lake each day.

Let us ride with Engineer Bill Barton in the cab of the 2024 out of Allouez. It is 5 A.M. Behind us reaches a long string of empties. We battle up the "hill" toward the range and Kelly Lake.

Arriving at the yard, Trainmaster Walter Elliot orders the crew to continue with our train to Calumet, to the west. The 2024 is coaled and watered at the roundhouse, and five minutes later we are on our way. Shortly after noon, with close to eleven thousand tons of iron ore behind us, we swing onto the main line of the G.N. at Gunn, Minnesota, and highball for Allouez, arriving at the lake front with a total of 240 mauling miles for the day's work.

Ore trains are dispatched as extras, operating under straight running orders. Little or no time is lost in taking sidings or in other delays that often slow rail operation.

Each carload of ore is weighed as it passes over a track scale. Yardmen work three shifts, with floodlights to aid night operations. When heavy fogs sweep in from the lake, a special radiophone device is used for communication between the cabs of switching engines and the yard crews. Often, in the fall and spring, the ore freezes solidly in the cars before it can be unloaded, and it is necessary to free it with steam.

We have already observed the manner in which the ore is analyzed and the cars grouped in the yards at the docks. The steel companies notify the railroad—in this case, the Great Northern—when their boats are to be expected, and include instructions regarding the type of ore required. The ship captain, twelve to fifteen miles out in Lake Superior, calls the dockmaster, using his ship-to-shore telephone, which allows the cars with the proper mix for this specific cargo to be spotted and their contents dumped into the ore pockets.

The Great Northern has four ore docks at Allouez, the longest of which is 2,244 feet, with a total of 1,352 ore bins. The full dock capacity at Allouez is 440,000 tons. One boat will take 160 to 250 carloads of ore. These are switched out of the some 3,000 hopper cars crowding the Great Northern's classification tracks at Allouez.

The Great Northern Railway, caught in the vicious maelstrom of war, had little time to build up its plant facilities. But, as did so many other railroads, it had prepared in the lean depression years to meet the turn of fortune that was bound to come, as witness the reconstruction in its shops of those twenty-five workhorse Articulateds that today are valiantly doing their part to supply the ore that makes for the building of the sinews of war.

When enemy submarines shut off the ore previously moving to the great steel plants at Sparrows Point, Maryland, from Brazil and other South American countries, America had to look to the Minnesota iron range for the added supply of which it was thus deprived.

As a result, *ninety-nine* per cent of the ore that went into the insatiable maws of American steel mills moved to the Upper Lake ports over the rails of the Great Northern, the Duluth, Missabe and Iron Range, the Northern Pacific, and the Soo Line, thence down the stormy inland seas that are the Great Lakes in the holds of our valiant fleet of ore boats.

CHAPTER X

THE PENNSYLVANIA SERVES THE NATION

Record Ore Move – Peak Passenger Travel

The American Railroads have provided a vital link in a wartime mine-to-mill transportation miracle that has poured necessary millions of extra tons of iron ore into the steel furnaces of the country. By so doing, the railroads have guaranteed an uninterrupted flow of steel for war, a flow that has reached the staggering total of nearly 182,000,000 tons of steel produced in United States steel mills during the two years that followed the declaration of war.

The Pennsylvania Railroad has played a leading part in this record-breaking ore move. The main supply of iron ore fed into the big steel mills of the eastern industrial states from Lake Erie ports moved over the rails of the Pennsylvania. In this dock-to-mill movement, this road, in the first ten months of 1943, transported over thirty-four per cent of the total tonnage of ore hauled by all railroads. During those ten months, which constitute the peak season, the P.R.R. hauled 13,462,006 gross tons.

The total tonnage moved by all railroads from Lake Erie ports in 1943 fell off slightly from the 44,136,495 tons handled in 1942, for the reason that the navigation season on the Great Lakes, as was pointed out in the foregoing chapter, did not open until late. However, when the lake freighters at last did begin to steam south from those far-northern ore docks, dock and railroad workers combined to unload and haul ore in a manner never before equaled. Yet, though there were some four to six weeks less in which to do the job, they came close to moving as much ore as was handled in 1942.

As an example, in November of 1943, a new record was established at the Pennsylvania ore dock in Cleveland, when 1,003 cars loaded with iron ore moved out of the dockyards in a single day. On May 9 of that year 898 cars were loaded with 57,811 tons over a twenty-four-hour period. Actually the dock machinery was in operation just twenty-one hours and thirty-five minutes, which reveals a picture of pretty close to forty-five tons handled every minute over that period. This is moving ore with a vengeance and is a striking illustration of the spirit of men on the civilian front.

Cleveland, Ohio, is the focal point for ore distribution, and to this port come the ore boats from the mines of the upper Great Lakes district. The ore movement from the Upper Lakes is today a far cry from those early times when iron ore was shipped in barrels in little schooners, which had to cope with the vicious rapids at Sault Sainte Marie, connecting the Upper and Lower Lake systems. Ore in those days was unloaded above the rapids; then reloaded in other small boats below the rapids. In 1855 the canal at Sault Sainte Marie was completed, and the efficient ore-boat movement of the present day assured.

The small ore boats graduated from schooner and brig to the whaleback; then to the modern bulk freighter of 15,000-ton capacity. The demands of today's war production program recently brought construction, under the U. S. Maritime Commission, of nearly a score of fine new boats. The new MacArthur lock at Sault Sainte Marie has been completed; thus the expanding ore fleet may sail speedily from the Upper Lake ports to Lower Lake destinations.

At Cleveland, the Pennsylvania Railroad maintains its largest single ore dock, which is the second largest in all of the Lower Lake "feeder" ports for eastern steel mills.

In 1943, nearly 85,000,000 tons of ore moved on the Lakes, and this Pennsylvania dock handled just under nine per cent of the total. Other large ore docks are located at Ashtabula, Ohio, and Erie, Pennsylvania.

We turn now to the unloading of an ore boat. The *Lehigh* has just been sighted coming through the breakwater. She has already been reported by ship-to-shore telephone, and everything is in readiness. Deck hands and dock hands are standing by.

Empty ore cars are waiting in what is known as the River Bed Yards.

As the *Lehigh* moves in and makes ready to tie up, we observe that all hatch doors have been rolled back in preparation for unloading. The boat now is virtually without a deck, and we see in her holds the red ore of the Minnesota iron range.

The workers on the dock are poised for action. Big clamshell buckets hover over the *Lehigh* like the open claws of birds of prey. As the lines are' made fast, the operators of the unloading machines start their tasks, every man jack with a personal pride in his ability to move ore with speed and efficiency.

The unloading operations are accomplished by a huge, steel-armed affair known as a Hulitt Machine. This machine features four electrically operated clamshell buckets, which go through their movements with mechanical wizardry and almost human performance, as they unload the ore from the boat into the waiting cars in one unbroken operation.

Each bucket is capable of taking a bite of an average seventeen tons, which it transfers into a scale hopper, or "Larry car," where the ore is weighed, then dumped into the waiting railroad car below. This entire operation consumes about one minute and five seconds.

The battery of four great buckets, with their steel-muscled arms and companion Larry cars, stand astraddle of four railroad tracks, reaching out along the dock. The Hulitt Machine itself travels on a 900-foot tramway. Loaded freight cars are moved out and empties moved in by a little narrow-gauge electric donkey called a "shunt." The shunt operates on an independent set of tracks, located between each pair of standard-gauge tracks.

These energetic "mules" dart in and out, as they perform their assigned work. They are equipped with mechanical arms, operated by compressed air, that fasten onto the ore cars and move them along the loading tracks as desired.

Some idea of the speed with which these unloading operations are performed can be gathered from a new all-time-record unloading that was established at the Cleveland dock on November 15, 1943. On that day, working under the late-season pressure of incoming boats, hurrying to beat the closing, icy jaws of winter on the Lakes, the machine operators, dock hands, and railroad yardmen teamed up to unload the James *Pichands* of 11,680 tons of red ore in three hours and fifteen minutes.

This involved handling nearly sixty tons a minute. Inasmuch as a small Pennsylvania hopper car has a capacity of about sixty tons, this meant that one of these cars was loaded, direct from the boat, on the average of about one a minute. Another page here for the book.

The handling of ore at the Cleveland dock is not a question of speed in spurts, but rather of steady day in and day out accomplishment, based on planning, co-operation, and the ability of the men of America to lick any job assigned to them.

Everything is synchronized. Never is there waiting or hesitancy. W. E. Newberry, dock superintendent, puts it this way: "All details to expedite the unloading have been worked out far in advance. A radiophone system is maintained between the incoming ore boats and shore officials. Information is exchanged constantly, which speeds up docking and unloading. The men know what is expected of them; they are always keen and ready. In spite of the manpower shortage, the Pennsylvania Railroad has performed a grand job in having cars on hand and the men to handle peak situations."

The arrangement of the Pennsylvania yards adjacent to the Cleveland dock meshes perfectly into the tempo of the wartime transportation demands. The tracks are arranged generally in a vast circle leading into and away from the dock. Empties are brought down the south rails into what is known as the River Bed Yards. Here they are classified, inspected, and moved onto the four tracks leading directly under the loading machines. The loaded cars, in turn, complete the trackage circle by coming out in the West Breakwater Yards, commonly called Whiskey Island. From here they are pulled out over the north tracks, ready for the road.

The entire dock and yard area is located on an island, and tied to the mainland by the big bridge over the Cuyahoga River. The circle of tracks on the island leads away from and back up to this bridge.

Clarence Frew, Assistant Road Foreman of Engines, has been

with the Pennsylvania forty years, and was the first man hired at the present enginehouse. Mr. Frew remembers well the old days when ore came to the lake ports in small schooners, and and was unloaded "with sweat and wheelbarrows." In those days the old H-2 and H-6 engines used to haul up to about 1,350 tons. Now the I-1s and N-1s, which are used extensively on the Pennsy ore trains, pull some 7,000 tons.

We learn from Yardmaster "Patty" Devine, a veteran of thirty-three years, that the yards have a track capacity for 1,000 cars, with plenty of additional trackage to work the ore cars. About 300 empties are held in constant readiness. An average of about 225 cars is required to handle the cargo of one 15,000-ton ore boat. Always Patrick Devine has his finger on the pulse of things, and he can tell you how many empty H-21s are on Track 7; how the G-27s are placed on Track 4; how many loaded G-22s are ready on Track 13. Yardmaster Devine stands as another human link in the stout chain of the Pennsylvania Railroad, of men who unite speed and safety in the wartime handling of iron ore.

In addition to Cleveland, the other Pennsylvania ore docks, as we have pointed out, are located at Erie and Ashtabula. Between them they handled, during the first ten months of 1943, which included seven of the eight principal navigation months, a total ore tonnage nearly equal to the total rail shipments going out of the dock at Cleveland.

Not all of the ore lifted from the boats is immediately transported to the steel mills, but is dumped in storage areas by a giant traveling crane, the big clamshell bucket of which operates independently of the Hulitt Machines. During the winter months when the Lakes are closed to navigation, these storage piles, together with those maintained by the mills, supply the necessary ore for the blast furnaces.

The rail-water transportation of the red earth of the mighty Iron Range is truly raw Victory, building up a tidal wave of steel that will one day smash forever the armies of our enemies.

PASSENGER PERFORMANCE

President Roosevelt was about to be inaugurated in March, 1937, for a second term. Pennsylvania Railroad officials had been planning for weeks how best to handle the rush of passenger traffic. It was estimated that some fifty thousand people would journey to the Nation's Capital for the Inauguration Day exercises. Concentrating every effort on the problem of providing smooth and efficient service, it was decided to halt freight traffic between New York and Washington for twelve hours, and concentrate on the operation of passenger trains.

When the rush was over, tabulations showed that the Pennsylvania had carried over the Maryland Division (Philadelphia-Washington) more than 68,000 persons in a twenty-four-hour period. Backs were slapped and everyone went around looking as smug and content as the cat that ate the canary.

President Roosevelt was inaugurated for the third time on January 20, 1941. The Pennsylvania carried 66,102 passengers. A nice bit of railroading, it was agreed.

Came then December 7, 1941. In the mad days that followed, passenger travel mounted by leaps and bounds. Servicemen traveled to Southern training camps; others came home on furloughs. High officials were scurrying back and forth. Frantic businessmen were rushing off to Washington and as promptly rushing home again. Troop trains were on the move; war trains were riding the rails. A shortage of tires and gasoline tossed other thousands of travelers into the overcrowded laps of the railroads.

Passenger traffic on the Pennsylvania skyrocketed clear out of sight. On Saturday, April 4, 1942 (the day before Easter), 103,430 passengers were carried between Philadelphia and Washington in twenty-four hours. The following Monday, 105,856 passengers rode the trains.

The Pennsylvania had already accomplished the "impossible." Now began the "miraculous."

Let us examine a few of the high lights of 1942:

Friday, July 3	110,513
Saturday, August 1	114,747

Saturday, August 15   124,377
Saturday, September 5   137,540

Came 1943, with yet even greater demands on the railroads; more record-breaking passenger travel on the Maryland Division. Saturday, February 20, found 141,950 passengers on the trains. Saturday, April 17, the count was 148,826. The following week the peak travel was 156,513, and then on April 26 (Easter Monday), it reached a new high of 158,953.

Pennsylvania officials were starting to pick at the covers when they went to bed. But, at least, they felt the limit had been reached. On Saturday, August 7, the vacation travel boosted the record to 160,229 for a twenty-four-hour period.

Passenger travel on peak days had more than doubled since that Inauguration-Day headache of 1937. Only a few days in 1943 when the Maryland Division carried less than 100,000 persons.

And then, on December 24, 1943, the present record of 178,-892 was reached.

Recently a member of the press rode the head end of the *Congressional Limited*, New York to Washington, and reported that in a span of three hours and thirty-five minutes a train was met or passed every two and one-half minutes. At times freight or passenger trains, or both, were moving simultaneously on all four of the railroad's main tracks.

This, indeed, is America's "hottest" stretch of track.

We list here a few of the methods employed by the Pennsylvania to meet the emergency of the wartime passenger haul on its Maryland Division:

Additional Tracks. Immediately that war was declared the Pennsylvania began to prepare for a greatly expanded traffic between New York and Washington, and the construction of new track got under way. This included sixteen miles of track between Baltimore and Gunpowder River, sixteen miles north; and six miles of track between Baltimore and Washington, which provided a three-track right-of-way between these two important cities. At present eight miles of track are being laid between Oak-

P.R.R. Engine #735, 2-10-0 Type Class I-1, en
route to Pittsburgh with 122 cars of ore on
the Erie & Ashtabula Division near Youngstown,
Ohio. The Pennsylvania, Pittsburgh & Lake Erie,
Bessemer & Lake Erie, and Baltimore & Ohio bring
thousands of tons of ore every day from lake
ports to the Pittsburgh district, where it will find
good usage against the Axis. Courtesy P. R. R.

The Pennsylvania's Trail Blazer #77 westbound on the New York Division near Princeton Junction, N. J., hauled by #4839 the famous GG-1. These are the electric engines that have been taking 16 to 20 cars every hour to Washington and been bearing the brunt of the heavy traffic between the nation's largest city and its capital. Courtesy of the P. R. R.

C. & O. Engine #1560, 2-8-8-2 Type Class H-7, with 6400 tons of coal between MX Cabin and Hilldale, West Virginia, on the Allegheny Sub-division. Eastbound. Courtesy C. & O. Railroad.

Early morning at Hinton, West Virginia, on the C. & O. eastbound coal train pulling out for Clifton Forge and Newport News with Engine #1241, Class K-3.

Pushing them up and dumping whole carloads of coal into the lake vessels at the C. & O.'s magnificent Great Lakes coal docks at Presque Isle, Toledo, Ohio, Hocking Division. Note the coal dust flying in the air from the overturned car at the farthest dock. Courtesy C. & O. Railroad.

Clear order board at Aikman, Kansas on the Santa Fe Middle Division for EB train. Photo snapped from a 5400 H.P. Diesel hauling G.F.X. (Green Fruit Express). The westbound train is #43, the northern California fast freight, with Engine 4109, 2-8-4 Type. Note the operator about to hoop up the orders. Courtesy Santa Fe Railroad.

ington and Bush River, Maryland, which, when completed, will provide three tracks for this vital section.

Double-Signaling. Contemplating the expansion of service, the railroad installed double signals on many of the vital links of the Maryland Division main line, with the result that signals are provided for trains traveling in either direction on all of the tracks. The ability to operate trains in this manner has proven helpful in the event of traffic interruptions during travel peaks in one direction.

Fast Turnaround. Through efficient operation at its terminals the railroad workmen clean, inspect, and service trains with such rapidity that the train can be turned and used again within fifteen or twenty minutes. This has been one of the major factors in the transportation of the record-breaking throngs. Before the last passengers have left an incoming train at New York or Washington, cleaners, inspectors, and other workmen are busy at their assigned tasks. Often these workmen are just completing their tasks when passengers are being loaded for the return trip. While the work of inspection is done quickly, it is also done thoroughly, and the fullest safety standards are maintained always.

In addition to tidying up the cars at terminals, the Pennsylvania employs scores of women as traveling cleaners on the New York–Washington trains. This reduces the time required to clean cars at terminals.

Women have played an important part in the actual operation of trains on the Pennsylvania. With many trainmen called into service, women trainmen have been employed to take over their jobs on some types of trains. This is particularly true as regards commuter trains. And these women have done, and are doing, a fine job of railroading.

Because of the pressing and ever increasing demand for passenger cars on the New York–Washington runs, standard make-up has been adopted on a majority of the trains. This, further, speeds turnaround time. Baggage service has been eliminated from certain trains, thus reducing station loading time.

The equipment problem has been acute, and the Pennsylvania hastily converted observation cars, parlor cars, passenger-baggage cars, and, in some cases, steel boxcars into coaches of various types in order to provide additional facilities for essential travel.

Aside from the physical operation of the trains, a contributing factor to the railroad's ability to accomplish this transportation miracle has been the wholehearted co-operation of the traveling public. People, generally, have heeded the Pennsylvania's advertised appeals to travel, whenever possible, during the middle of the week.

Extra sections have been added to trains whenever cars and locomotives were available; hundreds of temporary ticket booths have been erected in important stations to assist in serving the ever increasing crowds; thousands of clerks, ticket sellers, ushers, and other employees have been trained to replace men gone to war. The railroad has left no stone unturned in its attempt to make rail travel comfortable for the public in wartime.

Just to gain a little clearer picture, a little better understanding of the enormity of the task that has been and is being accomplished, let us examine for a moment a few astronomical figures, and if they make you slightly dizzy, think of the officials of the Pennsylvania, and the trainmen and the yardmen and the ticket sellers, faced with the task of providing transportation for these breathless, hurrying souls.

During 1942, the number of passengers arriving and departing at the Pennsylvania Station, New York City, was 77,293,500. This figure topped 1941 by better than 16,000,000. The highest total for a single year prior to 1942 stood at 69,662,810. The total for 1943 was 98,855,676.

More than 900 trains a day enter and leave the Pennsylvania Station every twenty-four hours.

In this chapter we have touched briefly on the ore move of the Pennsylvania and the passenger-transportation on the New York–Washington line. These are highlights of a railroad at war and reveal but a small part of the activities of the great Pennsylvania System, with its 9,914 miles of track and more than 4,500 locomotives, roaring to Victory down the steel rail.

As this is written, there are 37,960 men and women of the Pennsylvania in the armed forces. Eighty-one have given their lives for their country.

CHAPTER XI

COAL ON THE C.&O.

Coal Drag – Coal Fields – Mine Run

Out of the "Coal Bin" of America, black diamonds flow endlessly on the Chesapeake and Ohio—to industry, to tidewater, to American homes.

One hundred and forty-four cars of coal—11,500 tons—double-heading out of Hinton, West Virginia, over the Allegheny Sub-Division, bound for Clifton Forge. Here, for eighty miles, is the toughest stretch of railroad on the C.&O. system. With exhausts roaring, two mighty 2-6-6-6 Mallets charge at the grade. They are the powerful Allegheny type, named for the mountains they were built to conquer.

The steel rail is heavy, the roadbed well ballasted. The signals are automatic color-light. We have received a "high green"—a highball—in the Hinton Yard. And now we are looking the Alleghenies squarely in the face. This is Extra 1609.

Steadily the rail lifts. We thunder through eleven tunnels, ranging in length from 276 to 6,501 feet. We cross the Greenbrier River three times, Dunlop Creek four times, Jackson River three times; 11,500 tons of coal. Slowly, toilsomely it is raised from 1,382 feet at Hinton to 1,665 feet at Ronceverte to 2,071 feet at Allegheny, the water divide between Chesapeake Bay and the Gulf of Mexico. The average grade on the west slope of Allegheny Mountain is .57 per cent; the average grade on the east slope is 1.14 per cent. The grades are not compensated for curvature.

Up, up and over—144 loads. At Allegheny the helper engine is cut off, after slugging it out with the 1609 for fifty tough miles, and returns to Hinton. Extra 1609 slides down to Clifton Forge, the second most important yard on the division, extending from Mile-post 276, through Clifton Forge, to Mile-post 280. It contains sixty-three miles of track, having a total capacity of 5,100 cars, with a classification yard of twenty tracks, ranging from 4,981 feet to 5,209 feet.

Extra 1609 snakes into No. 5 track in the receiving yard. The caboose is detached on the thoroughfare track and runs by gravity for a distance of about two miles to the "hack track"—the happy home of cabooses awaiting the call to duty. The engine is cut off and slips away to the roundhouse to be readied for its return trip to Hinton.

Car inspectors check the coal train in Track 5. A hump engine moves the train onto the hump. Classification begins. The cars are weighed, as they pass over a track scale, while in motion.

A new train is made up—160 cars; 14,000 tons! The train and engine crews are called. A Class K-3, 2-8-2 type engine is assigned, and soon backs on. The coal train pulls out over the James River Sub-Division—either a solid Potomac Yard train, or inland train, handling loads for Lynchburg, important connections at Richmond, and industrial and tidewater coal destined for Newport News.

There are four classifications of loaded trains operated eastbound from Clifton Forge on the James River Sub-Division; namely: *Manifest, hot tide, inland,* and *Pot Yard.*

Briefly, these are as follows:

Manifest freight. This includes eastbound trains Nos. 92, 94, and 98 on the Allegheny and James River Sub-Divisions, and Nos. 90 and 92 on the Mountain Sub-Division. Trains westbound are Nos. 93 and 95 over all three subdivisions.

A typical manifest eastbound out of Clifton Forge would consist of up to 160 loads, including perishables, Government impedimenta, and coal. The coal would be a "fill out" to make up the tonnage.

The *hot tide train* supplies coal for dumping into boats at Newport News—coal destined for points along the Atlantic Seaboard.

The *inland trains* handle coal for Richmond for city delivery and interchange with the Atlantic Coast Line, Seaboard, and

Southern. These trains handle 160 cars of coal, of 13,000 to 15,000 gross tons. They normally maintain a full coal bin for industries in New England, Virginia, and South Atlantic coastal states.

The *Pot Yard* trains are solid coal trains. During the war emergency, a considerable number of these trains is operated from Strathmore, on the Rivanna Sub-Division, over the Virginia Air Line, thence over a portion of the Piedmont Sub-Division to Gordonsville, Virginia, thence over the Washington Sub-Division through Orange over the Southern Railway tracks to Potomac Yard. These trains carry coal billed to the District of Columbia, States of Maryland, Delaware, Pennsylvania, New Jersey, New York, and the New England States. The full tonnage of 13,000 to 15,000 tons is maintained over the James River Sub-Division, and over the Rivanna Sub-Division to Strathmore, where the loads are reduced to be handled over the heavier grades north of this point.

Interchange. In October, 1942, an average of 287 loaded cars was interchanged daily with other carriers, including 10 at Charlottesville with the Southern, 62 at Waynesboro with the N.& W., 4 at Staunton with the B.&O., 94 at Lynchburg with the N.&W. and Southern, 15 at Glasgow and Buena Vista with the N.&W., and 102 at Bartow with the Western Maryland. The interchange at Bartow included a large amount of coal for New England.

So the coal trains roll, and so will continue through the years, for again we are faced by the fact that no other transportation agency can ever hope to snatch up some 14,000 tons, deep in the Coal Bin of America, and rush it to industry, to tidewater, as quickly and as efficiently as the better-than-one-mile-and-a-quarter-long coal trains on the C.&O.

COAL-PRODUCING DISTRICTS ON THE C.&O.

Four general coal-mining districts are served by the Chesapeake and Ohio. They are the New River, the Kanawha, the Kentucky, and the Hocking. They include vast reserves of both high- and low-volatile coal. We will briefly review them, remembering that the oil and gasoline of tomorrow may today lie buried deep in these black treasure vaults of America.

NEW RIVER DISTRICT

In this district, with but few exceptions, the mines are low volatile, and have produced on the average about 12,750,000 tons per annum for the past fifteen years. It lies in the easternmost portion of southern West Virginia, on the main line of the C.&.O., beginning near Meadow Creek, West Virginia, and extending westerly to a point near Mount Carbon, West Virginia. It also covers large sections north and south of the main line, which are served by the Piney Creek, Winding Gulf, Gauley, Nicholas, Fayette, and Greenbrier branch lines, and by several smaller but important branches projecting from the main line at various points. There are three distinct fields; namely:

Greenbrier Field. This field, lying north of the C.&.O. main line, is located for the most part in Nicholas, Fayette, and Greenbrier Counties of West Virginia. It was opened in 1921, and since that time has increased production each year. The principal seam mined is the Sewell. However, there is some mining in the Fire Creek and Pocahontas seams.

Practically all of the operations in this field are equipped with modern screening plants for the preparation and shipment of various prepared sizes. "Greenbrier coal" is synonymous with high quality because of its low ash content and high B.T.U.'s. While this field is young in years of production, its coal is fast becoming the standard product in many markets.

Greenbrier Field has a total of twenty mines, all of which are active. The current effective production rating is 248 cars per day.

New River Field. This is one of the most important of the great smokeless fields of West Virginia, lying in Fayette and Raleigh Counties. It produces annually 10,000,000 tons of the famous New River low-volatile coal from Beckley, Sewell, and Fire Creek seams. The volatile content ranges from 16 per cent to 25 per cent, with a fuel ratio within the limits as fixed by the

134

United States Government of 2.5. It is low in ash content, which ranges from 2.5 per cent to 6 per cent. There is just a trace of sulphur. It is very high in carbon, averaging 15,000 B.T.U.'s. The chief uses include steam, domestic, by-product, metallurgical, coking, brick and tile burning, and smithing, ranking as one of the superior coals for the latter purpose.

The mining industry in this field has been brought up to the highest state of efficiency through the installation of modern equipment for handling, preparation, and treatment for dust. Its product is sold in lump, egg, stove, nut, pea, nut and slack, slack, and run-of-mine sizes.

Since 1872, when the Chesapeake and Ohio first entered this field, this coal has moved freely to markets demanding superior fuel. New River has a total of fifty-five mines, fifty-two of which are active. The current production rating is 885 cars per day.

Winding Gulf Field. Since its development thirty years ago, this field has successively increased production. It is located principally in Raleigh and Wyoming Counties, West Virginia, just south of the New River Field. Operations here are concentrated on the Beckley and Pocahontas seams, recognized as superior bituminous coals throughout the world.

This field covers approximately 250,000 acres, or about 400 square miles, with potential resources of one billion tons of coal —sufficient to perpetuate development for a hundred years. An average of 8,000 men is regularly employed, mining in excess of 11,000,000 tons annually, at the present rate of production. The seams mined are the standard measurement of by-product coals, being equally suitable for coking, brick and tile burning, metallurgical purposes, and domestic uses, and are the premier smithing coals of the world.

At many of the mines, the coal is washed and cleaned and the noncombustibles removed. The product of this field is sold in approximately the same sizes as those of the New River Field.

Winding Gulf Field has a total of fourteen mines, thirteen of which are active. The current effective production rate is 435 cars per day.

KANAWHA DISTRICT

This district lies immediately west of the New River District, occupying the westerly portion of southern West Virginia, and is entirely high-volatile coal, producing on the average for the past fifteen years about 27,300,000 tons annually. It begins near Mount Carbon, West Virginia, on the main line of the Chesapeake and Ohio, on the Kanawha River, and extends westerly to a point beyond St. Albans, and includes several large and important branches and many smaller subdivisions of these branches on the headwaters of Paint Creek, Cabin Creek, Coal River, and the Guyandot River.

The Kanawha District includes three fields: Kanawha, Coal River, and Logan.

Kanawha–Coal River Field. These combined fields are located principally in Kanawha, Fayette, Raleigh, Boone, and Lincoln Counties of West Virginia. This field is the oldest of the West Virginia fields, coal having been discovered in 1842. The records of mining for local use go back as far as 1817.

Operations on a broad commercial scale began immediately after the War between the States, or in 1865, water transportation being the earlier medium of access to markets.

Development increased rapidly, until the present daily production of 50,000 tons was reached. The Coal River portion of this field began production in 1905. At that time only 12,625 tons were mined. A peak of approximately 8,000,000 tons was reached in 1927. Subsequently about 6,000,000 tons annually have been produced. This field includes ten seams of commercial value, the principal seams being Powellton, Eagle, No. 2 Gas, Chilton, Winifrede, No. 5 Block, Stockton, and Cedar Grove.

The hard-structure, lumpy coals, years ago, were given the name of "Kanawha Splint." Under this name they have won an enviable reputation for malleable iron, steaming, gas, and domestic purposes. The No. 2 Gas, Powellton, and Eagle seams are of a softer structure, and are in extensive demand for steaming, gas, coke, and, particularly, by-product purposes. From 10,000,000 to 12,000,000 tons are produced annually in this field. The Kanawha–Coal River Field has a total of fifty-three mines, fifty-one of which are active. The current production is 1,132 cars per day.

Logan Field. This field is located principally in Logan County, West Virginia. Here thirty-one coal-producing companies, operating fifty mines, produce from 12,000,000 to 22,000,000 tons annually. The principal seams mined are the Island Creek, Eagle, Chilton, Alma, Draper, and Winifrede. These seams produce steam, gas, by-product, metallurgical, and domestic coals of a high quality. With hardly an exception, the mines in this field are equipped with shaker screens, picking tables, and loading booms. In a number of instances, cleaners are installed in order to insure a completely prepared product.

Logan Field has a total of fifty mines, all of which are active. The current effective production is 1,614 cars per day.

KENTUCKY DISTRICT

High-volatile coal is produced in this district. For the past fifteen years an average of about 9,200,000 tons per annum has been produced. This district lies in the easternmost portion of Kentucky, along the headwaters of the Big Sandy River and its tributaries, extending from Ashland and Big Sandy Junction, on the main line, and the Ohio River, just west of Huntington, West Virginia, to a point near Hitchens, Kentucky, on the Lexington Sub-Division of the Chesapeake and Ohio, thence southerly to the Virginia state line, near Elkhorn City and Jenkins, Kentucky. This district includes the entire Big Sandy branch line and several important tributary branches and subdivisions. The Big Sandy–Elkhorn Field is included in this district.

Big Sandy–Elkhorn Field. Here are about 1,750,000 acres, with approximately 12,500,000,000 tons of recoverable coal suitable for present economic needs. Comprised in this field is a total potential coal bin of twenty-five *billion* tons.

The first production began in 1906, when 124,570 tons were produced from a small number of mines. Annual production reached its peak in the year 1927, when 11,321,830 tons were produced, exclusive of mines on the Lexington Sub-division, and more than doubling the output of 1918, or the production at the end of World War I.

The principal seams mined are the Millers Creek and Elkhorn seams Nos. 1, 2, and 3, the composition ranging from a high-grade splint to an exceptionally good by-product coal, adaptable to many uses.

By reason of its hard structure, low ash content and nonclinkering tendencies, the Millers Creek seam is one of the preferred coals for domestic use, and is equally suitable for many other purposes, coming from the "fall," under normal conditions, in large blocks.

The Elkhorn seams, because of their peculiar structure and composition, are known as the world's greatest all-purpose coals, being of an extremely hard, lumpy, and free-burning nature. These coals have gained especial favor in the by-product coke and gas-making industries, for which they are particularly adapted. They also rank high among coals used for stationary and locomotive boilers, gas production, metallurgy, kiln, and cement burning. There are several mines producing cannel coal in this field. Cannel coal is used principally for forging purposes and open-grate burning.

There is a total of sixty-one mines in this area, sixty of which are active. The current production rate is 937 cars per day.

HOCKING DISTRICT

Production in this area is entirely high-volatile coal. Approximately 1,200,000 tons annually have been produced during the last fifteen years. The district lies in southeastern Ohio, on branch lines of the Chesapeake and Ohio, extending from Columbus, Ohio, to Pomeroy, Monday Creek Junction, and Athens, Ohio. It is located in Athens, Hocking, Jackson, Vinton, southern Meigs, and eastern Gallia Counties, Ohio.

It is comprised of three separate fields: Hocking, Jackson, and Pomeroy. Seams No. 6 and 7 are mined in the Hocking Field. Limestone seam No. 4 is mined in Jackson Field, and No. 8-A is mined in the Pomeroy Field. The latter, however, is an entirely different structure from the No. 8 coal mined in eastern Ohio.

In the Hocking Field all of the larger mines are equipped with the most modern screening devices, such as shaker screens, picking tables, mechanical slate pickers, et cetera. The installation of a number of washers has resulted in the production of a high-grade domestic and steam coal.

No. 6 seam is an excellent domestic coal and a high-grade steam coal, especially adapted for gas-producing purposes and particularly suitable for use in the burning of clay wares.

In Jackson Field, Limestone seam No. 4 is an excellent coal for either steam or domestic purposes.

Pomeroy Field produces extremely large and blocky coal, high in heat units, free from soot, making it one of the best domestic coals produced in Ohio. As a steam coal, it is equal to the No. 8 Eastern Ohio. The larger mines in the Pomeroy Field are electrically operated, and equipped with up-to-date tipples, shakers, screens, loading boos, and washers.

There are seventeen mines in the Hocking District, fifteen of which are active. The current production rating is 92 cars per day.

Coal! Something like five thousand cars a day moving out of the four coal-mining districts previously listed. This is probably the largest movement of coal originating along one railroad in the world.

In the year 1943, 62,607,378 tons of bituminous coal started its journey on the Chesapeake and Ohio. The C.&O. received from connections 15,099,303 tons, for a total of 77,706,691 tons hauled. And that is moving coal with a giant-handed power beautiful to behold.

Carload and less-than-carload merchandise freight reached 23,768,696 tons in 1943, making a grand total of all freight moved down the steel rail on the C.&O. in that year 101,475,377 tons. That is something for the book. That is an American Railroad. E pluribus unum—one of many. Theirs is the Big Parade.
. . .

MINE-RUN ASSEMBLY SERVICE

The vast network of feeder or branch lines delivers coal from mine tipple to assembly yards; thence to the make-up yard, where it is weighed, classified, and dispatched to always clamoring, yawning barges, steamer holds, bins, reserve piles. Coal to fuel war machines; coal for home industry; coal to sail the seas; coal for your hearthstone.

On each of the branch lines serving the coal fields in the New River, Kanawha, and eastern Kentucky districts, assembly yards are strategically located. These assembly yards serve as a base from which train operations are conducted to and from the mines, and to and from the intermediate train yards and/or the concentration points lying on the extremities of the coal-originating territory.

Here loaded coal cars are assembled; here the empty coal cars are received and will be distributed by the mine-run crews. Geographical conditions in mine territory are, for the most part, such that there are only limited track facilities. Consequently, it is necessary to switch and classify the cars outside of the coal fields.

At the assembly yards the loads are classified as between eastbound and westbound and short-haul, and built into trains for movement to concentration points. So far as possible, coal is moved from assembly yard to concentration point in solid trainloads. Most of the mine-run crews consist of five men—engineer, fireman, conductor, and two brakemen. Occasionally a third brakeman is required. In some instances, due to heavy grades, two locomotives are necessary, which adds, of course, an additional engine crew.

Each day the mines advise the number of loads ready or expected to be ready at a certain time; also the number and size of empties required for the next day's loading.

Let us follow a mine-run crew out of Thurmond over the Loop Creek Sub-Division to mines located on the White Oak Sub-Division, a distance of about ten miles from Thurmond, West Virginia.

This is Extra 1465. The date is June 14, 1943. Conductor C. B. Morris and Engineer McFadden, called at 10 A.M. Engine 1465 is coupled to train at 10:55, departing from Thurmond at 11 A.M. with thirty-nine empty coal cars. Arrives at Glen Jean at 12:10 P.M. Ten minutes to take water. Train proceeds to Carlisle interchange, arriving at 1:20. Thirty-two empties are switched out. The train arrives at Scarboro Yard at 1:55, picking up twenty-three empties. It moves to Whipple Mine, arriving at 2:40 P.M., setting off twenty-three empties.

The crew takes twenty minutes for lunch; then switches out twenty-five loads of coal. This work is finished at 4:10, and the train departs for Carlisle interchange, and between 4:50 and 5:25 one Virginian load is set off and thirty-six loads picked up. Scarboro at 5:35 P.M., with a short stop for air-brake test. Depart from Scarboro at 5:43, arriving at South Side Junction at 6:43. Seventeen minutes to turn down retainers at the top of a fall-away grade of 2.5 per cent. Between 7 and 7:28 P.M. cars are placed in the east yard at Thurmond. The crew is relieved at 7:28 P.M.

A total of sixty-two empties and sixty-two loads has been handled on the trip. So we have a brief picture of what is happening all through the vast coal fields. Big steel empties rolling to the mines; groaning loads of coal—fifty-, seventy-, and ninety-ton hoppers—moving from hill and dale out to join the mile-and-a-quarter-long trains on the main line of the Chesapeake and Ohio. Cars of the C.&O.; foreign-line cars of the Erie, the Nickel Plate, the Pere Marquette, the Pennsylvania, the B.&O., the Clinchfield, the Norfolk and Western, the Louisville, Nashville and Virginian.

Some mines load as many as 125 cars in a twenty-four-hour period. The daily car rating of the three coal fields that comprise the Kanawha District totals 2,747 cars. Effective May 10, 1944, the mine ratings were based on fifty-ton car units.

Coal moves from the mines to assembly yards, thence, so far as possible, in solid trainloads to concentration points at Russell, Kentucky, and Clifton Forge, Virginia. These yards are especially designed for handling the immense volume of traffic that flows through them continuously.

Russell is the concentration point for westbound coal, with a capacity of 9,300 cars, and is one of the largest railroad freight yards in the country. Clifton Forge, with a capacity of 5,100 cars, is the concentration point for eastbound coal.

CHAPTER XII

FREIGHT DIESELS OF THE SANTA FE

Moving Freight Across the Arizona Divide

The Diesel-electric freight locomotive is here to stay. It has proved itself under the most severe wartime conditions. This writer is a steam locomotive enthusiast, and has ridden thousands of miles in the cabs of American engines. We love them, but we offer no apology for our admiration of this new type of motive power that is trumpeting down the steel rail.

East and west, north and south, two-, three-, and four-unit Diesel-electric freight locomotives are hauling great trains, loaded to their maximum tonnage with war materials for the battle fronts throughout the world.

We find them on the Atlantic Coast Line, Seaboard, Southern, Burlington, Baltimore and Ohio, New Haven, Boston and Maine, Rock Island, Milwaukee, Great Northern, Northern Pacific, Rio Grande, Western Pacific, Missouri Pacific—and the Santa Fe.

Diesel-electric locomotives are particularly well suited for operation on the Santa Fe, due to the necessity of long hauls by tank cars of water for steam engines in the mountain and desert districts of Arizona and southern California.

From Winslow, Arizona, to Barstow, California, the big Diesels handle 3,500 tons both east- and westbound over the Third District of the Albuquerque Division, and the First and Second Districts of the Arizona Division, a total of 460 tough miles. On occasion, they are used between Barstow and Bakersfield, California, over the famous Tehachapi Mountains; also over the First and Second Districts of the Albuquerque Division, Albuquerque to Winslow.

In the writer's opinion, that 460 miles between Winslow and

Barstow compares with the Southern Pacific Sacramento Division, as boasting the finest operating performance of any division on any railroad anywhere in the United States. It would be difficult to find greater physical ruggedness, tougher operating conditions, higher traffic density, and more helper districts.

And, remember, everything routed east and west on the Santa Fe System Lines moves over this stretch of right-of-way.

All of the forty-eight Santa Fe freight Diesels are of the four-unit type, with a horsepower of 5,400 pounds. They are watered and fueled, between Winslow and Barstow, at Seligman, Arizona, and Needles, California, and are serviced at Barstow and Winslow. They receive general repairs and overhauling at Winslow, where the Santa Fe has installed extensive Diesel shops, platforms, and tracks.

Motor 127, as they are called on the Santa Fe, has been ordered for 11 A.M. at Winslow. We will climb aboard this blue and yellow Titan of freight service, coupled at the head of sixty-seven cars—3,467 tons. At 11:47 we get the highball, and the motors roar up. The driving wheels bite the steel rail, and some 7,000,000 pounds of war freight is on the move.

Westbound out of Winslow there is a ninety-six-mile helper district for freight trains to Supai, and the ruling grade for the entire distance is 1½ per cent. If we had been riding one of the big 3,800- or 3,900-class 2-10-2 Santa Fe type, the largest steam power used in this territory, and next to the most powerful road engines on the Santa Fe, a helper locomotive would have been required all the way to Supai.

At 11:55 we are on the main line and passing West Winslow. At 12:40 we are passing Canyon Diablo telegraph office, twenty-seven miles to the west. We are skirting the Painted Desert world, the land of the Navajo and the Hopi. This is high country, the great mesa land of northern Arizona. At Winslow the elevation was 4,856 feet.

We strike a steel song from the trestle across the Canyon Diablo—5,421 feet. We are climbing into the sky, a roaring man-made meteor. Angell, Winona, Cosnino—6,464 feet. Off there to the right, the silver-tipped crown of Arizona—San Francisco Peak, lifting to a glorious 12,611 feet. This is God's country!

Flagstaff, 6,894 feet. Winslow is fifty-nine miles behind the markers of our waycar. The Flagstaff operator "OSes" us by at 2:15. At 2:50 we are fighting our heavy train past Bellemont, 7,130 feet.

Now it's 7,335 feet. The Arizona Divide! The highest point on the Santa Fe, west of Glorieta. The top of the world. And we are riding this mountain steel to the steady pull of those 5,400 iron-lunged horses in this deep-chested GM Diesel-electric locomotive. Vital materials behind us, hurrying over the Santa Fe iron to pulsing West Coast war plants, to ports of embarkation on the Pacific.

Suddenly we get a jolt; the brakes go on. Back on his high perch in the waycar, the alert conductor thinks he can detect something dragging on the nineteenth car from the rear end. He is taking no chances, and pulls the air, which means that he has used the conductor's valve in the caboose to apply the brakes. The train grinds to a reluctant stop. A quick inspection reveals everything OK, however. The entire train is checked by hurrying trainmen. We get a highball, and resume our westward flight.

At 3:28 we are pounding through Williams. The track arches past famous old Bill Williams Mountain. 3:40. Our train comes to a stop at Supai. Retainers are set up. This takes eleven minutes, and at 3:51 we are crawling cautiously down the mountain, where the descending grade on the westbound track is as high as 161 feet per mile, at little more than ten miles an hour.

At 4:40 we stop at Daze, twelve miles west, to turn down the retainers, cool the wheels, and again inspect the train.

Our Diesel-electric locomotive, as is all motive power of this type, is equipped with a dynamic brake. In mountain territory its use eliminates the necessity of turning up the maximum number of retainers that would otherwise be required. It means less hot wheels, less wear and tear on brake-shoes.

Eight minutes at Daze, and our train is rolling again. We pass Ash Fork, in the valley, 5,126 feet elevation, and soon are slamming at another lifting grade of 1½ per cent on this our westbound track, which extends to Crookton, eighteen miles. Here we hurl our 3,467 staggering tons at one of the country's greatest horseshoe curves. We look straight across it at our waycar.

144

Santa Fe Motor #122, 5400 H.P. freight Diesel, with C.T.X. Calif.-Tex. fast freight, climbing the 1.5% grade east of Kingman, Arizona, on the First District of the Arizona Division. Photo by Delano, Office of War Information.

Draftees alight from train to view Santa Fe mixed main loaded on the rear end with tanks for front lines. Courtesy U.S. Army.

Southern Railway #48, all coach luxury stream-liner the Southerner running between New Orleans and New York, northbound near Greenville, South Carolina, on the Charlotte Division hauled by one Electro-Motive Corp. 2000 H.P. A-unit. This train has carried thousands of U.S. Army personnel to and from the many camps along its route. Courtesy Southern Railway.

From Crookton the descending grade drops from seventy-five to ninety-five feet per mile to Seligman. Here we pull into the yards. It is 6:15 in the cool evening, and our day's work is done. The Arizona Division crew takes over.

Our engineman, R. L. Mitchel, has done a grand job. To him it is just another run, an average trip, judged by Santa Fe standards. When they wheel through, Winslow to Seligman, under six hours, General Manager E. E. McCarty, of the Santa Fe Coastlines, and Division Superintendent A. B. Enderle beam with approval. The boys are railroading, out there on the Arizona Divide.

My good friend "Happy" Baxter, one of the best engineers we have ever ridden with, has made this run in five and a half hours with 3,500 tons. The mileage is 142.7. They are hard miles, mountain miles—and mountain miles are long and tedious and tough.

On this run one of those big 2-10-2 type steam locomotives would have required a helper all of the way, Winslow to Supai, and another, Ash Fork to Crookton. There would have been stops for water at Angell and Williams, and fuel would have been taken at the latter point. Steam-engine trains must be inspected every sixty miles; Diesel locomotives equipped with their dynamic brakes can run seventy-five miles without stopping.

In the old days the Santa Fe used to haul some three hundred carloads of water into Ash Fork every day for locomotive boiler consumption. With these big Diesels running through, only thirty water cars are required. Needless to say, this releases many tank cars for the hauling of precious wartime oil.

On the trip, Winslow to Seligman, we had no helper at any time, and the trim and powerful Diesel handled those sixty-seven cars almost as easily as though they had been the lightweight Pullmans of the *Chief*.

Let us now journey east over the Third District with a preference train. We are riding Motor No. 109, hauling the C.T.X. —California-Texas—fast freight. We have 3,690 tons—sixty-six cars—out of Seligman. We drop eleven cars of oil at Ash Fork. From Ash Fork to Winslow the train consists of 3,542 tons—

fifty-five cars. A Santa Fe type helper is coupled on for the pull up the 2.0 per cent grade. Ash Fork to Supai, a distance of twenty-three miles via the eastbound track.

The following is our log of the trip.

Leave Seligman	6:10 P.M.	MT
Arrive Ash Fork	7:15	Helper coupled on.
		Left 11 cars of oil.
Leave Ash Fork	7:42	
Arrive Supai	9:05	Cut off helper.
Leave Supai	9:10	
Arrive Williams	9:30	Crew ate. Inspected train.
Leave Williams	9:50	
Pass Riordan	11:00	Met 19 sixteen minutes late.
Arrive Angell	11:37	
Leave Angell	11:45	
Stop Canyon Diablo	12:05	Red home signal.
Leave Canyon Diablo	12:11	
Arrive Winslow	1:05 A.M.	MT

Total time over district, including detentions, 6 hours, 55 minutes.

With steam power, in addition to the helper, Ash Fork to Supai, this train would have required the additional service of helpers, Seligman to Crookton, and over the long drag of twenty-eight miles, Williams to Riordan.

So we have a pretty good picture of what a Diesel-electric freight hauler can accomplish on a rough, tough mountain run.

Now we are going to face west from Seligman. The First District of the Arizona Division is downhill all the way to Needles, California. We are dropping down, down to the great muddy river, the Rio Colorado. The westbound track in places is a 2 per cent descending grade, with only about ten miles less than 1.5 per cent.

Here again we find the dynamic brake doing its work with its customary efficiency. The huge Diesels are constantly handling their trains at the maximum fifty-mile-per-hour speed limit. They are big, romping playboys now. The distance, Seligman to Needles, is 149 miles. The run is usually made in from four and one-quarter to four and three-quarters hours.

Going west, wheels are singing; the slack is bunched; hurrying, impatient cars are crowding hard behind the blue and yellow locomotives.

But eastbound—ah, that is another story. The slack is dragged out, the iron-fisted couplings are straining, groaning, and every last car is hanging back like a balky mule.

Needles to Seligman. This is the longest sustained grade in the United States—149.7 slogging miles. Never has this stretch of track received the attention of which it is worthy. Little is known about it beyond the horizon of the Santa Fe operating department.

But right here is where the Santa Fe's GM Diesel-electric locomotives get their real baptism of fire. This is where they prove themselves over 150 miles of the shaggy old Santa Fe Trail.

The elevation at Needles, California, is just 476 feet above sea level. Seligman, Arizona, stands at 5,234 feet in the clouds. Almost one mile straight up. The grade is 1.5 per cent for 126 miles, Needles to Yampai, with the exception of twelve miles from Louise to Walapai, where it varies from level to a trifle more than 0.5 per cent. The last twenty-three miles, Yampai to Seligman, varies from 1.5 to 1 per cent.

The Santa Fe freight Diesels haul 3,500 tons up this long, punishing pull alone in from six to seven hours, moving right along at between fifteen and twenty miles an hour with maximum tonnage. Below we record an average eastbound trip with one of these trains.

Motor 116 is called for 1:30 P.M., with L. O. McLermen, engineer, and David L. Klatt, fireman; both of Needles. The train consists of 3,080 tons, with fifty-eight cars.

Leave Needles	2:41 P.M.	
Leave Topock	3:20	5 minutes detention behind work train.
Pass Yucca	4:15	
Pass Harris	5:17	

Pass Kingman	5:35	
Pass Louise	5:47	
Leave Berry	5:55	Inspection.
Pass Walapai	6:16	
Pass Hackberry	6:36	
Pass Truxton	7:10	
Arrive Peach Springs	7:32	Inspection.
Leave Peach Springs	7:40	
Pass Yampai	8:30	
Arrive Seligman	9:05	

This is a remarkable performance, with no stops for fuel or water. Only the largest articulated steam locomotives in this country could have pulled this train, Needles to Yampai, without a helper. This, further, is the longest steam helper district in the country.

The Electro-Motive Division of General Motors, which designed and built these Santa Fe freight haulers, can well be proud of their performance on this grueling run. Summer temperatures around Needles are surpassed by only one spot in the United States, and that is Death Valley, which is in itself additional proof of the ability of these Diesel motors to stand up and take it under adverse conditions.

And right here we would like to say a word for the men who maintain the four 1,350-hp engines that make up one of these freight locomotives. Theirs is one of the toughest jobs on the road. They work in stifling heat amid a ceaseless crashing thunder, breathing the hot fumes of oil, sweating it out, as they keep the roaring motors turning; even repairing breakdowns without interrupting the flight of the train charging down the steel rail. Soldiers of the iron road—the men on the fighting line of the Santa Fe.

CHAPTER XIII

WAR SERVICE OF THE SOUTHERN

War Transport – 727th Railway Battalion

The Southern Railway System, in addition to its vital job of transporting war freight and troops, was privileged to be the first railroad in the United States selected for the "on-the-ground" training of Railway Operating Battalions of the Transportation Corps, Army Service Forces.

This training was begun in 1942 on the New Orleans and Northeastern Division of the Southern, operating between New Orleans, Louisiana, and Meridian, Mississippi. Working shoulder to shoulder with veteran railroaders, members of the 727th and 715th Railway Operating Battalions received the training and experience necessary to take over and run a military railroad in a "theater of operations."

The first battalion to complete its training was the 727th—the Southern's own. It was sponsored by the Southern Railway, and commanded by Lieutenant Colonel Fred W. Okie, former Superintendent of the road's Birmingham Division. Two-thirds of the officers of this battalion are out of the ranks of the Southern.

Having completed its training, the 727th went overseas, and has participated in the North African, Sicilian, and Italian campaigns. The 727th Railway Battalion has been cited for its work at the front in the Tunisian Campaign, and many of its officers and enlisted personnel have been decorated for bravery under fire.

Colonel Okie himself has had numerous honors bestowed on him, including the Soldier's Medal, Legion of Merit, honorary officer of the Order of the British Empire, to name a few. Our hats are off to this railroad colonel and his men. They are soldiers of America, tough, resourceful, unbeaten.

Commenting on the work of the 727th, Colonel Okie has said: "Sometimes we didn't know how they rolled, but they rolled. We lost some locomotives in Tunisia. Then we mounted anti-aircraft guns on the trains. As soon as the Germans discovered that we had stingers, they left us alone. At Enna, we were practically running our trains into the lines. The boys said it was the first time they had brought up ammunition and then heard the infantry shoot it off."

Here in America, Colonel Okie's 45,000 former co-workers of the Southern Railway System view with infinite pride not only the battle-line accomplishments of the 727th, but also their own job of keeping 'em rolling on the Southern. They know that their work, too, has a "sting" in it for the enemy.

Down there on the Southern, they are bringing up the ammunition—even though they cannot hear the infantry shoot it off.

To try to detail fully the mighty transportation job the Southern Railway System is performing in World War II is impossible in the limited space at our command. A Hollywood publicity agent, dipping his prolific pen in fire, might write in lights the words, "colossal," "gigantic," "stupendous," and still fail to blazon adequately before the public eye the task accomplished by the Southern.

Long strides in rail transportation have been made since the "Best Friend of Charleston," the first locomotive built entirely in this country, rode the track on the South Carolina Railroad, now a part of the Southern. Out of every war has grown a new transportation era. Witness the enormous quantity of oil, moving from New Orleans to the Eastern Seaboard behind mighty Diesel-electric locomotives like the Southern's 6100. In meeting the challenge of war, the Southern and other lines are setting the pattern of the railroad of tomorrow.

Never in all of its history has the Southern Railway hauled so great a volume of freight or so many passengers. Originally built to serve an agricultural South, the rails of the Southern today hum not only with trains of vital food products, but also with a roaring parade of trains carrying war freight and fighting men.

The territory served by the Southern Railway network includes much of the vast area south of the Ohio and Potomac Rivers and east of the Mississippi. Every state in this vast territory, except West Virginia, carries the steel rail of the Southern.

Out of Louisville, Kentucky, the Southern reaches across Indiana and Illinois to the Father of Waters at St. Louis. Washington, Cincinnati, Louisville on the north; St. Louis and Memphis on the west; the bustling ports of Norfolk, Charleston, Savannah, Brunswick and Jacksonville on the Atlantic; Mobile and New Orleans on the Gulf of Mexico.

The steel of the main line stretches from Washington through Charlotte, Atlanta, Birmingham, and Meridian to New Orleans; from Washington to Jacksonville via Columbia and Savannah. The steel rail of the Southern serves Knoxville and Chattanooga. The list is long. Roaring metropolis and sleepy hamlet, linked close.

Perfumed magnolias, lacy Spanish moss dressing up great oaks, kinky-haired pickaninnies. Vast fields of tobacco; snowy fields of cotton; old plantations; lovely gardens. You can hear the singsong chant of the tobacco auctioneer; voices singing Negro spirituals; the songs of the South, dear to every American. This is Dixie. Here you ride the trains of the Southern.

Yes; "The Southern Serves the South."

Green and gold steam locomotives, thundering through a scenic wonderland. Green and gold Diesels weaving in and out of great industrial centers. Burden bearers of the South. The Southern is the largest carrier of cotton and cotton textile products in the world.

A land of enchantment, of romance; a world rich in history and legend; a country steeped in tradition; a people imbued with the principles of solid Americanism. A rock in the foundation of the Nation.

This is the land that gave birth to Robert E. Lee and Stonewall Jackson. Here the high cries of the locomotive whistles of the Southern stir echoes from valley and mountainside, as they shout their defiance at our country's enemies.

Some idea of the size and importance of the Southern in the Nation's rail network can be gained from the following statements:

In miles of road, the Southern ranks twelfth in the country. It is the third largest railroad east of Chicago and the Mississippi. It ranks seventh in gross revenues. It ranks seventh in freight revenues. It ranks fifth in passenger revenues, and sixth in passenger-miles. In ton-miles, the Southern ranks ninth.

The road mileage of the Southern Railway System totals approximately 8,000 miles. This mileage breaks down as follows: The Southern, 6,513 miles; the Cincinnati, New Orleans & Texas Pacific Railway (the first railway in the United States to be completely protected by automatic signals), 336 miles; the Alabama Great Southern Railroad, 315 miles; the New Orleans & Northeastern Railroad, 204 miles; the Georgia Southern & Florida Railway, 396 miles. Also, a number of short lines.

Through a consistent program of improvement and modernization in the period between World War I and II, the Southern has been brought to a high state of efficiency. Lines of heavy traffic density have been double-tracked, roadbeds improved, old bridges replaced by steel and concrete structures, passing tracks lengthened, automatic signals and other safety devices installed. Mechanical coal-handling plants have been provided; large classification yards, new engine terminals, and modern shops constructed at a number of important points.

In 1938, the Southern had a total of 1,701 locomotives, 848 passenger cars, and 47,079 freight-train cars. At the beginning of 1944, the Southern owned 1,590 locomotives. Of these 291 were steam passenger engines; 10 were Diesel passenger haulers; 1,009 were steam freight locomotives, with 8 Diesel freight locomotives; 240 steam and 32 Diesel switching locomotives completes the list of motive power. Early 1944 found the Southern with 978 units of passenger-train equipment and 57,588 freight-train units.

Thus, as compared with 1938, the System owned fewer locomotives but a larger number of freight and passenger cars.

Not to be overlooked, in view of the important part they came to play in handling an enormously inflated passenger load, are the six Southern streamliners placed in service between August, 1939, and May, 1941. These trains are as follows:

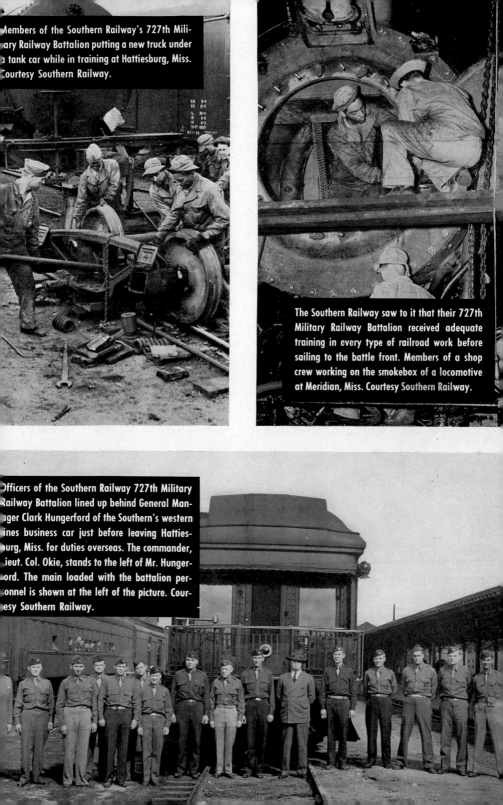

Members of the Southern Railway's 727th Military Railway Battalion putting a new truck under a tank car while in training at Hattiesburg, Miss. Courtesy Southern Railway.

The Southern Railway saw to it that their 727th Military Railway Battalion received adequate training in every type of railroad work before sailing to the battle front. Members of a shop crew working on the smokebox of a locomotive at Meridian, Miss. Courtesy Southern Railway.

Officers of the Southern Railway 727th Military Railway Battalion lined up behind General Manager Clark Hungerford of the Southern's western lines business car just before leaving Hattiesburg, Miss. for duties overseas. The commander, Lieut. Col. Okie, stands to the left of Mr. Hungerford. The main loaded with the battalion personnel is shown at the left of the picture. Courtesy Southern Railway.

Name of Train	No. of Trains	Normal Consist	Placed in Service	Operated Between	Daily Mileage Per Train
*Southerner	3	8	3-31-41	New York-New Orleans	924
**Tennessean	3	9	5-17-41	Washington-Memphis	619
Vulcan	2	2	8-24-39	Chattanooga-Meridian	591
Cracker	2	2	10-11-39	Atlanta-Brunswick	550
Goldenrod	1	2	9-24-39	Birmingham-Mobile	528
Joe Wheeler	1	2	9-24-39	Oakdale-Tuscumbia	497

*Operated over the Pennsylvania, New York to Washington.
**Operated over the Norfolk & Western, Lynchburg to Bristol, Va.

The Southern is manned by earnest and loyal employees, proud of the road, proud of the more than five thousand men and women in the armed forces, and, above all, prideful of Lieutenant Colonel Fred W. Okie and the 727th Railway Battalion.

In 1938, the Southern handled six and a quarter billion ton-miles of freight; in 1939, seven and a quarter billion; in 1940, eight billion; in 1941, ten and one-half billion. The figure leaped to thirteen and one-half billion in 1942. The Southern was fighting a war—a war of transportation. In 1943, the road hauled fifteen and one-third billion ton-miles of freight!

The same spectacular increase occurred in passenger-miles, due, in a large degree, to the fact that more than half of all the larger military, naval, and air-training stations were located in the territory served, directly or indirectly, by the Southern. In 1943, the road carried 14,678,774 passengers an average distance of 177.5 miles to produce 2,605,816.163 passenger-miles, an increase of 195.85 per cent over 1926, and 438.59 per cent over 1939.

Better than two and one-half billion passenger-miles. In 1938, men would have said, "It can't be done!" In 1943, cold statistics proved that it could. In this man's war, the railroads of the country were doing the "impossible" every day—doing it with trains and locomotives and an intestinal fortitude on the part of the personnel that was characteristic of the men of the iron road. It held a lesson for a lot of us. For, you remember, there were in this country certain defeatists who were crying that the war was lost before a shot was fired.

There was a day when our first line of defense was the American Railroads. They were ready that Sunday morning of December 7, 1941. They were ready when the big push came. Cotton and oil and sulphur moved out of Galveston and other Gulf ports by boat, but Hitler and his submarines stopped that. Folks sitting on their porches on the Florida coast watched tankers burning at our doorstep, watched American boats and American seamen die. Peacetime America and a wholly inadequate peacetime Navy were helpless. Those were dark days, which we remember with a shudder.

It remained for our peacetime railroads to stave off total disaster until Uncle Sam could build the guns and the ships and train the men to fight back.

Casey Jones was at the throttle of the last word in railroad motive power—motive power built by free enterprise during the years when America was asleep at the switch. Casey Jones was riding the rail behind the keen, gleaming blade of the headlight of an American locomotive—a blade that struck hard at the awful blackness of that first fearful year when the bandits of Berlin and the triggermen of Tokyo were winning on every front.

To return to the Southern Railway, and the fact that the road had fewer locomotives in 1943 than it had in 1938. In earlier pages, it has been repeatedly revealed that the railroads of the country had fewer engines at the start of the second World War than in 1917, and yet were prepared to haul a far greater tonnage.

This fact calls to mind the prediction made a century ago by Horatio Allen, pioneer locomotive builder and the first chief engineer of the South Carolina Canal and Railroad Company, a part of the present Southern Railway System.

Said Mr. Allen: "From my observation, I do not think there is any great probability of material improvement in the breed of horses, but the man is not living who can tell what the improved breed of locomotives will accomplish in the future."

Horatio Allen, from his seat in the high tower of the Terminal in the sky, no doubt, is smiling because of the beautiful and efficient Iron Horse that today is roaring down the railroad in America. He watches the Union Pacific's mighty 4000-class 4-8-8-4 locomotive storming across the Wasatch Range with its yellow reefers, the M-4s, of the Duluth, Missabe and Iron Range, roaring through with their ore trains, the great 2-6-6-6 Articulateds, the Allegheny-type, hauling mile-and-a-quarter-long coal trains on the Chesapeake & Ohio, the Santa Fe's 3776-class 4-8-4s, high-balling the *Chief* at ninety miles an hour, the green and gold Diesel-electric locomotives beating out the miles on his own Southern, the South's No. 1 carrier, and we can see him nodding and murmuring, "I knew it."

In 1938, the average locomotive on the Southern ran 33,179 miles. In 1942, it ran 43,863 miles. In 1943, it ran 44,242 miles.

In 1938, the average number of tons of freight in each train was 433.14 tons; in 1942, 566.96 tons; in 1943, 607.64 tons.

In 1938, each loaded freight car carried an average of 19.55 tons; in 1942, 27.32 tons; in 1943, 29.06 tons.

In 1938, the average ton was hauled 206.37 miles. In 1942, it was hauled 223.01 miles. In 1943, it was hauled 247.79 miles.

How well the Victory parade kept rolling on the Southern is illustrated by the statement that, in 1943, the percentage of bad-order engines to total ownership was only 7.33 per cent, and of bad-order freight cars only 1.37 per cent—the lowest in the company's half century of service.

In appraising the job the Southern has done, and is doing as this is written, it must be remembered that this road and the Southern Pacific, because of their location, have borne the brunt of the troop movement, as well as a large share of war freight.

Because of its many natural advantages, the South was chosen to play a leading role in the Nation's war program. Before Pearl Harbor, and afterward, millions of dollars were spent for the construction of new, and the expansion of existing, cantonments; for training fields, airports, airplane factories, powder plants, ammunition depots, shell-loading plants, small-arms plants, quartermasters' depots, as well as naval bases and shipyards.

Immediately that war was declared, all of the South's vast industrial facilities went into capacity war production. The South has a climate favorable to the year-round training of troops. These circumstances combined to thrust a tremendous burden onto the Southern Railway System, but the road was ready.

One of the first demands made of the Southern called for the movement of an entire division west from a southern cantonment. This, perhaps, sounds simple—a matter of a few extra trains, you say. Wait a minute.

A division is made up of some fifteen thousand men. Every fighting man moving to the front requires about eight tons of equipment, or just twice as much as the soldier in the first World War. An armored division requires seventy-five trains.

Less than seven days after the so-called Sons of Heaven struck at Pearl Harbor, the Southern was faced with the task of moving sixty-nine trains over its rails, and this in addition to all other roaring war trains rushing back and forth.

Pullmans, coaches, baggage cars, boxcars, flatcars—1,543 all together—started west. In three days and three nights the job was done. Sixty-nine trains. Of these the Southern handled fifty-two. The Louisville & Nashville hauled the rest. The trains were made-up, loaded, and stormed away in less than one-hour intervals.

Yes; the railroads were ready. On the Southern, as on other railroads, there was efficiency, perfect operating technique; trained men on the job, and no better-trained men exist than your railroader. Your engineer, train dispatcher, conductor, switchman, is a cog in a machine—a cog reaching ultimate perfection only after years of experience.

Before the end of the first year of the war, freight cars were being loaded to the roofs; passengers were crowding the aisles. Every piece of equipment that was safe to run was pressed into service. Out of the rip track, the railroad's "Skid Row," came old locomotives, old coaches, old dining cars.

The predominating color scheme of the Southern's coaches became almost entirely Marine green, Navy blue, and Army olive drab. The niceties and usual luxuries of train travel went by the board. Passengers, however, as a whole, were tolerant of inconveniences and discomforts.

President Ernest E. Norris, of the Southern, mopped his brow, as he said, "I never thought I'd live to see the day when I had to beg folks to please not ride our trains unless the trip was absolutely necessary."

The men in the road's Dining Car Department suffered a continual headache, and grew gray and bald before their time. Where once they served 70,000 meals a month in 1939, before

156

the end of 1943 they were serving an average of 350,000 meals monthly.

Experienced chefs, stewards, and waiters were called into the armed forces. Rationing came into effect. The high quality of the Southern's traditionally excellent cuisine suffered. Further, it was necessary to remind patrons tactfully not to linger over their coffee and cigars, for other hungry passengers were waiting. Certain of the dining-car headaches were eased somewhat through ingenuity and resourcefulness; others will be eliminated only when the war is won.

In handling the passenger load, outstanding records have been made by the two streamliners, the *Southerner* and the *Tennessean*, which were placed in service on March 31 and May 17, 1941, respectively.

In the year ending June 30, 1943 the *Southerner* traveled 846,592 miles and carried 209,099,936 passengers one mile. From March 31, 1941 to June 30, 1943, the train-miles were 1,905,347 and the passengers carried one mile were 433,240,010.

The *Tennessean*, for the year ending July 30, 1943 traveled 531,297 miles and carried 205,159,900 passengers one mile. From May 17, 1941 to June 30, 1943, this train ran up 1,126,658 train-miles and carried 288,394,743 passengers one mile.

With the coming of World War II, the many capital expenditures made by the Southern through the years for improvements in plant and facilities, for better utilization of rolling stock and power proved of inestimable worth. The money spent, the co-operation of passengers and shippers, the "know-how" of officials and the men and women on the line—all add up to the most phenomenal transportation job in the history of the railroad.

The final word of this chapter belongs to Lieutenant Colonel Fred W. Okie and the 727th Railway Battalion. It is reported that within four hours after their landing on Sicily the boys of the Southern, together with other railway units, in spite of land mines and demolition damage, had steam up in Italian locomotives, were repairing track and preparing to railroad in the good old American way.

No soldier in the world so quickly adapts himself, more readily throws off the cloak of brotherly love, and wades into the thick of the fight than the American doughboy. In North Africa, the boys were new to the battle line. The Germans were pouring it on, and it was a tough baptism of fire.

You will remember, perhaps, that the tide of battle had turned against our troops at Kasserine Pass. Certain combat forces were compelled to withdraw, with the result that considerable rolling stock operated by the 727th Battalion was trapped behind the German lines.

Colonel Okie was furious, and we can well imagine that this former superintendent of the Birmingham Division of the Southern stirred up a breeze. They needed that railway equipment, needed it badly.

Lieutenant Colonel Fred W. Okie called for volunteers. Men of his outfit rallied around—American railroaders. They infiltrated the enemy lines, grabbed something like thirteen trains, and came back, with the angry and amazed Germans throwing everything they had at them.

They needed those engines to bring up more ammunition for the infantry.

Railroad men of the Southern Railway System are doing a great job over here—and over there. . . .

A book will be written one day on the operations of the Railway Battalions of the Transportation Corps of the Army Service Forces. Railroad men of America are fighting a war on every continent, and under every conceivable condition—from battle-torn Italy to Guadalcanal, from Burma to Alaska; in England, China, Iran, France. They are operating more different kinds of motive power and rolling stock than many of them, in their wildest dreams, could vision. And they are doing a job of it in the hell-bent American fashion.

Home guards and boomers. . . . Engineer, fireman, brakeman; official, operator and conductor; section boss, track worker, yard brakeman, and machinist.

They, and others, are writing a page in railroad history on the world's battle lines. They are engraving in steel the story of American railroad achievement all up and down the face of this war-ravaged earth. They are highballing trains on the toughest "rawhide" runs this world has ever seen.

And to the American railroader, wherever he hangs his hat, we pay humble tribute.

CHAPTER XIV

EASTBOUND PERISHABLE ON THE UNION PACIFIC

Vitamin C Rides the Rail in Wartime

As an abundant source of Vitamin C, oranges and other citrus fruits are in even greater demand in wartime than in peace. In spite of the staggering load of vital war material handled by the railroads, there must also be transported those essential fruits so necessary in maintaining the health of soldier and civilian alike.

The Union Pacific serves a large part of the Western territory that produces great quantities of citrus fruits—oranges, lemons, grapefruit. Modern "freezers," or refrigerator cars, provide the protective transportation that maintains these fruits in orchard-fresh condition.

The supplying of proper foods in wartime is considered as of primary importance. To gain a more intimate knowledge of this little-known task in the transportation field, we are going to ride a Union Pacific perishable train, eastbound, Ogden, Utah, to Council Bluffs, Iowa.

Note the clocklike precision with which everything moves, the infinite care with which a fruit train is handled as it rushes toward the Eastern markets. Remember, too that what the U.P. is doing in getting these long trains of yellow and white "reefers" over the road is being duplicated by the Southern Pacific, the Santa Fe, Atlantic Coast Line, Illinois Central, Southern, the Seaboard.

This is April 12, 1943. We are in the yards in Ogden, Utah. RV 36 and CN 24 Fruit Blocks of the Pacific Fruit Express are being consolidated. RV symbol covers green fruit originating at Roseville, California. CN symbol represents a train originating at Colton, California.

U. P. Engine 3950-3961, latest 4-6-6-4 Type built for that road, in Echo Canyon, Utah on the Eighth Subdivision of the Wyoming Division.
Courtesy Union Pacific R.R.

The fruit still rolls east despite the war. U. P. #4019 near Echo, Utah with eastbound fruit block, on the Eighth Subdivision of the Wyoming Division. Courtesy Union Pacific.

U. P. #812, first of that road's 4-8-4 Type, with #28, the San Francisco Overland Limited, east of Cheyenne, Wyoming on the Fourth Subdivision of the Nebraska Division. This famous train has been doing more than her bit in carrying military personnel and war workers to and from California's northern metropolis. Photo by Preston George.

The first train came over "The Hill," the Sierra Nevadas, behind those snorting cab-ahead 4-8-8-2's on the Southern Pacific; the latter train stormed across El Cajon Pass on the Union Pacific.

RV 36 arrived at Ogden at 8:55 A.M. CN 24 pulled in at 10:19, Mountain Time. RV 36 headed into icehouse track No. 4. CN 24 was spotted on icehouse track No. 2, and its inspection was completed at 10:40.

Waybills have been checked for direction, diversion, manifest, and classification. Now they are delivered to train order case for train order movement to be worked up into the train on which they will leave, and a permanent record is made.

These two Fruit Blocks are consolidated into one train by the Ogden Union Railway and Depot forces. The train is ordered to leave with 3,100 to 3,200 tons, not to exceed seventy cars. Car inspectors turn in reports of any bad-order cars; the manifest clerk checks reports of cars to be used in consolidation.

The yardmaster hands the switch list to the engine foreman, instructing him as to make-up of consolidated train on Track 7. Switching is performed from both ends. The consolidation is accomplished. Engine 4015, a big 4-8-8-4 type, backs onto the train. A final inspection is made, including inspection of roofs for loose running boards, loose top handholds, et cetera. Comes the inspection of running-gear, brake-rigging and all parts of the cars. The air brakes are tested.

The conductor has received his waybills, and checks train orders with the engineer. It is 1:15 P.M. The big freight-hauler gives a deep-throated cough; the drivers take hold of the steel rail, almost stop, but, with a mighty effort, keep moving. Steam is hissing; the engine takes a deep breath, barks again. The slack starts to run out; the caboose gives a jerk; the fruit train is under way.

The perishable arrives at Echo, Utah, at 2:51 P.M., and pulls out at 3:14. The engine has received coal and water. The conductor comes up to the head end, and stands there as the train moves slowly past him, making a running inspection. He catches the caboose grab-irons and waves a highball.

Evanston, Wyoming. We pull in at 4:50, and depart at 5:10.

A busy twenty minutes, with engine dopers servicing this big truculent 4-8-8-4. The sand-dome has been filled. A new engine crew says, "Howdy." They perform their chores and settle down to doing a hitch with Eastbound Perishable.

Carter, Wyoming, at 6:26 P.M. This is a hungry brute, a thirsty one. Coal and water. Service. Highball at 6:37. Eleven minutes. They don't fool around. The Army needs Vitamin C.

We pull into Green River at 7:50. They head us into the yard, and uncouple this 4000-class engine, which is assigned to the 8th Sub-Division, comprising territory between Odgen, Utah, and Green River. The grades are heavier on this stretch, and it takes a real engine to bat these fruit trains through.

Switching here involves the removal of two short loads and one bad-order car. The 3961 backs on. This is a new 4-6-6-4 locomotive, a honey of an engine. She looks as though she was capable of giving Vitamin C a ride.

We flicker our tail-lights at Green River at 9:40 P.M., and do a little fast running. And here is Bitter Creek coming at us. The brakes bite, and we stop at 11:40. Coal and water, and train inspection. We're out at 11:51, roaring on across Wyoming.

We stand at the switch in Rawlins at 2:15 A.M. This is April 13 now. We're in the yard at 2:35. The engine receives the customary attention, and car department employees check the train. We run into a delay here. This fruit train normally would be in Rawlins only thirty minutes. However, we pulled in ahead of a fleet of eastbound passenger trains, and there is not sufficient time between them to try to go anywhere.

It is 5:20 A.M. when we leave Rawlins. There are sixty cars —3,050 tons. We beat out the miles to Hanna, arriving at 6:31. The engine takes on coal and water, and we are outbound at 6:47. Here the conductor and head brakeman inspected the train, the head-end man walking back until met by the conductor; then they crossed over and checked the opposite sides as they returned.

Water at Rock River at 8:00 A.M. Out at 8:02. That is fast work.

We arrive at Laramie at 9:05. Here Pacific Fruit Express men make an inspection, but no cars require icing. Some cars are dropped; others picked up. We leave at 11:10 with 45-18-3000. That is 45 loads, 18 empties, for a tonnage total of 3,000.

A two-minute stop at Buford at quarter past one involves testing the air before starting down Sherman Hill.

There's Cheyenne out there on the prairie. We are looking past the big boiler of the 3961 at the sprawl of this plains city. We swing into the yards at 3 P.M. RV Fruit Block 34 has arrived ahead of our RV 36 and CN 24 and is being worked.

It is 5:20 when we pull down through the east lead and onto main track at the east end of Cheyenne Yard. We have forty loads and twenty-three empties now. The empties are foreign cars en route home. Our tonnage is 2,785. We are puffing east at 5:30, with engine 9056, a 4-12-2 Union Pacific type.

We pound away at fifteen to eighteen miles an hour up the grade to Archer, Wyoming, eight miles from Cheyenne. The big, mauling freight engine starts to pick up speed, and we hold fifty miles an hour until approaching Pine Bluffs, Wyoming. The engineer makes a ten-pound air reduction; then a second reduction to pull the train down to twenty-five miles an hour for the yard limit board.

We are at the coal chute at 6:28. While coal and water come aboard, trainmen are focusing their lanterns on wheels and undercarriage of the cars. These frequent inspections of running-gear and equipment are primarily for the purpose of nipping possible trouble in the bud. Journals heating or broken parts might easily lead to delay and consequent damage to consist.

The engine is oiled and greased, and, with everything in shape, the highball is given at 6:42 P.M.

Immediately after the departure of the train, the operator at Pine Bluffs makes his report to the train dispatcher at North Platte, giving the time, the number of loads, empties, and tonnage; the number of perishable and manifest cars. The dispatcher immediately telephones the operator at Sidney, Nebraska, advising the approximate time the train will arrive there. The call boy at Sidney then calls a train and engine crew to operate this train from Sidney to North Platte.

Our train passes Kimball at 7:15. The operator on duty makes a running inspection, as he stands in front of the telegraph office, watching for smoking journals or anything that might be dragging or throwing fire. It is "all black."

We're at Sidney at 8:10, stopping at the coal chute. The new crew takes charge. Again train and engine receive an inspection, and the big locomotive is serviced. Car department employees make what is called a "Class C" inspection at this point, walking down both sides of the train. Our caboose is taken off; another is coupled on. The new conductor receives his waybills. The engineer makes a twenty-pound reduction of air with brake-valve, and carmen see that all brakes are applied; make certain then that they release properly. Blue protection lights are removed from both ends of the train, and we pull out at 8:30 P.M.

The roaring exhaust beats at the night; those twelve drivers are rolling faster and faster, and soon we are traveling at the maximum of fifty miles an hour. We boom through Julesburg, Colorado, at 9:46, and rush on toward Ogallala, Nebraska, thirty miles away. Approaching Ogallala, the engineman makes an initial application of approximately ten pounds of air, and, when the brake-valve quits blowing, follows up with two additional applications of eight pounds, bringing the train to a standstill clear of the head-in switch.

The head brakeman hurries to open it. We stop at the coal chute at 10:30, and there is another inspection. At 10:46 Union Pacific Train No. 102, the *City of San Francisco*, breezes past.

We head out, and 31.4 miles from Ogallala pass O'Fallons, where the operator makes a running inspection, giving the train crew a lantern signal that tells them everything looks all right. Now we're approaching the west switch of North Platte Yard, and the speed comes down to yard limit requirements. Already a switchman has lined the iron for us, and we're in at 11:50 P.M. At 12:20 A.M. the train has been spotted at the ice dock, and the head-end brakeman cuts off the Union Pacific 4-12-2. Through yard leads the engine makes its way to the roundhouse. Here it is prepared for the return trip west.

Marker lights are removed from the caboose. The conductor turns his waybills over to the billing clerks and registers the time of arrival and the time of tie-up. Pacific Fruit Express employees put out protection signals and the process of icing starts.

All cars containing perishables are re-iced, as big cakes of ice are conveyed from icehouse on raised platforms and put in the car-bunkers by hand. When this work has been finished the protection signals are removed and switch engines attack both ends of the train. Cars for Kansas City go into one track, and the cars that will move east to Council Bluffs go into another. Twenty-six switching movements are required.

Now there is insufficient tonnage for eastward movement, but the Chief Dispatcher at Grand Island has already made his plans for the make-up of the train. RO 12, fast stock, has arrived from Denver, Colorado, and thirty-one cars of eastbound livestock and two cars of manifest are placed on the head end to fill out the train.

Train and engine crews have been called for 4:10 A.M., to leave North Platte at 4:40. Engine 5060, a 2-10-2 Santa Fe type, lumbers from the roundhouse lead and backs on. Protection signals are put out, the air lines coupled up, and a Class A inspection begins. This includes lifting the lids on each journal box to make sure that all journals are in proper shape as regards grease and packing.

The conductor registers at the yard office, receives his waybills and instructions. He delivers train order tissues to the engineer, compares time with the engineer and head brakeman; then heads for the caboose with his waybills. Each car number, contents, destination, routing, and all waybill instructions are recorded in his train book.

The rear brakeman places the marker lamps in position on the caboose, the protection signals are removed, and the train pulls out of the North Platte yard track at 5:30 A.M., crossing over to eastbound main track with sixty loads and no empties.

We are through Gothenburg at 6:37 A.M. There is a stop at Lexington, Nebraska, for water at 7:05. The engineer looks over the locomotive, and the conductor and head brakeman make a walking inspection. The flagman is called in, and we depart at 7:17. We pass Kearney, 35.3 miles away, at 8:06; Gibbon at 8:25; Wood River at 8:40.

The train pulls into the Grand Island Yard at 9:10 A.M. The engine is cut off, and engine 5032, another 2-10-2 type takes over. Cabooses are changed. There is another Class C inspection. Still sixty loads, no empties, 2,597 tons. The departure is made at 9:45.

Approaching Chapman, trainmen on the rear end think they see a smoking journal and swing us down. There is a walking inspection, but it was a false alarm. Central City at 10:35. Columbus. Coal and water, and three cars of livestock behind the engine are set off. We're rolling at 11:45. Fremont slides past at 12:45. At Valley, Nebraska, fourteen cars of livestock are set out for feed and water.

We leave Valley at 1:18 P.M. At Summit, 2.3 miles west of Seymour, Nebraska, we drop four cars of livestock for South Omaha and one car with a routing, Omaha, Chicago, St. Paul, Minneapolis & Omaha. We highball out of Summit at 2:03, and arrive at the ice dock at Council Bluffs, Iowa, at 2:20. The engine is cut off. Switch engine and crew relieve our conductor and rear brakeman. The conductor goes through the routine of checking out. The caboose goes to the buggy track, and Pacific Fruit Express Company men put out protection signals.

The perishable cars are re-iced. When this is done, the switch engine couples onto the train, moving it to the Council Bluffs yard, a little over a mile away. Here the train is broken down, with cars being made up in trains that will soon be rushing away over various railroads. You will see these white and yellow reefers that have earlier rolled over "The Hill" and El Cajon Pass in far-off California hurrying on their way, north, south, and east —oranges, yellow as the California sun, lemons, grapefruit.

Vitamin C, for the Nation's health—for civilians, for fighting men. Day in and day out, citrus fruits are on the move. Wars may come and wars may go, but life-giving Vitamin C rolls down the iron road forever. It will aid in the rebuilding of wounded soldiers, it will nourish and provide health for babies, for the sick.

John Smith and Sam Jones feel they could not start the day without that glass of orange juice, that luscious grapefruit, for breakfast. And they will have it while guns are thundering, and after the lights go on again all over the world. The American Railroads will see to that.

166

The story of the refrigerator car in wartime goes further than the transportation of fruits and vegetables from the West Coast area. One of the problems presented by the acute shortages of rolling stock has been that of the foreign boxcar returning home empty, and in particular the empty refrigerator car. This reefer, moving east from California, Idaho, Arizona, Nevada, Utah, with a full load, had been traveling back empty.

Those home-bound coolers were loafing on the job, and so, acting at the request of the Office of Defense Transportation, the Interstate Commerce Commission, amending its Service Order No. 104, made it mandatory instead of permissive for the railroads to substitute up to three refrigerator cars for every boxcar for certain types of westbound shipments.

These empty reefers were the only remaining reserve of unused freight car equipment, and the country was crying for transport. Here, for example, was the traffic manager of a national publication confronted with the problem of getting tons of magazines out to the West Coast. The empty refrigerator car proved the answer to a prayer.

Under the original order, only cars of the Pacific Fruit Express and the Santa Fe could be used, but this was amended to include all westbound refrigerator cars eligible for such loading, if and when there was freight to be transported and the facilities were suitable.

All of which bears out the old adage of, "Where there's a will there's a way." In days gone by, the utilization of a westbound reefer was limited to the hobo who stowed away in the ice bunker. But all of that is changed. No longer is the homeward wending refrigerator car a deadhead, but is a burden bearer, working its passage.

CHAPTER XV

RUSSELL TERMINAL DIVISION

Hump Yard – Coal Classification

Russell Yard and the Grand Canyon have nothing particular in common, except largeness. Viewing Russell for the first time, one is reminded of the cowboy who, making his initial visit to the rim of the Grand Canyon, remarked, "It is sure pretty, but it would be an awful thing to jump into."

Russell Yard, by far the largest and most important freight yard on the Chesapeake and Ohio Railway, is one of the largest yards in the country. It is, further, unique in that it has a hump yard that is used entirely for the classification of westbound loaded coal cars.

Russell Yard is located at Russell, Kentucky. In excess of seventy-five per cent of all coal traffic originating on the Chesapeake and Ohio moves westbound through this yard, and records reveal that a total of 14,538 cars have been handled through Russell Yard in one day, divided 7,207 cars received and 7,331 forwarded, with a monthly total of 186,914 received and 186,895 forwarded.

All westbound coal, except for Huntington, Ashland, and local points, is concentrated at Russell. Coal trains from Handley, St. Albans, Whitesville, Danville, Sproul, Peach Creek, Shelby, Martin, and other points in the coal fields are run direct to Russell, where the cars are weighed, routed, billed, classified, and made up into trains for movement either to Parsons Yard, Columbus, or Toledo, via Columbus, and Stevens Yard, Cincinnati. Empty coal cars returning from Columbus and Cincinnati gateways are inspected, made up into trains for forwarding to the mines.

So important is the function performed at Russell, it constitutes in itself a separate operating division, known as the Russell Terminal Division, and is in charge of a Division Superintendent.

The Russell Division consists of 149.8 miles of track, divided, 7.1 miles of first, 7.1 miles of second, 5.3 miles of third main track, and 130.4 miles of yard tracks and sidings. It extends from MP 523 through Russell Yard to MP 530, the beginning of the Cincinnati Division. The main tracks are equipped with color-light automatic block signals and laid with 130- and 131-pound rail.

Russell Yard has a capacity of 9,300 cars, and is divided into four operating sections; namely: the eastbound yard, capacity 3,560 cars; the westbound receiving yard, capacity 1,575 cars; the old westbound classification yard, capacity 1,360 cars, and the new westbound classification yard, capacity 2,805 cars. The westbound receiving yard is connected with both the old and new classification yards.

All of the switching leads and switches are laid with 130-pound rail. There are 422 switches in Russell Yard. Two modern interlocking plants are located between the east and west ends of the yards, governing the movement of trains operating on the main tracks and controlling switches leading from the yard tracks to the main tracks.

As the coal is "humped," or switched, in this great westbound coal classification yard at Russell, classifications include coal trains for the Pennsylvania Railroad at Columbus, the Erie at Marion, the Nickel Plate at Fostoria, commercial loads for Toledo, and Lake consignments.

Classifications are also made for the Baltimore & Ohio at Vauces, Ohio, and the Detroit, Toledo & Ironton Railway at Greggs, Ohio. And for the Chicago Division of the C.&O. and the Chicago Division of the Big Four; also the Big Four's Toledo Division.

Big Class T-1 locomotives walk 160 coal cars—13,500 tons—out of Russell for Columbus and Toledo. 2-10-4s, they are, the Texas type, which weigh 566,000 pounds and have a tractive effort of 93,350 pounds, and with booster, 108,625 pounds. The coal capacity of the tender is 30 tons; the water capacity, 23,500 gallons. Class K-3 locomotives, 2-8-2s, handle 143 loaded coal cars—11,000 tons—for Cincinnati.

The returning empty coal cars are all handled in the eastbound receiving yard. They are switched, classified, and run to the various coal fields, as directed by the Chief Car Distributor at Huntington.

Now, before we proceed with coal classification and the other activities at the great Russell Yard, let's examine a typical modern hump yard, with its car retarders, power switches, and other facilities for the make-up of trains in peace or wartime.

HUMP YARD

A hump yard is not new. The first "hump" came into use around 1893, and yardmasters, who had the reputation of hating everybody, no doubt went around kissing boomer switchmen. When the apple hit Sir Isaac Newton on the head, the hump yard principal was born, for a hump yard is ruled by gravity.

Today, in a hump yard, a switch engine moves a freight train to an elevated section of track, or "hump"; then a car, or a cut of cars, is nudged over the lip of the hump, and gravity couples on. In the early days of the hump yard, switchmen and car-riders, or "hump jockeys," directed and braked these cars or cuts to their destination in the various tracks of the classification yard. This against the time when each car or cut was herded around the yard by a switch engine, manned by an engineer, fireman, and three or more yardmen.

Switching in the old days was a slow, tedious process, requiring a lot of time, sweat, and profanity. To the layman, a big freight yard is still complicated. However, it has been vastly simplified and the work expedited, until today we find a great classification center such as Russell Yard capable of classifying 4,000 cars in a twenty-four-hour period. Often, under the press of wartime urgency, as many as 1,465 cars have been classified in one eight-hour shift.

During World War I railroad traffic suffered severe congestion and delays through the inability of make-up yards to clear expeditiously the flood of cars that deluged them. Many a harassed yardmaster would have preferred to be at the front dodging bullets rather than freight cars in his own backyard.

If the methods employed in 1917-18 were in use today, our entire transportation system would be seriously crippled. Greater road speeds, improved locomotives and cars, modern signal systems, improvements to track facilities—all have united greatly to increase the flow of traffic. The long forward strides made by the railroads would largely be annulled if the classification yards could not adequately handle the volume of traffic moving in from the main line.

To obtain the full benefit of high train speeds and longer trains, freight yards should have the capacity and facilities to accept trains immediately upon their arrival, reclassify the cars promptly, and send them on their way without delays. And, for the most part, they are doing that little thing—doing it in spite of the war burden and the resultant manpower shortage.

How they have done it is one of the miracles of the times. They certainly could not have done it without gravity yards, car retarders, and power switches. No; not any more than many of the railroads of the country could have cleared up serious bottlenecks without Centralized Traffic Control.

In the interval between the first and second World War, the car retarder was developed and applied to forty highly important classification yards on twenty different railroads. These yards include a total of 1,367 classification tracks, with at least 69,677 rail-feet of retarders and 1,431 power-operated switches.

Numerous railroads have reported phenomenal performance records for car-retarder yards installed on their properties. Before going farther, it might be better to learn first what a car retarder is, how the yards are laid out, and how they are operated. It will then be more readily understood just why such remarkable performances are possible.

The hump, or raised portion of the yard from which cars are dispatched, must be constructed high enough for an empty car to move—by gravity—down through the switches to a point at least several car-lengths beyond the clearance point of any classification track under the most adverse conditions of running

171

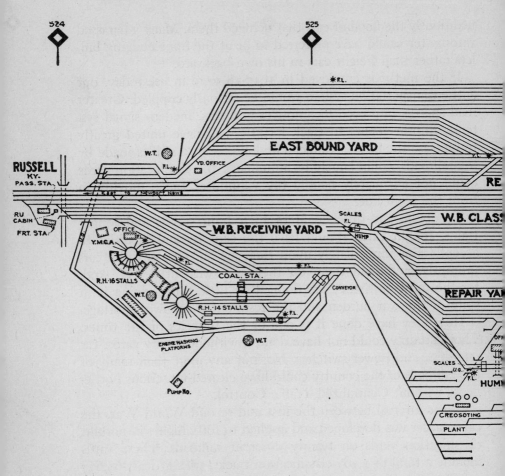

or drifting. However, with such a hump, the heavily loaded car under the most favorable conditions would accelerate to an unsafe speed.

Hence, car retarders are used to compensate for differences in weights of cars and running conditions. Computations for the correct height of the hump take into consideration slow-rolling cars, adverse winds, and cold weather, which reduces the effectiveness of journal lubrication. The amount of retardation available in a yard must be adequate to brake a hundred-ton car under the most favorable running conditions, passing through any route, to a safe coupling speed on the classification track. The most modern car retarders are constructed in units that can be

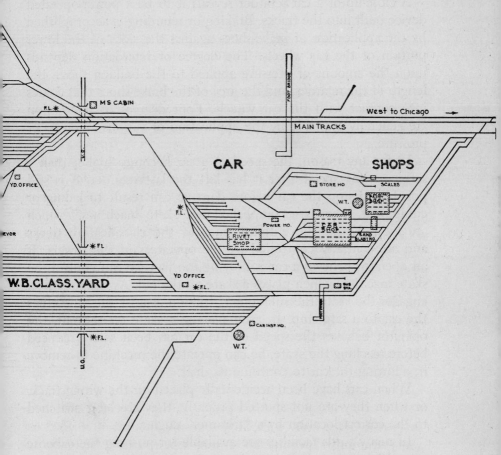

applied to the track in varying lengths, thus affording variable braking power according to particular yard requirements.

It is the usual practice to control the retarders and power switches from two or more towers, depending on the size of the yard. One tower generally houses the control machine which regulates the retarders on the main hump lead and the power switches over which movements are made to the secondary lead tracks. The retarders and power switches on these lead tracks are controlled by machines located in towers that are erected near the entrance to the classification tracks. The operator in the tower on the main hump lead has a master control over the hump signals.

A close-up of a car retarder reveals it to be a power-operated device built into the tracks. Braking or retarding is accomplished by the application of brake-shoes against the sides of the lower portion of the car wheels. The degree of retardation depends upon the amount of pressure applied to the braking shoes, the length of the retarder, and the area of the brake-shoes that comes into contact with the car wheels. Four degrees of retardation are generally available by the application of various amounts of pressure.

If, for any reason, the speed of a car becomes higher than a safe coupling speed after it has left the last retarder, it is still possible to stop the car before damage can result to lading or equipment. This is accomplished by "skate machines," which are located near the entering ends of the classification tracks and are centrally controlled by the operators in the towers. If an operator believes a car is moving too fast, he can control the skate machine, which places a skate on the rail. As the car wheel engages the skate the subsequent friction against the rail brings the car to a safe stop. If, after placing a skate on the rail, the operator believes the speed of the car has been safely reduced before reaching the skate, he can operate the machine to remove it, allowing the car to continue its drift.

When cars have been accidentally placed on the wrong track, or when they are not spotted properly, they are later switched to the correct location by a "trimmer" engine.

In many yards facilities are available for pushing the caboose over the hump and allowing it to proceed through the retarders and switches and couple itself to a train that is made up. In such yards it is the practice to couple the road engine to the cars in the classification yard rather than switch the train to a departure yard.

There are two general types of car retarders—the electro-pneumatic and the electric. The electro-pneumatic type utilizes four different air pressures in the operating cylinders to provide the four degrees of retardation. In the electric type the degree of retardation is effected by changing the distance between the brake-shoes with a consequent variance in the spring pressure against the shoes.

Complementing the car retarders, as necessary adjuncts to maximum yard efficiency, are the power-operated switches over which the cars move from the hump track to the various classification tracks. These power switches may be either the electro-pneumatic or the electric type. The fastest electric machines operate in approximately one second, and the electro-pneumatic switch machines snap the switch-points into position in a fraction of a second, or almost instantaneously.

The familiar ladder-track layout is not employed in car-retarder yards because in such a layout a separate retarder would be required for each track. Instead, groups of four to seven classification tracks are connected to secondary leads, with a retarder on each lead controlling the car speeds before they reach the classification tracks. Groups of these secondary leads are joined to major leads, which in turn branch out from the main hump lead. Retarders control the car speeds on each of the major leads and secondary leads, as well as the main hump lead. Power switches operate the various switches in this network of lead tracks.

At night adequate yard illumination is provided by means of floodlights, enabling the operators to observe humping operations. Such illumination also permits the men in the yards to work with safety.

All right; so far so good. A long freight has pulled into the hump yard. The road engine and caboose have been cut off, and a switch engine has dragged or pushed the train onto the hump, as the case may be. Here are cars for a dozen or more destinations. Now you say, "How is this sorting accomplished? Who knows what goes where?"

The conductor of the incoming freight has turned his way-bills over to the yard clerks in the yardmaster's office. Switch lists are made up, and these go to the men in the towers and the hump conductor. In most car-retarder-equipped classification yards, a printing telegraph system is installed between the yard office, towers, and hump conductor. Over this the switching lists are transmitted; also operators are advised as to car weights, which assist in giving each car the proper retardation.

In several yards classification of cars is further expedited by communication systems between the yard engines and the hump conductor. Either "one-way" or "two-way" communication systems are available. One well-known and highly successful type employs the track rails, together with auxiliary wires, to carry the communication currents between the sending and receiving apparatus in the locomotive, and similar apparatus in the control office.

In operation, it is not unlike police radio calling systems. However, it is not a radio system, since its field of operation is restricted to the area covered by the rails and the associated wires. A type of telephone instrument is used in the yard office. In the locomotive, the engineman receives his instructions through a loudspeaker. If two-way communication is in effect, the engineman speaks through a hand set that resembles a house telephone.

These yard communication systems are especially valuable during fog or other adverse weather conditions that may make it difficult for the engineman to observe the signal indications. Too, more detailed information can be given by the conductor, and there is far better control of humping speeds.

In yards where signals—usually of the light type—are incorporated in the layout, one signal is located at the hump and others are located along the approach to the hump at sufficient intervals to provide the engineman with a distinct view of at least one signal at all times. These signals are controlled—usually by the hump conductor—from a controller located at the top of the hump.

A sorting clerk in a post office holds in his hand a big bundle of letters. These represent the cars in this train on the hump. Before the clerk are pouches for various cities. These represent the tracks in a classification yard. The postal clerk scales a letter into a Boston pouch, three into a New York pouch, two into an Albany pouch. A car is cut from the slow-moving train on the hump. An operator in a switch tower guides it into a track where a train is being made up for Boston. Now three cars come drifting down, and they are turned into a track of a New York

The Union Pacific's own Type 4-12-2 engine 9030 with a westward extra east of LaSalle, Colorado on the Northern Subdivision of the Colorado Division. Photo by H. W. Pontin Railroad Photographs.

Another view of a great engine running on superb track. U. P. 4002, 4-8-8-4 Type, westbound at Peterson, Utah on the Eighth Subdivision of the Wyoming Division. The operation is left-hand. These locomotives have contributed a major share to the U. P.'s fine war effort. Courtesy Union Pacific R.R.

C. & O. retarder control panel at Russell yard, Kentucky. Note the switch list. Courtesy Union Switch & Signal Co.

Car inspection of journal boxes as cars a pushed up the hump at Russell, Kentucky. Cou tesy C. & O. Railroad.

Car starting down the hump at the C. & O.'s Russell yard at Russell, Kentucky. Note the retarders. Courtesy Union Switch & Signal Co.

Weighing them in as the cars pass over track scales in the C. & O. scalehouse at Russ Courtesy C. & O. Railroad

Wartime coal for our northern states. The great C. & O. T-1 engine #3002, 2-10-4 Type, with the standard tonnage of 13,500 and 160 cars heading for Toledo, Ohio from Russell, Ky., near Robbins, Ohio coaling station on the Russell Division. Photo by H. W. Pontin Railroad Photographs.

Double humping them at the C. & O.'s Russell, Ky. westward classification yard looking west from the hump. Scalehouse at lower left with car going over scales—retarder tower in background—yardmaster's tower in far background. Courtesy Union Switch & Signal Co.

Sante Fe #8 Fast Mail and Express east of Grants, N. M. on the First District of the Albuquerque Division. The engine is 4-8-4 Type 3776 Class and is running through from Los Angeles to La Junta. Photo by Otto C. Perry.

train in the making. Two now for Albany. The car retarders adjust their speed, and they roll to join cars that will soon be on their way to Boston, to New York, to Albany. As simple as that.

The long train on the hump dissolves with magic speed. Another train then replaces it, and so the work of classification continues, all around the clock. Coal, oil, foodstuff, war material. This is how traffic is kept on the move; this is how wars are won.

Highly significant are the figures that attest to the speed and efficiency with which cars are handled in classification yards equipped with car retarders and power switches. Even though the volume of traffic passing through such yards has increased from thirty to one hundred per cent or more over prewar levels, the cars are still being classified without delays and congestion.

The power-equipped yard's greatest contribution to the war effort has been its ability to classify trains promptly upon their arrival, even during peak hours. This is possible because car retarders permit practically continuous utilization of the hump. Because of the quick action of the switch machines in throwing switches, it is possible to space cars closer together, as they roll from the hump to the various classification tracks. Further speed and efficiency are obtained by voice-communication systems between the yard office, the hump conductor, and the locomotive, thus providing closer co-ordination of yard movements.

A yard free of congestion prevents delays out on the road. This allows of a more intensive utilization of cars and locomotives, releasing badly needed equipment for service elsewhere. So moves the battle of transportation.

One railroad, which has four yards equipped with retarders, reports that a yard can be operated twenty-five per cent faster than if manual braking was used in controlling car speeds. In one instance, a train consisting of 110 cars was classified in twenty-three minutes, or at the rate of 5.2 cars per minute. This was accomplished with a humping speed of 2.6 miles per hour, with an average of 1.4 cars per cut.

In another yard, the normal amount of traffic handled per month before the war was approximately 29,530 cars. Under war conditions this figure was increased to 62,140 cars per month.

Still another yard classified approximately 4,600 cars weekly during 1930. During May, 1942, 15,792 cars were classified each week. With freight trains arriving at average intervals of one every fifteen minutes, cars were kept moving over the hump at an average rate of one every thirty-eight seconds throughout the twenty-four-hour day.

When one railroad completed a car-retarder yard several years ago it was estimated that 3,000 cars per day could be handled. During 1942 this yard frequently humped 3,500 cars daily, with all road trains departing on schedule. When certain trains arrived behind time, the speed of yard operations was stepped up to a point where the classification between arriving and departing trains occupied less than thirty minutes.

Thus we have the picture of the general make-up of an average hump yard as it operates today. Now we will return to Russell.

COAL CLASSIFICATION

It was in 1918 that the Chesapeake and Ohio constructed a hump yard at Russell, Kentucky. It was equipped with power switches, but at that time employed car riders to brake the cars. In 1929 car retarders were added.

The present westbound receiving yard for coal consists of eight tracks, having a capacity of 115 cars each, and nine tracks, with a capacity of 88 cars each. The classification yard includes twenty-one tracks, most of which can accommodate 120 cars. There are in service twenty-one electro-pneumatic double-rail retarders, with a total length of approximately 1,313 rail-feet. To compensate for variable weather temperatures, inert retarders are placed in the classifying tracks approximately thirty car lengths apart.

Since Russell Yard has been equipped with car retarders, it has been available for humping operations practically continuously at its 240-car-per-hour capacity. For this reason it has been possible to keep the yard free of congestion, even though at times a considerable proportion of the entire day's volume of traffic arrives within a short interval of time.

Humping operations are directed by a three-indication color-light signal at the apex of the hump, with a repeater signal 3,000 feet in advance of this signal. Trimmer operations—the switching out of cars accidentally placed on the wrong track, as previously indicated—are directed by a similar signal, located at the throat of the yard and facing the classification tracks.

The retarders and switches are controlled from three towers. Tower 1, situated near the apex of the hump, controls the adjacent retarders; also the power switches over which movements are made to various sections of the yard. Tower 2, located on the south side of the yard, controls switches and retarders on the south side. Tower 3, situated to the north of the yard, controls switches and retarders in the north section.

Direct communication between the towers and the hump yardmaster's office is established by a loudspeaker system. In addition, a telephone equipped with a loudspeaker is in service at the base of Towers 2 and 3 to facilitate communication between car repairmen, the yardmaster, and car retarder operators.

Where formerly it was necessary to halt humping operations at frequent intervals to return car riders to the hump, it is now possible to continue humping as long as cars are available in the receiving yard.

There is, however, more than the matter of simple classification involved, as we will see, and includes weighing and billing.

In order to expedite the weighing and billing of cars passing through Russell, each car is moved from the mine on the authority of a "mine card." The car initial and number, point of origin, the name of the shipper and consignee, and the destination of the car are shown.

When the coal train arrives in the westbound receiving yard, mine-card bills for the entire train and a switch list of the train are on the engine. These are delivered to the Route Clerk, who routes the cars on the switch list. The switch list then goes to the Yard Clerk, who marks the tracks into which the coal is to be classified. He then makes a mimeographed copy of the switch list and sends copies of the list to the Tower operators, the weighmaster, and the hump conductor. Mine-card bills move to the weighmaster on a two-way belt conveyor.

The weighing of each car is accomplished as it rolls down the hump, passing over a 400-ton plate fulcrum scale, equipped with a Streeter-Amet automatic weight-recording device. The scale track is 72 feet long, a distance sufficient to retain the car on the scale for 3.5 seconds, or long enough to complete weighing operations. As each car passes over the scales it is automatically counted by a counter, located in the superintendent's office, approximately a mile away. The counter is operated by a circuit passing through the contacts of a circuit controller, actuated by the depression of a bar by the wheels of each car.

After the cars are weighed and the weights stamped on the bills, the bills are returned to the billing office, where the rates are applied, freight calculated, and total revenue shown. Bill clerks then make out the revenue bills, with the exception of C.&O. Lake-coal shipments. On the mine-card bills for the Lake-coal, the rates are applied, the bills photographed, and the original mine-card bills accompany the cars to the Lake at Toledo.

Trains are built up in the classification yard, checks are taken, showing the cars as they stand in the train. Wheel reports are made on typewriters and the bills lined up in station order and placed with the wheel reports. These are delivered to the conductor when he reports to the office, where he examines, and signs for, bulletins and checks his watch with the Western Union clock. He then goes to the caboose on his train and is ready to highball.

All westbound coal moves into the westbound receiving yard, which is connected with the old and the new humps, and the cars are inspected, journal lids raised, and the packing set up. The waybills have been moved forward to the locomotive and are dispatched by pneumatic tube to the hump office. As the train passes the yard entrance a man calls off each car's initials and number, and its tare weight. These facts are recorded by Telecord on cylindrical records in the hump office, so that before the train has come to a stop in the receiving yard, a check list can be made for comparison with the waybills. When the trains are handled over the new hump, the cars are given underneath inspection from a pit located on the east slope of the hump. This pit is equipped with powerful lights that illuminate the underbody and running-gear of the cars. An oiling system is installed on this slope, and car oilers with air guns apply lubrication to the journal boxes as the cars are humped; then close the lids.

So the coal trains move in and out of the great yard at Russell—coal in an amount that is bewildering, unbelievable. And yet for all of the enormity of this coal tonnage, Russell Yard assimilates and classifies and dispatches it with the complete competence and assurance characteristic of your American railroad and your American railroader.

Besides the grimy coal trains moving in and out of Russell Yard, there are the hurrying manifest jobs—No. 99, two sections of 95, two sections of 93. No. 97, with perishables from the South, in for re-icing. From the Cincinnati gateway, Nos. 92, 94, 98. From the Columbus gateway, No. 92 and two 94s. There are also two pick-up runs from the Huntington Division—one in the morning and one at night.

The eastbound trains are flat-switched from both ends in the eastbound yard and classified in station order, leaving Russell for both the Huntington Division and the Big Sandy Sub-Division.

Westbound manifest trains are handled in the old classification yard, which has twenty tracks. Bills are thrown off as the train pulls by the Yard Office, and the closely meshed gears of things begin to turn. As the trains pull in, a Class B or running inspection is made by carmen, who watch for dragging equipment and loads with lading shifted.

After the train comes to a stop, a twenty-five-pound air reduction is made, followed by an air inspection; then the air is bled from the train line. A switching list is made out for the yard conductor and brakemen, and the switching begins from both ends.

When the switching and classification have been completed, the Mechanical Department takes over. Hose couplings are hooked up, and the "yard air" is coupled to the train line and the pressure built up to seventy pounds; then the brakes are applied and each car is inspected. Follows a release of the brakes, and another inspection is made to see that all brakes have released properly. Now the road engine backs on, and the engineman applies and releases brakes, making certain that he has full control.

There are train orders and a clearance, and another train pulls out of Russell Yard to go booming down the C.&O.

OFFICES AND FACILITIES

At Russell Yard, the three-story brick yard office building lifts above the maze of tracks, there on the south side of the new hump. On the first floor are the offices of the General Foreman, together with a lunch room, shower baths, and washrooms. On the second floor are the Fuel Forwarding Agencies, weight-report separating and forwarding rooms, a darkroom for developing films, meeting room, Machine Foreman's room, stationary and file rooms, ladies' rest rooms. The third floor has a Route Clerk's room, Record Clerk's room, Bill Clerk's room, a Yard Clerk and wheel-report room, Conductor's room, offices of Yardmaster, Assistant Terminal Trainmaster's office, Timekeeper's room, Car Tracer's room, and the Freight Service Agent's office.

A pedestrian underpass beneath the new hump connects the office building with a parking lot to the north of the hump. A footbridge links the third story of the building with the top of the hump itself.

The Locomotive Department at Russell maintains two round-houses, having a total of twenty-nine stalls—fifteen in the old and fourteen in the new house. Between them is located a well-equipped machine shop. This locomotive terminal can dispatch 125 large locomotives daily.

Each roundhouse has a separate turntable. Run-around tracks make it possible to move locomotives from the roundhouses to the eastbound yard without interfering with main-line or yard movement. A modern power house is located near the engine terminal, joined to which is a locomotive boiler washing system.

Both eastbound and westbound yards are equipped with air lines so located that trains may be charged with air and the brakes inspected and tested before engines are coupled to trains. This is a time-saving feature of the utmost importance.

Repair tracks, located on the south side of the new hump, are so arranged that cars from the two westbound classification yards can quickly receive light repairs and be returned to service. The modern repair shops at Russell are equipped to rebuild and make heavy repairs to all classes of freight cars, and have a capacity of forty-five rebuilt cars a day.

The Maintenance of Way Department has a well-equipped shop at the new hump, which includes facilities for repairing and rebuilding car retarders and equipment.

Ample water storage facilities are provided at Russell, which consumes one and one-half to two million gallons daily, or enough water to supply a city of some 30,000 to 40,000 population. A treating plant conditions and filters this water, which flows through five and one-half miles of mains to the water columns located in the various yards.

The American Creosoting Company, with storage facilities for one million ties, maintains a tie-treating plant at Russell Yard.

A vast, bustling freight car metropolis. Day and night, come rain or shine, fog or blizzard, eternally jostling cars form rank. Boxcars, coal cars, loaded cars, empty cars, cuts, and trains. Iron hands locked tight, slack running out, mighty road engines, black plumes waving, shouting lustily. That is Russell Yard, in war or peacetime.

CHAPTER XVI

THE RAILROADS CARRY THE MAIL

Santa Fe Fast Mail – Wheat and Stock

The mailing and receiving of letters, parcel post, and express matter have become so much a part of everyday American life that few of us give a thought to the vital part the railroads of the country play in speeding the United States mail to your door and mine.

There is no class of service rendered by the railroads in which they take more pride than that of the safe and swift transport of mail and express, and this in spite of enormous burdens imposed by wartime traffic. The movement of mail, from the days of the Pony Express and the stage coach to the present time, provides a highlight in American history, as well as being one of the marvels of the world.

Probably the most famous and the fastest of the great trains that literally and figuratively "carry the mail" are the Santa Fe *Fast Mail and Express* trains, Nos. 7 and 8. These trains operate between Chicago and Los Angeles, via Kansas City, La Junta, Colorado, and Albuquerque, New Mexico. They are the only regularly scheduled daily trains that run through under one management, carrying mail and express exclusively, west of the Missouri River.

Before the United States' entry into World War II, *Fast Mail* Nos. 7 and 8 were scheduled in the public folder, with the notation that this train would carry a limited number of coach passengers in the combined car used for a crew rider on the rear end. This service, of course, was limited because of the many people who wanted to ride Nos. 7 and 8. One man we know in particular—a man in a position to occupy a stateroom on the best trains if he so desired—looked forward with boyish enthusiasm to his annual trip out to the Coast when he could ride the *Fast Mail,* even though it necessitated occupying a common coach seat.

Because of the distance they cover, Nos. 7 and 8 have accumulated more car-miles than any other trains of this type in the country.

Now let us examine a small part of the important detail of moving the United States mail between the East and the West Coast. Scores of roads serve as feeders in the delivery of mail to the big trunk lines that rush it through.

No. 7 makes connections at Barstow, California, with trains bound for San Francisco. The Chicago–Washington State mail is handled from Chicago to St. Paul and return by Milwaukee Nos. 56 and 57, crack mail trains. On the Great Northern it is Nos. 27 and 28, east and west, between St. Paul and Seattle. Burlington No. 15 carries most of the San Francisco mail and express from Chicago to Union Pacific Transfer at Council Bluffs, thence it moves by the U.P.'s crack No. 9 to Ogden, where it is turned over to the Southern Pacific. Eastbound, the Union Pacific's No. 6 receives mail and express from the S.P. and delivers it to the Burlington.

Other solid trains of mail and express in the East are the New York Central's No. 159, No. 35 and Second 35, the latter carrying express and sleeping cars for Detroit. From the Boston & Albany comes No. 9. All of these trains make connections with Santa Fe No. 7, Milwaukee No. 57 and the Burlington's Second 15. These trains also carry Chicago mail and express.

Eastbound, and making connections from these roads, are Nos. 14 and 32 of the Central, with the *Century* carrying a through working mail car. The Pennsylvania's No. 13 carries mail, New York to St. Louis; also No. 11.

Timetable records reveal that the Santa Fe operated No. 17 as early as September 12, 1897, for the purpose of carrying mail. On June 8, 1901, No. 17 became No. 7, and was designated at first as *Mail and Express* to Kansas City, from which point it was the *Mexico and California Mail and Express.* Then for many years it was known as the *Fargo Fast Mail;* then it became the

Fast Mail. In later years, No. 7 was the *Fast Mail and Express,* as it is known today.

This service, which is maintained daily, has shown continuous improvement, meeting always the demands of traffic and the demands for expedited service, for which it was originally established. This is shown in the reduction of the running time from Chicago from sixty-six hours and ten minutes, as of February 7, 1915, to forty-seven hours in 1935, a schedule held rigidly until 1942. Then, because of heavy war traffic on the road, it was increased to forty-nine hours and twenty-five minutes, the present running time.

Eastbound No. 8 carries the same class of equipment as No. 7, and operates on a schedule of fifty-three hours and twenty minutes, Los Angeles to Chicago. Since the United States' entry into the war, No. 7 is operated in two sections daily, the first section being limited to eleven cars and a rider for the crew. So far as possible, No. 8 is limited to twelve cars, but there are days when she handles fifteen or sixteen. This applies for the most part east of Albuquerque, and at such times as she is not being run in two sections.

Every possible attention is given to the motive power and equipment that handle Nos. 7 and 8. When they are due, everybody on the line is on the lookout for them. The dispatcher will run them around anything on the road, for in wartime their on-time performance is vital. The high lords of the steel rail, for they are Government trains.

This writer has ridden the locomotives that haul 7 and 8 over every mile of the Santa Fe upon which they operate. Rarely are they late. The newest and finest engines are theirs—the beautiful and fast 3460-class east of La Junta, with rare exceptions; the 3776-class, La Junta to Los Angeles, or, possibly, a '65-class 4-8-4.

The Santa Fe's 3460-class 4-6-4 or Hudson-type locomotives have 84-inch drivers and carry a boiler pressure of 300 pounds, and they *do* "carry the mail." To ride one of these engines, handling Nos. 7 and 8 over the First District of the Colorado Division between La Junta, Colorado, and Dodge City, Kansas, is an experience that lives with you a long time. Here is probably the equal, if not the fastest, of any stretch of track in the country. The distance is 201.4 miles. Here I have ridden both steam and Diesel locomotives faster than anywhere else in the United States.

No. 7's average time, Dodge City to La Junta, is 61.9 miles an hour. Eastbound, No. 8 averages 55.2 miles an hour. The westbound *El Capitan*, the *Super Chief*, and the *Chief* average 73.7, 72.9 and 55.8 miles an hour respectively. Eastbound, the *El Capitan* averages 71.2, the *Super Chief*, 71.4, and the *Chief*, 68 miles an hour. These figures are on-time performance.

To the layman, averages, like statistics, often make little impression. However, the motorist who, in normal times, averages thirty-five miles an hour, must drive fifty and fifty-five miles an hour whenever possible to maintain this average for the trip. It is the same on a railroad. To mark up an average of seventy-odd miles an hour over a 200-mile run, your engineer must run around one hundred miles an hour wherever he can. This to compensate for slowdowns and stops en route.

The *Chief* and *Fast Mail*, for instance, make a five-minute stop at Syracuse, Kansas, halfway over the Division, for engine service. This applies to both east- and westbound, as these trains are hauled by steam locomotives. No. 8 also has flag stops at Lamar, Colorado, and Garden City, Kansas. There are, of course, many places where war-traffic conditions at times cause delays. But the Mail goes through. Note again those average speeds of sixty and seventy miles an hour.

The Santa Fe 3460-class is one of the three 4-6-4s in the country boasting 84-inch drivers and 300-pound boiler pressure. The other two are the Chicago & North Western Class E-4 and the Milwaukee's F-7, having tractive efforts of 55,000 and 50,000 pounds respectively, against 49,600 pounds for the 3460-class. However, for fast-running with a train up to seventeen cars, they would, I believe, have some difficulty in staying with the 3460s.

I have ridden the 3460-class ahead of sixteen mail and express cars, loaded to the roof, and for mile after mile the speedometer needle was never below one hundred miles an hour. The Santa Fe has the roadbed and the rail, and they really wheel them on this Division, as elsewhere. I have seen "slow orders" received on engines on the Santa Fe to reduce speed to seventy miles an hour. And that is something for the book.

To watch them pick up and deliver mail at these high speeds provides a thrill. However, you exercise extreme caution in watching it, for the mail bags, there in the mail crane, fairly skim the running board. It is there—and then it is gone, all in a heart beat. Swish, bang, presto—your letter, with its three-cent ticket, has started its journey as United States mail.

The riding qualities of the 3460-class locomotives are exceptional, and you come to accept a meteor-like 100-mile-an-hour speed as you did a mere dawdling sixty. The 3460 tenders ride like a baby in a cradle. They have six-wheel trucks and carry 20,000 gallons of water and 7,107 gallons of fuel oil.

Another feature of these engines is their vision, which is the best of any steam locomotives I have ever ridden. When you are in the cab of one of these big Hudsons, walking down the railroad at one hundred miles an hour, the world's your oyster.

It was one of these 3460-class—the 3461—as perhaps you remember, that made the all-time-record run between Los Angeles and Chicago without being cut off, except at the usual servicing stops, and to cut cars in or out of the train. The train was No. 8, the Santa Fe's *Fast Mail*.

I was riding the engine of Great Northern's No. 28, their Fast Mail, from Minot, North Dakota, to New Rockford, over the Second Sub-Division of the Minot Division, 108.8 miles, when the engineer, as have many others, asked me why I spent so much time riding locomotives. I gave him five primary reasons, which I will set down here.

(1) To observe at first-hand the all-around operation of the railroads. And certainly there is no finer grandstand seat than in the cab of an engine, for there you are at center ice. (2) To watch the performance of American locomotives, which from boyhood have held the greatest fascination for me. (3) To look at the railroad itself. (4) To become better acquainted with the railroad geography of the United States. (5) To see song and game birds, birds of prey, and the wide variety of both domestic

and wild animals that pass in review as you ride in a locomotive cab.

A few minutes later, we pulled into New Rockford. The Great Northern runner climbed down, motioning for me to come along. "Farrington," he said, "speaking of birds—up here on this road, we get more of 'em with a locomotive than a lot of folks get with a gun."

We walked to the front of the engine, and there on the pilot was a Hungarian partridge, a prairie chicken, and a pheasant. I had seen birds on locomotives before, but never a mixed bag like this.

Some time later, I was telling the story to C. D. "Spike" Eberhart, of the Santa Fe. Spike lives in La Junta, Colorado, and runs the *Fast Mail* eastbound and the *Chief* westbound, to and from Dodge City. That he is a crack engine runner goes without saying. He is, further, a great sportsman, and the secretary of the La Junta Isaac Walton League of Colorado.

Being an outdoor man and a bird lover, Mr. Eberhart remarked that it was unfortunate so many game birds were killed by locomotives. He also revealed the interesting fact that the two varieties that seldom or never contested the right-of-way with a locomotive were magpies and crows—the birds most despised, but the smartest.

Hawks, Spike went on to say, occasionally fell prey to the locomotive, together with many species of ducks, often owls, and a few doves, with pheasants the worst sufferers. Doves, he told me, next to magpies and crows, appeared to be the smartest when it came to keeping out of the way of a rapidly moving train.

The point of this digression is that Mr. Eberhart apparently knows his birds, as he knows railroads and locomotives. He has been running engines on this Colorado Division "speedway" for forty years. He is representative of the high type of men who handle trains in the United States—alert, keen-eyed, competent. Behind them the traveler and the U. S. Mail ride fast and safely.

WHEAT AND STOCK

Wheat marketing, for the past fifteen years, has become an increasingly difficult problem for the railroads. Approximately one-fourth of the Nation's staple food product, wheat, is produced in that great bread basket, largely included in Kansas, Oklahoma, and Texas. Climatic conditions are closely akin, and here the crops are harvested and ready for market in a tight span of three to four weeks. This period has steadily been shortened by the increasing employment of the combine-harvester, which cuts and threshes wheat in a single operation.

In prewar years, the railroads were in a position to assemble empty boxcars from all parts of the country to meet the demands for carriers for this deluge of grain. These cars were rapidly shuttled back and forth between shipping points and great wheat terminals at a speed limited only by the inspection and unloading facilities of the terminals. Railroad men and shippers, working in close co-operation, were able just about to keep pace with the increasing tempo of the harvest when a new factor appeared on the horizon.

Through the aid of Commodity Credit Corporation loans, the wheat surplus of recent years was carried over from one harvest to the next in storage on ranches, grain elevators, and at sub-terminals and terminals. Millions of bushels of this wheat came into Government ownership just ahead of the harvest season. The railroads then were faced with the task of moving this stored wheat from wheat-raising districts to tidewater storage at the same time that the new crop was being harvested. It seemed a superhuman task, but, through the close co-operation of railroads and shippers, it was accomplished, as all available empty boxcars were rushed in from north, south, east, and west.

However, when the wartime industrial production hit its stride, the railroads and the shippers found themselves in difficulty. Industry and the demands of a nation at war created a serious car shortage. No longer was it possible to make-up and store the necessary boxcars for the wheat rush. As a consequence, it was necessary to erect new farm and elevator storage for the crops of 1942 and 1943. In many localities, it was impossible to provide inside storage and outdoor wheat piles sprang up, pending the day this wheat could be assimilated in the markets of the country.

The demands of war increased the use of wheat and wheat products. The vast wheat surplus dwindled, creating a demand for Canadian wheat. This, instead of materially relieving the pressure on American Railroads, thrust on them a further burden, because of the fact that it was necessary to supply cars for the movement of this Canadian wheat.

The result was that while we were supplying 250 cars daily to aid in the movement of Canadian wheat, great piles of American wheat remained on the ground throughout western Kansas, Oklahoma, and Texas. Fortunately, because of a normally dry climate, there was little deterioration.

In the Southwest, 250,000,000 bushels of wheat are produced annually. Of this, the Santa Fe moves 105,180,000 bushels—70,120 carloads—together with 33,500 cars of flour and 16,500 cars of millfeeds. Thus we find the Santa Fe, owning 35,121 boxcars, moving 120,120 cars of wheat and its products, in addition to the thousands of other commodities required by a nation at war.

To sum it up, the car-loading of grain in 1943 was the heaviest in years. It was handled, however, without addition to the boxcar supply, which because of the demands of war has not been built up in appreciable numbers.

Like the mail, the grain trains must go through.

The transportation of livestock from the range country of the Southwest to market requires, possibly, as high a degree of efficiency and know-how as anything else connected with the railroad business.

To the shipper of livestock, quick handling and prompt delivery is often the margin between profit and loss. Buyers on the livestock markets usually hold the arrivals down to the number they expect to slaughter each day. The daily production of the processor is, so far as possible, held to a strict schedule. Animals arriving on the market after the buyers have finished for the day must be held over until the following market day. This involves feeding costs and, often, a decline in the quality of the animals offered for sale.

The problem of the railroad is to make certain that the stock arrives on time. This applies to Iowa hogs—only a few hours from the Chicago market—exactly as it applies to cattle from Texas and sheep from Colorado and New Mexico and Wyoming. The longer the haul, the greater the difficulties of the carrier. By law, animals in transit must be unloaded, fed, and watered after they have been en route thirty-six hours. This is a costly operation for the stockman, and he is continually seeking routings and service that will eliminate these stops so far as possible.

The bulk movement, however, of cattle and sheep from the range country does not move directly to market, but has for its destination the pasture and pens of the "feeder," where the animals receive their final fattening.

Stock movements come in seasonal surges, further complicating the transportation problem. The Santa Fe, for instance, has some 7,900 stock cars. The annual spring movement of cattle from the Southwest to the Flint Hills' pastures of Oklahoma and Kansas requires upward of 7,500 cars. At the same time that this movement is in progress, lambs come from Colorado and Western Kansas, hogs from the Corn Belt, and fed cattle from all parts of the Middle West—all to become a part of the daily stockyard movement.

Another animal migration takes place in the fall, when the Flint Hills' pastures begin to dry up. Cattle fattened on the lush bluestem grass of that area start their drift to packing houses and to feed pens in Missouri, Iowa, and Illinois. Here again the peak movement joins with the normal marketing of other meat animals, which provides one grand rush.

The Iowa and Illinois farmers, the Missouri cattle feeders, the New Mexico sheepmen, the Texas cattlemen, and the Kansas grazers all want their animals delivered at the stockyards, unloaded and fed before eight A.M. Any later delivery brings an immediate protest, and a noon delivery is likely to result in a damage claim.

In peacetime, everything is rosy, and the stock trains are scheduled and storm through with reasonable dispatch. But in wartime it is another story and another headache for the harassed railroads. Texas cattlemen, moving their beeves to Flint Hills,

...Angeles (4-8-4 type, the first steam locomotive to be run through from Los Angeles to Chicago. On #8, the fast mail and express, east of Lamar, Colorado on the Colorado Division. Photo by Otto C. Perry.

Union Pacific #6 Mail and Express at sundown east of Grand Island, Nebraska, on the First Subdivision of the Nebraska Division. Engine 829, 4-8-4 Type. Note the 14-wheel tender. Photo by H. W. Pontin Railroad Photographs.

N.Y.C. #9, fast mail, with one of the early 4-6-4 Type Class J-1C, running over the water pan at East Palmyra, N. Y. It is only on the rarest occasions that they do not get a full tank. Courtesy New York Central.

Great Northern #27 Fast Mail between St. Paul and Seattle hauled by #2511 4-8-2 Type, Class P-2 descending grade at Belton, Montana. Photo by Otto C. Perry.

Santa Fe Extra 5004 West with 4200 tons and 81 cars of wheat and stock for the Pacific coast running over the Pecos Division near Vaughn, N. M. The engine is a 2-10-4 Type 5001 Class. Photo by Otto C. Perry.

The ever ready co-operation of the railroads with the war effort is illustrated here when a break occurred in the big inch pipe line during high water of the Arkansas River at Little Rock in the spring of 1943. J. D. Farrington, chief executive officer of the Rock Island, granted permission allowing pipe line engineers to construct an emergency line across the railroad bridge and in less than 99 hours oil was again flowing to the eastern seaboard. Courtesy of Rock Island Lines.

New 5400 horsepower Rock Island freight Diesel running over the Electro-Motive test track at La Grange, Ill., before delivery in April '44 to do her bit for the war effort. Courtesy Electro-Motive Corporation.

once were given the right of way over other traffic that they might reach their destination before the expiration of the thirty-six-hour limit. Now they go into the hole to allow troop trains and fighting equipment to roar by.

The manpower shortage requires the operation of longer and slower trains, delays in terminals are more frequent, and, to top it all, the headache of all headaches is the problem of unloading at the stockyards. Here, as everywhere else, we find the lack of experienced workmen is responsible for much lost time.

The stockman howls and fumes, and is met with the cry of, "Don't you know there is a war on?" This makes the stockman very happy, and he says sweetly, "Yes, by the humpbacked Judas Priest, I know there is a war goin' on, and I'm in it!"

The amount of livestock being produced on the vast ranges of the West and Southwest is about fifteen per cent above normal. However, feed shortages in the Middle West are reducing the finish and final weight of the animals to the point where it is claimed that this increase is almost entirely lost. But this fact in no way alleviates the transportation problem, for, fat or lean, a steer occupies just so much space in a stock car. And time marches on, entirely disdainful of war traffic and the manpower shortage.

Yet, the railroads have to deliver, and do—somehow.

Rail movement of livestock in 1943 was heavier than in 1942, heavier than any immediately preceding year before the ambuscade at Pearl Harbor. Although there was no increase in the number of stock cars in service, an average increase of car movement was registered in 1943 to the tune of 2,000 cars a week, and this with only occasional and minor delays.

Add to the movement of United States mail, the movement of grain and the livestock trains—all vital to the life of the Nation; all thundering down the steel rail on the Union Pacific, the Southern Pacific, the Great Northern, the Rio Grande, the Rock Island, the Santa Fe, and other railroads of America. All performing miracles, doing the "impossible," in the transport of peace- and wartime commodities—with peacetime plant and equipment.

CHAPTER XVII

WAR TRAINS OF THE ROCK ISLAND

Troop Movement – Train Escort – Military Police

Within a matter of a few hours after bombs began raining down on Pearl Harbor that Sunday morning of December 7, 1941, more than twelve hundred crack mile-a-minute passenger trains were standing on terminal tracks in the United States, ready to begin the movement of the largest military force in American history the greatest average distance.

Great road engines had been assembled, trains made up, crews called, tracks cleared. In those few scant hours, the decks of American Railroads had been cleared for action, and twelve hundred passenger trains were ready to roll.

The Rock Island Lines occupied a prominent place among those railroads that were "standing by," for included in this list of twelve hundred trains were fifteen Diesel-powered streamliners from the Rock Island's famous fleet of speed queens of the rails —the Rockets.

The cry had been raised that the railroads of the country were done, that they were close to being down and out. With the coming of World War II, the railroads tossed this charge back into the teeth of the croakers and the critics. The Iron Horse and a steel rail have come to stand as the Nation's first line of defense.

At the beginning of the second year of World War II, a troop movement, as has been revealed in the opening chapter, was starting every six minutes. And for every soldier moving down the steel rail, there must be eight tons of equipment. Twenty-five hundred special trains thundering over the railroads each month. Millions of tons of impedimenta rolling hard on the heels of

194

the boys in O.D.—guns, ammunition, tanks, half-tracks, jeeps; clothing, food, blankets; planes, parts, oil, gasoline.

Twenty-five hundred special troop trains, transporting approximately two million soldiers, sailors, marines. Almost as large a military personnel traveling aboard scheduled train movements.

During 1943, the railroads carried more than ten million troops in these special trains and their special cars. This tremendous transportation load was reflected in the record-breaking performance of all railroads. In the case of many systems and networks, spinning their web across midwestern states, linking North and South and East and West, every existing record went by the board in that second grim war year.

The Rock Island, for example, with more than eight thousand miles of track in fourteen states, stretching from Minnesota nearly to the Gulf and from Memphis and Chicago to New Mexico, carried the greatest freight tonnage and the largest number of passengers in the road's entire history.

During 1943, according to J. D. Farrington, chief executive officer, much of this immense volume of traffic consisted of men and materials of war. Rock Island passengers, carried on regular troop trains during the year, totaled more than 15,466,653, for an increase of over 73 per cent above 1942, and 300 per cent above that carried previous to the war in the year of 1939.

During the second year of the war, the Rock Island Lines' carloading showed an increase of 76,724, or 6 per cent over the loadings for 1942, and 43 per cent over 1939, while the revenue ton-miles increased 29 per cent over 1942, and 121 per cent over 1939.

During 1943, this railroad carried over 42,380,395 tons of revenue carload freight, or double the volume of 1939. This increase was handled in only 10 per cent more carloads by increasing the average freight loading from 23 tons per car in 1939 to 30.2 per car carried during 1943, and increasing the average car miles per day from 45 to nearly 63.

The foregoing facts and figures eloquently attest to the stability, the dependability of the great carriers of America. These Rock Island Lines' figures give some idea of the huge transportation job accomplished. During the prewar years, the harbingers of despair little realized that more than ten billion dollars were being spent by the railroads on new roadbeds, heavier rail, track realignment, which reduced grades and curvatures, as well as the acquiring of the most modern streamliners and the incorporation of breath-taking fast freight schedules.

Between 1937 and 1940, the Rock Island brought out its fleet of fifteen famous Rocket trains. These trains have proved up, and readily forecast the construction of future lightweight passenger equipment.

In setting the 1943 passenger record on the Rock Island, the road's many steam-powered and conventional-type trains, particularly the *Golden State Limited* and the *Californian*, were loaded to peak capacity throughout the year.

Officials of the Rock Island Lines, as have the officials of other railroads, immediately realized the importance of extending every possible courtesy and service to the men and women traveling in uniform. If motives other than patriotic duty were needed, the fact that the troops of today are the shippers and travelers of tomorrow would have been sufficient.

Since these troop movements began, employees have been repeatedly instructed to exercise every care to provide the type of service that will be remembered after the war. It is human nature to remember the bad rather than the good. And yet the latter will linger in the back of the human mind, like a smoldering, almost forgotten spark, needing only a small thing to revive its hot flame. The important thing is the creation of a spark that will live.

To quote from a handbook, published by the Rock Island and containing instructions for their train "escorts" (the railroad representatives who accompany troop trains): "When the wheels of the last troop train have stopped, and the last soldier has returned to his home, it is to them that we must turn; for their patronage will mean the difference between success and failure."

Rock Island officials, early in 1941, set up a special military department, the function of which was to supervise the movement of troops over the System, to see that all matters pertaining to these movements were handled according to the regulations set down by the War Department.

Since this railroad provides direct main-line service from the north-central states to the Southwest, where a great number of military camps are located, troop movements, movements on special trains, as well as those movements included in regular service, have been largely to and from that area. The Golden State route, which originates in Chicago, with branch-line connections to the North and the South, runs to Tucumcari, New Mexico, where it connects with the Southern Pacific Lines, reaching on across Arizona and California to the Pacific Coast.

Two through trains, the *Golden State Limited* and the *Californian*, are operated over this route daily. These trains have been booked to capacity, largely with military personnel, a great part of the time.

Between Memphis and Tucumcari, the Rock Island route is almost as the crow flies. Across Arkansas, Oklahoma, the Texas Panhandle and into Tucumcari, New Mexico, reach the silver rails of the Rock Island. This route is of vast importance in the movement of troops and war materials. In another chapter we have reported on the war activities of the Southern and its important network reaching out to the great war camps and training grounds of the South. It is at Memphis that the Southern and four other important lines of the Atlantic states make junction with the Rock Island. Still other roads link its western terminals in Texas and New Mexico.

The great number of flying fields in the Southwest have been provided with excellent passenger service through both this and the Golden State route.

The movement of a special troop train, from its point of origin to its destination, usually requires the track facilities of two or more railroads. Each road supplies its own locomotive, caboose, train crew, and Passenger Department escort. Such movements, particularly when they involve several railroads, require close co-ordination and include a vast amount of detail. It is remarkable, however, how simply and directly the procedure has been worked out.

All railroads have shown the highest degree of co-operative effort in the delivering and accepting of trains, even when burdened to the utmost with the endless rush of war transport. The same is true concerning relations between carriers, the Association of American Railroads, and the military agencies of the Government.

Let us now examine something of the detail of troop movement, where it originates and how it operates, once the intricate wheels have been set in motion.

All troop movements originate with the General Staff of the Army, which sends out an order specifying the nature of the movement to the Army's Services of Supply. It is then turned over to the Traffic Control Section of the Army Transportation Corps for advance planning. This information is then sent by teletype to the Railroad Military Bureau involved.

These bureaus are a part of the regular passenger association, and are located at New York, Chicago, and Atlanta. Routings over one or more railroads are then assigned, a number called a "Main" number is given the route, and the railroads that are to handle the movement are notified. The individual roads, however, are familiar only with the details of the movement over their own rails—the time the train may be expected and the destination or the connecting line to which it is to be delivered.

After the railroad, in this case the Rock Island, has been notified of the movement, an escort from the Passenger Department is assigned to accompany the train. This escort works directly with the train commander during the time the train is on his particular line.

The Rock Island has about twenty-five passenger representatives available for this work. During emergencies, this group is supplemented by members of the Freight Traffic Department. As frequently happens on the Rock Island, an escort may leave Chicago, ride a troop train to Denver, and, upon his arrival there, be assigned to another train destined for Kansas City. There he may immediately be assigned to another troop train.

After being assigned to a "Main," the escort contacts the Operating Department of his railroad. Here he ascertains the time of arrival—if the train is to be received from a connecting line—or the time the train is scheduled to leave, if it originates on his line. When the train arrives, he confers with the train commander, or with the officer in charge of the train, regarding any details of service that may need attention. Although the escort has no jurisdiction over the troops themselves, he acts as the railroad's representative and does everything possible to assure the safe and efficient movement of the troops and their officers.

The escort's first duty is to check the tickets held by the train commander, which cover all of the men aboard. He then makes a careful inspection of the train, making certain that there is adequate water, ice, cups, also a supply of towels. When a diner is provided, he confers with the commanding officer and steward to complete arrangements for the serving of all meals. Where kitchen equipment has been set up in baggage cars, adequate supplies of nonperishable food for the entire trip are usually stocked at the point of origin. The troop commander, however, can wire ahead to emergency supply points (regular military installations) where he may replenish his supply. Fifteen such supply stations are located on the Rock Island Lines, and it is seldom necessary to procure supplies from other sources.

All military movements, of course, no matter how small, are handled with the utmost degree of secrecy. The escort's association with the troops aboard is of a necessity limited. Ordinarily, the men do not know their destination, and a new escort is immediately a target for "leading" inquiries. Unless he is constantly alert, he may unwittingly find himself revealing military secrets.

For instance, there is the casual, "Say, Mister, where we goin'?" Or there may be the approach in which some homesick kid speaks of his home town, his folks, and finally says, longingly, "Gee, we ain't goin' any place near there are we?"

On runs west from Memphis, your Rock Island escort finds that most troops, particularly those in the Air Corps, believe they are bound for Texas, and are mainly interested in the possibility of seeing cowboys.

Many of these kids often find themselves traveling through a country familiar to them. But regardless of how near they are, there can be no visit with the home folks, even during an extended station stop, not even by telephone. Sometimes other means are found for the expression of some bit of homely sentiment. There was, for example, the Oklahoma kid who was so overjoyed when he discovered himself in the old home state that he asked permission to get off the train at a small station—just to stand in his bare feet on "good old Oklahoma earth."

Often there is some personal problem that the friendly train escort can help to solve, as in the case of the troop train traveling across Arkansas when a soldier literally lost his shirt. The window was open, as they often are on a troop train, and the boy's shirt, which contained $112 was blown out of the window.

He reported his loss to the escort on the fast-running Rock Island train. The escort stopped the train at the next station and wired the station agent at the depot nearest the point where the soldier had lost his shirt. The agent enlisted the aid of the section foreman, who boarded a section car and started out in search of the missing garment. It was found and forwarded to its owner at the camp for which the troop train was destined.

It's all in the life of a troop-train escort, and never a trip that does not provide at least one little human episode for this important member of the railroad's personnel to file in his memory book.

Perhaps the escort has a boy of his own in service; perhaps there is a neighbor's kid in the Army or Navy or Air Corps. Perhaps there are youngsters from his home town whom he knew intimately—the boy who used to fill the gas tank of his car, the boy next door who played on the high-school football team, the kid who roared down "Main Street" in his hopped-up jallopy, now driving a tank in the red, screaming hell of the battle line. The train escort is just another of the rank and file of home folks—a man always willing and anxious to be of help to our boys in service.

MILITARY POLICE

Besides the fighting men who ride the troop trains, there are other thousands of soldiers, sailors, and marines who ride the Rock Island's regularly scheduled trains. For them there is no train escort, and it becomes the duty of the employees of the Rock Island—and all other railroads—to extend to these men and women in service every possible courtesy.

Since the military personnel so traveling on the Rock Island and other railroads are not accompanied by escorts, they are in charge of the conductor of the train, and, of the utmost importance to the railroad, the Military Police or Shore Patrol, or both.

In carrying out the enormous military movements, the railroads recognize the contribution of the khaki-clad Military Police and the blue-clad Shore Patrol. These men aid in the efficient transportation of millions of troops and servicemen. Wherever there are trains, you will find the polite, intelligent, specially trained members of the armed forces, who wear the arm brassards, "M.P." or "S.P.," that represent military authority.

You find them on the trains and in the jam-packed railroad stations. They are of inestimable help to the GI Joes and Josephines, as they offer aid to the thousands of military personnel who find themselves in strange cities.

"Where is the USO Canteen?"

"What train do I take?"

"I've lost my money and ticket. What shall I do?"

Your M.P. or S.P. man knows all of the answers. His duties go far beyond "police duties," and he likes to help the bewildered soldier or sailor who finds himself in difficulty. They go far in supplementing the service of station officials and information clerks.

The men of the Military Police assigned to ride passenger trains, particularly those operating between heavily traveled terminals, perform countless tasks important to the expediting of train movement. They patrol the platform before the train departs, directing servicemen and checking tickets. Before the departure of the train, they present a copy of their orders to the conductor of the train to which they have been assigned. Upon the departure of the train, and operating in pairs, they go through the train with him, as he picks up tickets, checking the passes and leave papers of the men in uniform. In this way, the least amount of annoyance is caused the serviceman; they are further available should any question arise regarding a soldier or sailor's transportation. If men are asleep, they move down the aisle of the car and awaken them, thus avoiding delay to the conductor.

Train patrols have jurisdiction over all service personnel, except members of the Merchant Marine, including command officers.

The Military Police receive the same basic training as all Army men, in addition to specialized training in police work. While they need not be large men, they must be fully capable of handling themselves if the occasion arises. Above all, they must be resourceful to the point of remaining master of any situation in a diplomatic manner, and without recourse to force, except as a last resort. For, first of all, your M.P. must be a gentleman, as he maintains the rules of conduct that govern the life of every man in uniform.

The police branch of the Navy Shore Patrol does not differ greatly from that of the Army, except that it has a smaller personnel, for the reason that the Navy is numerically smaller than the Army. These men selected for the Shore Patrol, however, must have had previous police experience.

Although the enforcement of discipline is a prime requisite, on trains, as elsewhere, your M.P. and S.P. man spends the greater part of his time in the performance of more agreeable duties. A serviceman is asked to button his blouse, to take his luggage from the aisle, to remove his feet from adjoining seats. A soldier, sailor, or marine is on parade before the public eye. Most of them are aware of this, and act accordingly; a few, however, must receive prompting from the M.P.

Military Police have been riding trains since the spring of 1942. Each commanding general of the nine service commands is responsible for the train patrols in his area. The Navy Shore Patrol was authorized by the Bureau of Naval Personnel in August, 1942, and was assigned to serve with the Military Police in joint operations. Both organizations are under the Provost Marshal General at Washington, D.C. This office maintains a number of command officers who ride the trains all over the United States and report on the conditions and the performance of duty by the Military Police and Shore Patrol in the various commands.

Only because of the efficient and intelligent co-operation of these organizations have the railroads been able to handle the enormous number of servicemen who ride the trains. They have rendered, and are rendering, a great service to the men in uniform, to the railroads, and to the American people. . . .

On the trains of America, on the trains of the Rock Island, we watch an endless parade of figures in olive drab and blue—on the Choctaw Rocket, on the Rocky Mountain Rocket, and many more. Blurred faces, waving hands. A fleeting moment we see them; then they are gone—except in our memory.

We see them at the great gateways of Denver, Des Moines, Chicago, Kansas City, Memphis; at busy junctions, at country depots—eager faces, sober faces, lonesome faces.

Boys earning their "Wings"; kids from "Boot" camps, like the Great Lakes Training Station; fledgling marines, San Diego bound—all hurrying to new stations, to new worlds. Thousands of men and women on furlough, returning for that all too brief visit home. Many for the first time see the great plains of the West, the Rocky Mountains; oil derricks, vast fields of golden grain, cattle on the range; Indians, cowboys.

Strange, new places; endless panoramas. GI Joe and Josephine have a front seat in the biggest theater on earth, and, in wartime, the grimmest.

Today these fighting men of the Nation are riding the Central, the Pennsy, the Santa Fe, the Rio Grande, the Southern—the Rock Island. Tomorrow they will be riding the troop transports on the Seven Seas. To them the train escort and all other men and women of the Rock Island say, "Bon voyage, and—hurry back."

CHAPTER XVIII

TROOP TRAIN ON THE MILWAUKEE

When Fighting Men Ride the Rails

There is something about a troop train—something fascinating, mysterious, grim. Soldiers are riding the rails. Where they are going, God only knows. You grin, you wave—you get a little lump in your throat. This business of war is hell!

It is spring—the spring of 1942. The air has that soft, balmy feel. Buds are swelling, trees are joining the Easter parade in all of their fresh, new finery. You gaze dreamy-eyed from the window; your feet are beginning to itch; you know that old restless feeling; you want to get out and away. Your glance swings to the railroad track, lingers there. What a day to climb aboard a train and rush off to those always greener fields around the bend. Why must you be shackled to a desk, to a machine—to a job?

An engine whistles; something tugs at you, deep inside. Sort of gets you, a locomotive whistle—kind of makes you want to climb aboard. A smoke plume pounding into the sky, jaunty, triumphant. The exhaust is chanting, husky-voiced. It is like the beat of a mighty drum. What is it saying? You listen to its impatient cry. Now you get it. Over and over that iron-lunged locomotive is shouting of its conquest of time and distance. The pulse of that big passenger-hauler—for it is a passenger, you see —is fast.

"*Hurrying-hurrying-hurrying!*" That is what it is saying, breathlessly.

A mighty boiler-front, flashing drivers, and side-rods. You can see the pale blur of faces now, faces framed in the windows, faces staring out at a new, strange world—lonely faces. A few are happy-go-lucky, unconcerned, but mostly they seem lonesome, lost.

Through those fast-moving windows you glimpse drab coloring. Olive drab! This is a troop train! You tighten up. You come down to earth—hard. Spring. Birds singing; flowers in bloom; warmth in the sun. These things you forget. Those boys are going to war!

You watch until the last car has hurried past. You are sober, thoughtful now. You pick up the thread of things; you go back to your job, working a little harder—harder than you have ever worked before, knowing that your efforts are needed to back those fighting men. You realize now how close the home front is to the battle front.

Yes; there is something about a troop train. . . .

The big maroon and gold 4-6-4 Hudson-type passenger rolled out of the lead track at the Western Avenue roundhouse of the Chicago, Milwaukee, St. Paul and Pacific, and moved down to couple onto its train in the Chicago terminal of the Milwaukee Road. It is 9:45 P.M. The night is warm.

A sister 4-6-4 engine is backing onto the famous *Olympian*. Green lights gleam high up on that big boiler-front. The crack limited of the Milwaukee tonight is running as the first section of a troop train—a "Main" train. Let's call it Main 109.

The *Olympian* pulls out of the train shed, and emerges from beneath the Chicago Daily News Building—the *Olympian*, carrying signals.

Something like ten minutes later, the second section highballs out. There are fourteen Pullmans, a baggage car, and two baggage cars converted into kitchen cars in charge of a Mess Sergeant. These kitchen cars contain field stoves and iceboxes, and each will feed from 200 to 300 men. Sometimes the men remain in their seats, and the food, the "chow," is brought to them. Again, they may file up to the converted baggage car, where they are served by the mess-stewards.

On a troop train, the railroad maintains liaison with the Army by means of a train escort, as explained in the previous chapter—a man who goes along to aid the Train Commander with matters pertaining to transportation, extra supplies, mail, special stops, and other things.

In a drawing room of a Pullman, we will find a G.H.Q. on

wheels. From this headquarters the Train Commander attends to all the details of his traveling Army camp, of which he alone knows the destination.

The sleepers are well stocked with linen and blankets, as the kitchen cars are well supplied with a satisfying variety of grub. Porters make up the berths as carefully as they would for any Pullman passenger. Taps are sounded at a time set by the Train Commander, and later than in camp.

There are thirty-nine men to a car, the Pullmans of this train being the standard car of twelve sections and a drawing room. Two men sleep in a lower, one in an upper. The Navy puts one man in a lower. But this is the Army.

Troops spend a goodly portion of their daylight hours at the windows—seeing America as guests of Uncle Sam. They average about six moves during the training period, and have an opportunity, perhaps, to view the Hudson, the Rockies, the Great Lakes; they ride into the deep South; they see the famous Florida and California beaches—wartime tourists.

"Gee, it's a big country!"

"Man, look at those mountains!"

"Hey, Joe, there's an Indian!"

But scenery sometimes doesn't mean much to a homesick kid —a kid like the boy in "Upper 4." There's no place in all of the world like Main Street back home; like the East Side in little old "N'York"; like Fulton Street, Brooklyn.

You are in the Union Depot, Chicago. The big 4-6-4 Hudson —790,000 pounds of steam motive power—has coupled on. The air-brake and signal-hose and steam-heat connections are hooked up. The brakes are tested. The train conductor comes up with the orders, and it is almost time to begin the run over the first engine district to Minneapolis, Minnesota, a distance of 420 miles.

The fireman has built up his fire; the engineer, a veteran of forty years on the Milwaukee, tries the water pump, injectors, the sanders, checks the lubricators. Back down the train a lantern waves a highball. The engineer reaches for the throttle. The side-rods start to creep; there is a bark from the exhaust; the

206

drivers bite hard at the sanded rail. A troop train is on the move. Main 109.

Through a man-made canyon, under viaducts. Faster, faster. The engineer makes a running test of brakes near Tower No. 2. The exhaust roars up again, hard, quick. The train clatters across the tracks of the Chicago & North Western. Approaching Mayfair now at fifty-five miles an hour.

A red signal. The engineer closes the throttle; the mechanical stoker is slowed down. The engineer curses the towerman. This is a troop train, the second section of the *Olympian*. The light winks from red to green. The exhaust barks angrily. This is the second red block that has checked the train's flight. The engineer looks at his watch. Four minutes have been lost. He hooks up the reverse lever, an eye on the valve pilot.

You are in open country. The fireman checks the water glass, the gauge cocks, opens the throttle of the feed water pump a little more. He gets down for a look at his fire. The speedometer registers seventy-five miles an hour. The whistle screams often for highway crossings.

Three hundred pounds the steam gauge registers. Smoke lies back over the train. The exhaust is singing its eternal refrain. *Hurrying-hurrying-hurrying!* The engine is burning coal—9,000 pounds an hour—coal that for a million years lay buried in the earth. Coal, now the burning energy that rushes a troop train westward through the night.

One o'clock. Milwaukee. The train grinds to a stop. The locomotive is serviced. A new engine crew climbs aboard. Again the highball. Signals are checked. Another running brake test. Everything is done with clocklike precision. You marvel. You know a little thrill. You are proud of American Railroads.

The Milwaukee is a great road. For ninety-two years it has played a part in the Nation's progress. The Milwaukee serves the Midwest, reaches across the plains, the mountains to the great Northwest. It links with steel twelve states, this Milwaukee Road —twelve rich and bountiful states.

A distant signal glimmers; the home signal is red. A switch engine is blocking the Milwaukee cut-off. The heavy train comes to a stop; the engineer whistles out the flagman—an angry long and three short. Now the track is clear. The flagman is called in. His lanterns are bobbing far back. His white lantern waves. You are moving.

There is a heavy grade up to Brookfield—eleven miles. You listen to the deeper, slower note of the exhaust. But the needle on the steam gauge, you note, is glued to the 300-pound mark. Right on the pin. The feed water pump is working at full capacity.

The train is over the hill now. The reverse lever is hooked up. Again the exhaust is saying, *Hurrying-hurrying-hurrying!* The speedometer needle crawls to seventy-five—seventy-five miles an hour. Eight pounds back pressure. The big drivers are turning over 300 times a minute. You are riding an iron thunderbolt, riding it to music—the music of steam and steel. Marshal music tonight on the Milwaukee, for this is a troop train.

Music to lull tired men to sleep, as they are cradled by the gentle movement of the big Pullmans. But not all of the boys back there are asleep. A kid in an upper, his eyes wide open, is staring at pictures in the dark. Pictures of home.

The boy in Lower 8, the one who is awake, listens to the slow, regular breathing of the kid beside him, to the noises in the night—the engine up ahead, the wheels, clicking off the rail-lengths. He is thinking of Dad and Mother, and that last letter from Mary. He wonders where he is going, how long before he will be coming back. How long?

You are living with those boys back there—the youth of America. Your neighbors' kids and mine. Murphy, Zelinski, Smith, and Jones.

The fireman calls, "Clear Signal!" The echo comes back from the right side of the cab, "Clear Signal!" If only those boys in the cars behind could be as safe tomorrow as they are tonight, riding the rails on the Milwaukee. . . .

Oconomowoc is rushing to meet you.

"Clear order board!"

"Clear order board!"

The fireman shakes some dead ashes into the ashpan, opens the fire-door to observe the operation of the distributing jets of the stoker.

Shore patrol examining liberty papers of naval personnel at Rock Island station in Memphis, Tennessee. Courtesy U. S. Navy.

Among their other duties the Military Police examine transportation and passes of Army personnel going on furlough. Courtesy U.S. Army.

Freight trains have speeded up the transportation of foodstuffs to feed the men and women in the armed forces. This Rock Island meat special is made up in Silvis, Illinois, each morning with fresh meats from the Southwest. The train covers the 174 miles to Chicago daily, delivering its important consist to connecting eastern lines at that point before 1.00 P.M. The engine is 5010, 4-8-4 Type Class R-67B. Courtesy Rock Island Lines.

Rock Island Extra 4026 West—a main loaded with Naval Personnel. The engine is 4-8-2 Type Class M-50 and was snapped running 60 miles per hour east of Goodland, Kansas. Photo by Otto C. Perry.

Milwaukee Land 222 West, advance section of the regular coast time freight #263, with a consist of machinery and armament material for the shipyards of Washington. The engine is Class S-1 4-8-4 Type. This picture was taken west of Portage, Wisconsin. Courtesy of the Milwaukee Road.

The Scenic Limited, Train #1 of the Rio Grande, carrying many members of the Ski Troops en route to their training quarters at Pando, Colorado; in the Royal Gorge just east of the Hanging Bridge on the Pueblo Division. The engine #1800 is the latest of the Rio Grande's crack 4-8-4 Type Class M-68. Photo by Otto C. Perry.

C. & O. Engine #602 with signals; 4-8-4 Type Class J-3; with first #47, the Sportsman, at White Sulphur Springs, West Virginia on the Allegheny Subdivision of the Clifton Forge Division. This train carries many a war worker from Tidewater, Virginia to Detroit. Courtesy C. & O. Railroad.

Three o'clock. Portage. The troop train stops. Lights are wink-, ing. Roundhouse employees swarm around the hard-breathing Hudson with power Alemite grease-guns. Their exhausts sound like triphammers. The engine is completely serviced, and again the long, dark line of cars rolls on. The train enters cab-signal territory, and signal indications corresponding to semaphore signals are visible in the cab.

There is a slowdown at Wisconsin Dells. Something jams in the crusher of the stoker. You watch the fireman working on it, grim, sweaty, profane. The coal is too far back in the tender for easy hand-firing. The engineer eases off on the throttle; the steam pressure drops to 205 pounds. You feel the nervous ten-sion. This is the second section of the *Olympian*. This is a troop train. Main 109.

The fireman finds a piece of scrap iron in the stoker, clears it. The stoker is again feeding coal; the fire brightens. But the water is low—only about an inch showing in the bottom of the glass. The feed water pump has been shut off while the stoker was dead to keep the steam pressure from dropping too much. The engineer is nursing the engine along, pampering it; watching the white dial of the steam gauge; looking at his watch.

He is eleven minutes late—better than twenty minutes behind the first section, the *Olympian*, carrying signals.

New Lisborn. Twenty-two tons of coal roar into the tender. Black diamonds. Highball! The engineer is hitting her hard—rapping the stack. The train smashes at the tunnel at Tunnel City, Wisconsin. The grade is descending now. The cab sways and jerks. You look at the steam gauge, the speedometer. Eighty miles an hour!

They are pinning back the ears of Father Time—making up time. La Crosse. The engine is serviced again. A new crew takes over.

The train crosses the Mississippi and you are in Minnesota. The track follows the river. To the left are the hills of the Mississippi Palisades. You are reminded of the New York Central's right-of-way along the Hudson. Some of the boys back in the Pullmans are thinking that too.

The cruising speed here is seventy miles an hour. It is a water grade, with frequent curves. The engine is being worked at about half throttle, which gives the engineer a chance to use the sludge remover, blowing water from the boiler, thus reducing the concentration of salts and other impurities.

You see thousands of Canadian geese in the river and on Lake Pepin. Now and then you notice a flock of mallards, resting in their northward flight. There are slowdowns at Winona, Lake City, Red Wing.

St. Paul Union Depot. It is a busy place. Trains are arriving or departing. The eastbound *Morning Hiawatha*, the Great Northern's *Empire Builder*, the Northern Pacific's *North Coast Limited*, the North Western's *North American*, the Burlington's *Zephyr*, and locals on the Omaha, Great Western and Soo Line. A North Country crossroads, St. Paul.

Your engine is uncoupled. Another big 4-6-4 locomotive backs on. This engine will handle the train to Harlowton, Montana, you are told—a distance of 915 miles. This is one of the longest, if not *the* longest, continuous runs for a coal-burning steam locomotive in the world. Almost one thousand miles! Immediately you have an even greater respect for this big passenger-hauler.

East of Minneapolis, the Milwaukee Road burns coal mined in Indiana. West of Minneapolis, on the main line to Harlowton, Montana coal is used. This coal is a distant relative of lignite, and it is a good fuel but difficult, in that it sparks very easily and thus becomes a fire hazard. Specially constructed front ends and ashpans are necessary.

The vast agricultural west begins at Minneapolis. The soil is being prepared for planting. Ducks in the water holes, and a kid back in the train sighs, thinking of that dog and gun at home. He is going hunting, but not for ducks, and the game he is after will shoot back.

There is a stop at Glencoe for water. Engine crews are changed at Montevideo. You notice a sign: "The only Montevideo in North America."

The rail is bad now; the drivers begin to slip, even at high speed. The engineer jockeys the throttle, one hand on the sanding valve. Low clouds; rain. The bottom has dropped out of the sky. Signals are difficult to see.

"Where the hot hell is that signal?"

"There she is! Clear signal!"

The engine slipping has caused the exhaust to tear holes in the fire. The steam pressure is down. The fireman is firing by hand, doctoring those holes through which cold air is rushing.

"Signal at forty-five."

An application of the brakes brings the speed down in preparation for a possible "stop" at the next semaphore. Two torpedoes. A soldier says, "Hell, they're shootin' at us!"

A flagman appears in the wet smother ahead, waving a red flag and a fusee. He catches the engine grab-irons and yells that No. 263 is stalled with a broken air-hose. The train crawls on, and follows 263 to the next siding. Twenty-three minutes late now.

The weather brightens up. There is a stop at Milbank for coal and water. Twenty tons of coal; 18,000 gallons of water. The fireman shakes the grates, opens the water sprinkler to deaden the ash and cinders, puts in a few scoops of coal, filling the back corners. The engineer and conductor check a "31" order just received.

Twenty miles of one per cent ascending grade out of Milbank. The fireman says, "Before we had mechanical stokers, a fireman got a real workout on this stretch." The engineer is giving the engine a merciless beating, trying to win back some of that lost time. He makes up three minutes on the hill. Descending, speed restrictions and a speed-recorder tape serve to prevent the man at the throttle from attempting to make up more time.

There is a stop at Aberdeen. The big Hudson is serviced, and the crew is changed. Leaving town, the exhausts are a little sloppy, and the engineman puts on the injector, thus aiding the feed water pump to get additional antifoam solution into the boiler. There are a few more blows from the sludge removers, and the water is finally conditioned to the point where the exhausts are dry and snappy.

You look at endless prairie, as far as the eye can see. There is no house, no living thing. Back in a Pullman, the kid from Brooklyn says, "My God, it makes you feel like you was never outdoors before." The boy from the East Side shakes his head. "Jeez, there ain't nobody livin' in the joint."

Coal at Roscoe, South Dakota. At Mobridge you adjust your watch from Central to Mountain Time. You are crossing the Missouri River now, the "Big Muddy," and entering the Standing Rock Indian Reservation. You pass through Wakpala, an Indian settlement. Stolid faces staring; faces at the windows staring back.

The sun is going down. The sun has exploded. Such color no man could ever put on canvas. "I wish my mother could see that," the kid in Lower 8 tells his bunkie.

A coyote lopes off at a skulking run. "Look at the dog," says a kid from Boston; "he must be lost."

The porter grins. "Dat's a kioty, boss."

Night draws the shades on a vast world in which no living thing moves. Someone says, "Gosh, it's a big country."

At Thunderhawk, South Dakota, you meet a one-hundred-car freight train. It is carrying lumber, mining products, a few carloads of sheep. You have met many such trains, reminding you that the Milwaukee Road is a mighty steel bond in Uncle Sam's great domain, a roaring artery of transportation, backed by 35,000 loyal and patriotic employees.

You try to visualize the amount of raw products alone hauled by the Milwaukee—cattle, sheep, wheat, lumber—and you are staggered. The eye cannot see, nor the brain comprehend, such immensity as is spread out along the right-of-way and beyond. The boys in the train are getting a geography lesson they will never forget. This is America. This is what they are fighting for.

North Dakota now. Bowman. The silver beam of the headlight reaching out like a glinting steel blade. The onrushing train crosses the Bad Lands, rolls down a long grade to stop at Marmarth. Your troop train is on schedule.

Again a new engine crew. Soon you are entering Montana, with the first stop at Baker, which, in years gone by, was one of the largest wool-loading centers in America. Coal and water at Mildred. Miles City, named after General Nelson A. Miles, Indian fighter. Yesterday's wild frontier town. You can see those dim false fronts, almost hear the pistol shots of celebrating cow-boys.

The stouthearted Hudson-type locomotive is serviced, and the last engine crew to handle engine 145 on its 915-mile run takes charge for the run to Harlowton. Low western stars; a beautiful night. And then, suddenly, the headlight picks up a running herd of wild horses. One or two are hit.

The locomotive is whistling for Harlowton, a shrill, trium-phant blast. It is 6:15 in the morning. The engine seems to re-lax, breathes easier. Nine hundred and fifteen miles! Service well performed. It is uncoupled and turned over to a hostler and his helper. It will be taken to the roundhouse for inspection and grooming for its return trip to St. Paul.

Newsboys are at the station to get their morning papers from Miles City. A few typical westerners are on the platform.

"Hey, Joe, look at the cowboy."

"I thought them guys was just in Western-story magazines."

"Heigh-o-o, Silver!"

A great Westinghouse electric locomotive backs onto the train. This particular unit, you are told, was run by President Harding between Deer Lodge and Missoula a lot of years ago, and now carries a bronze plaque on each side of the cab to that effect. This locomotive has really seen service.

You climb aboard. Except for the blower fan in the heating boiler compartment and the hum of the traction motors, every-thing is quiet. Highball! Your troop train is moving. There is no booming exhaust, no clatter of reciprocating parts, no roaring firebox. The glamour and romance of railroading, as dreamed by almost every small boy whose highest ambition is someday to become a locomotive engineer, is somehow missing.

And yet here is power, silent power that picks up the heavy train and moves it with the invisible might that is electric energy. Main 109, the second section of the *Olympian*, is swinging into its steel stride on the Rocky Mountain Division of the Mil-waukee Road, hauled by an electric engine.

In the far distance ahead are snow-capped mountains—the Rockies! Off there is the Continental Divide—the rock-ribbed backbone of America. There is something about that first glimpse of the Rockies that sends a thrill dancing down your spine, something that makes you want to shout, "This is God's country!"

You see green, irrigated valleys; thousands of fine-looking cattle grazing. Beefsteak on the hoof. Funny, you never really appreciated beefsteak until they started to ration it. At Martindale, you glimpse some elk not far from the right-of-way.

The train winds through a sixteen-mile canyon, through narrow passages that seem to threaten to rake the sides of the cars. Sharp curves, high trestles, tunnels. In these tunnels, you really appreciate the fact that you are riding an electric locomotive. No stifling smoke and steam, no choking gas.

Ringling. Lombard. You cross the Missouri River again. The Big Muddy? The Missouri never got that name here, for the mountain water is crystal clear. Your train follows the Madison River to Three Forks, Montana. You can actually see trout in the river.

Back there, the kid from Maine says, "Holy smoke!" He did his first fishing as a bare-foot boy, with a home-made willow pole, and strung his fish on a forked stick. Mallard ducks and a few redheads on the river. Cattle and sheep along the banks.

At Three Forks another engine crew, and soon you are speeding through picturesque Jefferson Canyon, following the Jefferson River. Here the real Rockies hit you right in the eye.

Climbing. From Three Forks to Continental Divide, a distance of fifty-five miles, you climb 2,285 feet nearer the sky—1,992 feet in twenty-one miles between Piedmont and the summit over an ascending grade of something like two per cent. The voltmeter shows only about 2,700 volts, instead of 3,000, indicating that a freight is climbing the eastbound grade.

Second No. 15 meets the freight at Donald, on top. One three-unit motor, with a tractive effort of 172,000 pounds, and a two-unit helper, having a tractive effort of 112,000 pounds, are handling the ninety-car freight drag.

You are looking at a black tunnel-mouth now. Pipestone Tunnel, 2,300 feet long. The electric engine goes into regeneration, converting the traction motors into generators, and the resistance holds the train at a predetermined speed down the moun-

214

tain into Butte. The fireman has read the K.W.H. meter and made the proper records in the book provided for that purpose. From these records and similar records maintained at substations, credit is obtained for current produced by regeneration.

You are told that, with the controller in "off" position and when a speed of thirty-five miles an hour has been attained, the combination lever is moved to third motor combination and the regenerating lever placed in regenerating position. At forty miles per hour the engineer moves the main controller handle into the first notch until the ammeter goes to zero, when the handle is rapidly advanced to the sixteenth notch.

There is no grinding of brakes, no brake-shoes smoking, no speed checks, and the only time the brakes are applied is when rounding certain curves when the speed must be reduced below that controlled by regeneration.

There is a stop at Butte, and you enter then fairly level country, running at around sixty-five miles an hour to Deer Lodge. Here are the headquarters' shops for the Rocky Mountain Division and Milwaukee electrified territory.

Once more a new crew. Deer Lodge stands at 4,508 feet altitude, and the train is now running on a practically water level descending grade for the next forty miles. Then you start to climb the Bitter Root Mountains. From Superior, Montana, to East Portal, the boundary between Montana and Idaho, the train lifts 1,425 feet in thirty-two miles, reaching an altitude of 4,170 feet at the entrance of St. Paul Pass Tunnel, which is 8,771 feet in length. There again the electric engine goes into regeneration, as the train rolls down to Avery, Idaho.

That is all for the electric locomotive. A nice bit of railroading over 442.7 miles. Hydroelectric power, born of the mountains—the Belts, the Rockies, the Bitter Roots—has carried a train over them. A troop train.

A whacking big 4-8-4 Mountain-type steam locomotive backs down. It was built in the Milwaukee Road's shops. It burns oil. This 4-8-4 engine has been overhauled recently and is right in the pink. It is waving a white plume. Kind of seems like a feather in her hat, just for the privilege of hauling United States soldiers.

You are riding now down the St. Joe—the Shadowy St. Joe.

215

The fireman watches the engineer, operating the firing valve according to the demands of the locomotive. Curves are frequent. The flanges squeal against the outside railhead; now and then the brakes take hold.

Deer are standing on the far bank of the river east of St. Maries, Idaho. Several times you have seen beavers at work on their dams. You are not the only one who has seen these brief pictures of American wild life. The eyes of the homesick kid in Lower 8 brighten; this is something to write Mother and Dad about.

The train stops at St. Maries for water. . . . Night. . . . Spokane Union Depot. . . . You are moving again. Main 109 is running right to the dot. Ten minutes away the *Olympian* is roaring through the blackness. You arrive at Othello at 1:25 A.M. Here, with a little twinge of regret, you take leave of this 4-8-4 steam locomotive. There is something about one of these big engines that stirs you, grips you. Truly, engines of war! Emblematic of industrial America and its fine transportation system, this mighty iron horse.

Whispering out of the gloom comes a General Electric locomotive. It has, you learn, the so-called bipolar-type motor. Slowly, ponderously it backs down. Iron couplers clasp, lock. The electric engine has a look of competence—a silent brute, performing its task with the ease of a soft-spoken giant. . . .

You are crossing the Columbia River, flowing strongly, quietly below you. Othello is an hour behind the marker lights of our troop train. It is moonlight. . . . You climb Beverly Hill in the Saddle Mountains . . . Ellensburg, Washington. . . . The train strums on steel; you are looking at the Yakima River. After a time the right-of-way begins to lift into the foothills. Up, up into clear, cold air. Snowy rims. The Cascade Range.

Snoqualmie Pass. Snoqualmie Tunnel, 11,890 feet through the mountain. The grade falls away; the engineer is using regenerative braking. Off to the left, Mt. Rainier lifts out of the mist —a giant ice cream cone against the sky. Your mind's eye brings into focus beautiful Puget Sound, the Strait of Juan de Fuca, Cape Flattery—land's end. The blue Pacific! Out there a war is

216

being fought—a grim and terrible war. These boys back in the train are going to join it. . . .

First No. 15, the *Olympian*, will continue on to Tacoma, Washington, the Western Terminus of the Milwaukee Road. Main 109 has as its destination another port city. It pulls slowly into the station, stops. The Milwaukee Road has delivered a troop train to the Pacific Northwest.

The soldiers detrain, fall in, march away. You watch them, a funny feeling inside—pride, heartache. There's the kid from Upper 4, the kid from Brooklyn, the kid from Lower 8. Hup! Hup! Hup! There they go. Murphy, Zelinsky, Smith, and Jones. Your neighbors' kids and mine. Yes; there's something about a troop train. . . .

CHAPTER XIX

BATTLE LINE OF THE C.&O.

Tidewater Coal – Signals – Military Move

Solid trains of coal are run through from Russell Yard to Presque Isle for dumping into the Lake freighters. The Presque Isle docks are located on Maumee Bay, near the mouth of the Maumee River, about seven miles from Toledo. Yard crews at Wallbridge move the trains of Lake coal over the trackage of the Toledo Terminal Railway to the Presque Isle Terminal, where it is placed in storage yards to await unloading.

Included in the facilities at Presque Isle are three Brown Hoist coal-dumpers, and we mean coal-dumpers. What these steel-muscled machines do with a 50-, 60-, 70-, or even a 120-ton car of coal is amazing. Here is revealed the two-fisted manner in which things are accomplished in "soft" America, the friendly, easygoing country that the little yellow men and the Prussian military machine thought they could lick.

From the yards at Presque Isle, the coal is switched to tracks serving the piers in cuts or groups of cars, commonly called "tides" or "cargoes," which conform to a particular shipper's requirements. Upon reaching these pier tracks, the cars are dropped by gravity to a point where an electrically operated "mule" can lay its muscular steel arm on them—the same kind of mule we saw in operation at the ore docks in Cleveland in the Pennsylvania Railroad chapter.

This mule propels the coal car up an incline and spots it on a huge cradle-like elevator. The hoist goes into operation, lifting the car and contents bodily between supporting steel towers. The cradle then is tipped, and the coal spills into the yawning mouth of a conveyor called a "pan." Steel aprons control the flow of coal, thus preventing breakage. The car is turned completely over; then the hoist gently, easily, returns it to the original position on the pier. It is "kicked" from the elevator cradle, and moves then by gravity down an incline to the "empty" track.

The coal in the pan flows through a big telescopic chute, or "trimmer," into the hold of the boat.

Each of the three coal-dumpers at Presque Isle has a rated capacity of fifty cars per hour. The low-level type of pier here has features of great importance to coal shippers and consumers, in that the breakage of coal through rough handling is almost entirely eliminated.

Coal from the vast mining districts along the Chesapeake and Ohio, coal from Russell Yard, coal from Presque Isle—coal on its way to industrial centers on the Lakes, to war plants, to greedy locomotives, to homes. The red-grimed ore boats carrying coal as a return cargo to the far tip of Lake Superior—to Duluth, to Two Harbors, to Superior.

In 1942, coal in the amount of 15,654,717 tons was dumped over the docks at Presque Isle—265,231 cars. On April 29 of that year, 1,957 cars—114,333 tons—roared into the yawning holds of those sturdy carriers, the Lake boats. This meant that one car was dumped *every forty-four seconds!*

While the combined capacity of the three coal-dumpers is 150 tons an hour, or 3,600 cars per day, it must be remembered that this represents continuous operation. Allowing for time lost in docking and movement of boats during loading, the actual loading capacity is estimated at sixty per cent of the rated capacity, or 2,150 cars per day, equivalent to approximately 118,800 tons.

NEWPORT NEWS AND NORFOLK TERMINALS

At Newport News, the chief Atlantic port of the Chesapeake and Ohio, the shipping facilities are the largest occupied entirely by one railroad. The yards and sidings have a total capacity of 10,300 cars. The terminal is situated on the north side of Hampton Roads at the mouth of the James River, and consists of the property east of NY Cabin (Mile Post 14), including coal, merchandise freight, and passenger piers, and the necessary receiving, classification, forwarding, and storage yards, and floating equipment. Included is a branch line of 8.2 miles, extending from Old Point Junction to Phoebus, Virginia, which serves the communities of Hampton, Langley Field, and Old Point Comfort, Virginia.

The Norfolk Terminal, on the east side of the Elizabeth River, is situated across Hampton Roads from Newport News in the business district of Norfolk. Traffic between the Newport News and Norfolk Terminals is handled across Hampton Roads by means of the passenger steamer *Virginia*, the steam tugs *George W. Stevens*, *F. M. Whitaker*, *Richmond*, the oil tug *Chessie*, and a fleet of tugs and barges. Interchange is made with nine railroads at Norfolk, using car floats between Newport News and connections with the Norfolk and Portsmouth Belt Line at Sewell's Point.

Of the two coal piers at Newport News, Pier No. 9 is of the high-level elevating type, and Pier No. 15 is of the low-level elevating type. Pier 9 is 1,200 feet long and 90 feet high, with docking space for six vessels. Pier 15 has berth space for one vessel.

The low-level operation of Pier 15 is the same as at Presque Isle, and it has a capacity of about thirty cars—1,500 tons per hour. It is designed principally to handle prepared coal with a minimum amount of breakage.

Pier 9 is for the fast handling of "slack" or "steam size" coal, with a maximum dumping capacity of 6,000 tons, or 120 cars, per hour. Three traveling cargo towers equipped with telescopic chutes and trimmers and one bunkering machine, designed to reduce hand trimming in the holds of the ships, are in operation on the downstream side of the dock.

Coal trains of 160 cars, arriving from the West, are pulled into one of the ten Receiving Yard Tracks, each of which is capable of holding an entire train. After the usual mechanical inspection, the waybills are checked to determine the consignee and grade of coal, each car is tagged according to its classification, and then the train is "humped," as the cars roll into various of the thirty-nine tracks. Coal that is not moved direct to the piers is switched to one of the storage yards. Of these the

Dawson City Yard, adjacent to Pier 9, is the largest, having a capacity of 1,800 cars.

During 1942, 4,283,000 tons of coal were dumped over the piers at Newport News, a total approximately sixty-three per cent of the previous five-year average. This reduction was due to war conditions. The record dumped during one year in the five-year period was 10,351,000 tons.

In normal times, this coal is for movement to Atlantic Coast points—including Philadelphia, New York, and New England —and foreign ports.

HUNTINGTON TERMINAL

Huntington, West Virginia, occupying a position at approximately the center of the Chesapeake and Ohio System, is the headquarters of the Western General Division. It is the largest city in the state and an important industrial center, with a population of 80,000. It was founded and laid out by and named for that great railroad builder—Colis P. Huntington.

Huntington is a terminal point for passenger crews, an interchange point with the Baltimore & Ohio and transfer point for the transshipment of coal to river barges. Exclusive of the C.&O. facilities, the city is the home of 175 industrial plants, which are served by the road. These include such nationally known names as the International Nickel Company, American Car and Foundry Company, Owens-Illinois Glass, and others.

Main-line track facilities through the terminals of Huntington and Ashland, Kentucky, which is 4.5 miles east of Russell, include three running tracks between Barboursville and DK Cabin, four between DK and HO Cabins, three between HO and KV Cabins, two over the Big Sandy Bridge, three between BS Junction and Clyffeside, four between Clyffeside and NC Cabin, and three between NC Cabin and Russell Yard. The three-track sections are equipped with color-light automatic signals for movements in either direction on any track without the use of train orders.

Huntington Yard switching territory extends from a point just east of Mile Post 501, Guyandot, West Virginia, to the point of connection with the West Huntington Belt Line, near Mile Post 506. Classification is handled at the 16th Street Yard, which has a working capacity of 500 cars.

Ten regular manifest trains pick up and set off cars at Huntington, together with eleven locals and "Bulldogs" operating east and west out of Huntington, and "Extras" moving through Huntington with loads from the mines and empties for them returning to the coal fields.

On an average day, something like 5,000 cars are handled in and out through the Huntington Terminal. A total of over thirty passenger trains is operated daily over the trackage here, including twelve branch-line trains and from two to six special troop movements. From 200 to 250 passenger cars are iced and watered every day at Huntington.

All passenger-train crews, except porters, terminate their runs at this point. The Huntington Freight Agency handles a large volume of l.c.l. transfer business. As an example, on May 8, 1943, forty cars of merchandise were loaded and thirty-two unloaded.

The heaviest tonnage handled at the Huntington Terminal is the coal destined for transshipment to Ohio River Barges. There are three river tipples, operated by the Ohio River Company, Island Creek Coal Company, and the American Rolling Mills Company.

The coal originates in the Kanawha, Coal River, and Logan coal fields, and moves as part of "Extra" trains bound for Russell Yard, and is set off at Huntington. Here the coal is weighed, humped, classified, and switched to the river tipples in cuts not to exceed sixty-five cars.

On May 8, 1943, 230 cars were set off and 219 cars were dumped at these three tipples. During the year 1942, the tipples dumped 3,981,436 tons, for a monthly average of 331,786 tons. In the first five months of 1942 an average of 365,174 tons per month were dumped, an increase of 9.5 per cent over the same period in 1941.

COAL FOR THE C.&O.

Coal, of course, is the fuel employed on the Chesapeake and Ohio for heating, for power houses, for thundering locomotives, and approximately 2,600,000 tons are used annually. This is about equal to 4½ per cent of the total tonnage originating on the line.

The distribution of coal to locomotive fueling stations and other points requires constant care and supervision. This work is directed by a Fuel Supervisor and his assistants.

A specially equipped instruction car moves to various terminal points, providing a means of instructing firemen as to the most efficient methods of turning coal into power. This contributes materially to the full utilization of locomotives and the prompt movement of trains.

And here we leave the coal fields and the mighty coal trains, booming down the rails of the Chesapeake and Ohio, and not without a feeling of regret. At the same time, we know a swelling pride, for this is America.

SIGNALS

The first automatic signals on the Chesapeake and Ohio were installed in 1910. These were of the electric semaphore type, and were put in operation on the main line between Newport News and Richmond, Virginia, a distance of seventy-four miles; also between Clifton Forge, Virginia, and Cincinnati, Ohio, a distance of 387 miles.

The color-light type of signal was developed around 1906, but its use was restricted at that time to tunnels until about 1913, at which time it was found practical for use at locations where long-range daylight indications were required. The use of this type of signal has progressed rapidly during the past twenty years.

In 1929, a progressive replacement program was begun over the system, which was completed in 1942. Again we see an example of progress on the C.&O. during the depression days.

There are several types of interlocking systems in service. These are located at junction points, crossings at grade with

RULE	INDICATION	NAME	ASPECTS A	B	C	D	G	H
281	PROCEED	CLEAR	G R			G → NUMBER PLATE		
282	APPROACH NEXT SIGNAL AT NOT EXCEEDING MEDIUM SPEED	APPROACH MEDIUM	Y G	Y G → NUMBER PLATE				
283	PROCEED AT NOT EXCEEDING MEDIUM SPEED	CLEAR MEDIUM	R G					
285	PREPARE TO STOP AT NEXT SIGNAL. TRAIN EXCEEDING MEDIUM SPEED MUST AT ONCE REDUCE TO THAT SPEED	APPROACH	Y R		Y → NUMBER PLATE			
287	PROCEED AT NOT EXCEEDING SLOW SPEED	CLEAR SLOW	G					
288	PROCEED AT NOT EXCEEDING SLOW SPEED PREPARED TO STOP AT NEXT SIGNAL	SLOW APPROACH	Y R					
290	PROCEED AT RESTRICTED SPEED	RESTRICTING	R Y	R Y → NUMBER PLATE				Y
291	STOP; THEN PROCEED IN ACCORDANCE WITH RULE 509-(a)-C	STOP AND PROCEED	R Y	R → NUMBER PLATE				
292	STOP	STOP	R R				R	

STANDARD SIGNAL ASPECTS, CHESAPEAKE AND OHIO RAILWAY CO. Office Supt. Telegraph and Signals, Richmond, Va.

First trick on the N. & W. C.T.C. machine at Roanoke, Virginia. This machine covers the operation on the Shenandoah Division from Roanoke to Stuarts Draft, Virginia, 96 miles. Note dispatcher's train sheet operating timetable and train order book left in foreground. These are used for non-C.T.C. portion of division. Courtesy N. & W. Railroad.

Santa Fe high-speed train order stand has proved an aid in wartime in eliminating the necessity of slowing up trains to pick up orders. Fireman hooping order from Engine 3227, 2-8-2 Type, at Isleta, N.M. on the El Paso District of the New Mexico Division. The lower hoop is for the conductor on the waycar at the rear end. Photo by Delano, Office of War Information.

other railroads, or other points where necessary. However, a number of these interlocking stations have been eliminated from time to time, and the switches and signals at these locations remotely controlled from adjacent stations.

Centralized Traffic Control, the great magician of modern railroading, and traffic locking between interlocking plants, under both of which systems trains are operated in either direction over a designated section of track or tracks by signal indications which supersede superiority of trains and without the use of train orders, are coming into use on the Chesapeake and Ohio. The present installations comprise a total of 70 miles of single track, 78 miles of double track, 20 miles of three track, and 1 mile of four track, or a total of 169 miles of road and 290 miles of track.

The locations of the major installations are as follows: Newport News to Oriana, Virginia; Ft. Lee to Richmond, Virginia; Gordonsville to Lindsay, Virginia; Walkerford to Tyree, Virginia; Covington to Alleghany, Virginia; White Sulphur Springs to Whitcomb, West Virginia; MacDougal to Gauley, West Virginia; Scott to Guyandot, West Virginia; West Hamlin to Ranger, West Virginia; Huntington, West Virginia, to Russell, Kentucky; Carntown to Stevens, Kentucky; Newport, Kentucky, to Cincinnati, Ohio; and Brighton to Cheviot, Ohio.

"Take siding" signals are in service at various locations, and are under control of the train dispatcher. This signal is of the position-light type, and the indication displayed consists of five white lights, arranged in the shape of a cross, and requires the train to enter the siding governed by the signal to meet or pass another train.

In recent installations of automatic signals, the signals have been approach-lighted, in which case the signal lights are normally extinguished and are lighted automatically by the approaching train. This results in a reduction in the cost of operation.

MILITARY MOVE

During wartimes, Newport News has been a point of embarkation and/or debarkation in every conflict in which the United

States has engaged since the days of the landing of John Smith.

Following Pearl Harbor, vast volumes of war materials and military personnel moved through the world-famous Newport News—guns, tanks, trucks, jeeps. Planes, bombs and bullets, and the men to fly them, and drop them, and shoot them.

Manifest trains, special trains, troop trains converge at Newport News. Frequently there are as many as twenty special trains handling military personnel pounding down the rails to Newport News in a day. From Fort Lee, from Fort Eustis, from Camp Patrick Henry, from Camp Peary they come—the fighting men of America.

During the years prior to World War II, the Chesapeake and Ohio built up a fine fleet of passenger trains—the *Sportsman*, the *Fast Flying Virginian*, the *George Washington*. A Virginia section of each is now operated as well as the Washington. The war, however, has made tourist travel unpatriotic, but it has brought to the C.&O. an unprecedented number of travelers concerned with the business of the war effort.

Military movements are handled in both regular and special trains. Because it required more trained traffic representatives on-line, the road closed its off-line offices and transferred these experienced agents to various points on the C.&O. Some of these men are assigned exclusively to military traffic originating on the road. Others maintain ticket offices at camps or military reservations. Still others accompany all special military trains over the system and are on continuous liaison duty between the Train Command Officer and the Railway Company. These representatives protect against such emergencies as rerouting, the securing of supplies, sickness, and many other details as they arise.

The Chesapeake and Ohio, together with all of the other railroads of the country, is today marching with Uncle Sam. Every thundering exhaust from the stack of a C.&O. locomotive is another shot for Victory.

The 740th Railway Battalion, formerly the 568th, is composed of approximately two-thirds of former Chesapeake and Ohio employees. And as of May, 1944, the C.&O. lists 4,357 in the armed forces.

They call it the "Battlefield Line"—these tracks of the Chesapeake and Ohio—for the road's main line reaches out from tidewater in Virginia, famous in Colonial and Revolutionary history, to pass through Williamsburg, the oldest incorporated city in America and the Colonial capital, and Richmond, the capital of the Confederacy, and Charlottesville, the home of Jefferson, to cross the Piedmont Valley, the beautiful Blue Ridge Mountains, the famous valley of the Shenandoah, and the high, tumbled summit of the Alleghenies. From here the steel rail of the C.&O. follows the lovely Greenbrier River, the turbulent New River, boiling through the Grand Canyon of the East, the placid Kanawha, flowing through the "Coal Bin of America," the beautiful Ohio to the "Queen City" of Cincinnati.

This is the iron road, the battle line of the Chesapeake and Ohio Railway, and its Executive Vice President A. T. Lowmaster is one of this country's finest railroaders.

During these grim days, the C.&O. is exercising every effort to maintain the high standards of comfort, convenience, and courteous service that earned the friendship of its patrons in happier times. When the curtain drops on the battle scene, the Chesapeake and Ohio will continue its history of pioneering improvements down the path of the Iron Horse.

CHAPTER XX

THE TRAIN DISPATCHER IN WARTIME

Train Dispatching on the Santa Fe

The train dispatcher is the man behind the gun on the railroads of America. He is the man with the "thousand track" brain; the man whose eye can see at a glance one hundred miles and more of steel rail; he is the master strategist; the sleepless, vigilant guardian of all trains. His is the power to command thundering locomotives, speeding limiteds, hurrying troop trains, flashing mail trains; trains of war material, trains of ore, grain, livestock. The *Twentieth Century Limited*, the *Tennessean*, the *Olympian*, the *Daylight*, the Santa Fe *Chief*—these and hundreds more of the crack trains of the country are as toys under the eye and the hand of—the Train Dispatcher.

Less than 5,000 train dispatchers direct the movement of all trains on all railroads of the United States. The immediate operation and the responsibility of safe movement of every last train in the country rest squarely on the shoulders of the train dispatcher, and not the slightest detail can be passed on to any subordinate.

Every minute of his eight-hour trick, the dispatcher is called upon to make instant and one hundred per cent correct decisions. There can be no hesitation, no appeal to someone else, no hedging or uncertainty. Never can he falter or withhold judgment; never can he err. He must know the condition of the track; the capabilities of all motive power; the character and experience, the whims and frailties of every engineer.

He knows, for instance, that the 3860 is a notoriously poor steamer and cannot be depended on to make the running time with full tonnage, even with "Highball" Bill Baldwin at the throttle. He knows, too, that "Flatwheel" John Smith will not make his time with the finest locomotive on the road. He must know these things and act accordingly.

He must be intimately familiar with every inch of track; the location of every siding, spur, signal, telegraph office—the distance between them; how long it will take certain engines to haul certain trains over that piece of rail under every possible weather condition. He must carry in his mind every engine and train moving in his district. He must know the location and speed of as many as twenty-five to one hundred trains traveling in opposite directions under their various classifications. He must know all of this, and more, for he is the man who keeps 'em rolling.

When the history of the second World War has finally been written, one of the outstanding chapters will record the record made by the railroads of the United States in handling 100 per cent more traffic than their manpower and equipment were designed for, even at peak rushes.

Many details of this enormous movement, for military reasons, are not available as this is written. You do not talk of the number of troop trains on the move, or the amount of guns, ammunition, tanks, and other war material in transit. These are war secrets, which your railroad man keeps under his hat.

The railroads are performing a far greater task today than during World War I. In 1917-18, the railroad transportation system bogged down. Uncle Sam took over, to discover at once that he had neither the experience nor the ability to bring order out of the chaos. Both the Government and the railroads learned a lesson then that they subsequently found of inestimable value when confronted by the problems of the present conflict.

Even today the obstacles are unbelievably great. There is a shortage of equipment, and it is wearing out. There is a shortage of manpower, and the men are wearing out. However, men and equipment somehow keep the war trains rolling. A few inefficient and inexperienced crews; a few poorly operated railroads could break down the whole transportation system.

It hasn't happened, and it won't happen, because every man, from call boy to president, won't let it happen. Certainly there is much to complain about and criticize, but the trains keep moving—the troop trains, the trains of war goods, fine trains for both civilian and the man in uniform.

And the man who holds the master key of it all is the train dispatcher—the man behind the man at the throttle.

A Draft Board official told a railway that a train dispatcher could easily be replaced in six months, a statement born of ignorance; certainly. If this "authority" had said six years he would have been nearer. Certainly a man would hesitate to employ mechanics of six months' experience to work on his car or build his house. Yet he would entrust lives and property to an "apprentice" in the dispatcher's office.

Only through years of experience does your train dispatcher acquire the judgment and ability necessary to the safe and efficient handling of trains. His schooling is long and arduous; he has to "grow" into the chair before the train sheet.

Regardless of how good a train dispatcher is, he can only guess at what is happening between stations. Once having issued orders, he can do nothing until the train with which he is immediately concerned arrives at the next telegraph office.

In single-track operation, the dispatcher must know the position of every train every minute, and so keep in touch with all trains always.

One of the most important developments of modern railroading has been Centralized Traffic Control. C.T.C. has increased the capacity of single-track lines where it has been installed fifty per cent and better. It has, further, eased the strain on the dispatcher. Nothing pleases your train dispatcher more than, after watching, guiding the progress of two opposing trains with C.T.C., to be able finally to direct one into a siding and slip the other by on the main track without holding either train.

The train dispatcher at his C.T.C. board takes infinite pride in the arranging and successful completion of such a nonstop meet. And it is surprising how often this is accomplished.

The first long-distance C.T.C. installation was placed in service on the McCook Division of the Chicago, Burlington & Quincy Railroad between Akron and Denver, Colorado, on what is known as the Colorado Sub-Division, over a distance of 111.5

miles. The dispatcher and his C.T.C. machine are located at Brush, Colorado, 24 miles west of Akron.

This dispatcher, like many of us—myself included—happens to be an ardent duck hunter. So every time he makes a nonstop meet, he has come to refer to it as, "Making a Mallard." The old "green head," so dear to many of us, is the prevailing duck in Colorado, and there yearly, in all of its splendor, gathers by the hundreds of thousands.

My friend, the dispatcher on the "Q," in using the expression, "Making a Mallard," has coined a phrase that is now used by many others operating C.T.C. machines on various railroads throughout the United States. I offer it here for the use of other dispatchers and railroaders who are duck-shooting enthusiasts.

TRAIN DISPATCHING ON THE THIRD DISTRICT OF THE SANTE FE'S ALBUQUERQUE DIVISION

The Albuquerque Division is part of the Santa Fe's main line to the Pacific Coast. It extends from Albuquerque, New Mexico, to Seligman, Arizona, a distance of 428.8 miles; from Dalies to Belen, New Mexico, 10.3 miles; and also the Fourth District, Ash Fork to Phoenix, 193.7 miles, with two branches, totaling 19 miles, in addition.

The Division headquarters and dispatchers' offices are located at Winslow, Arizona. The First District Dispatcher takes over from the New Mexico Division at Isleta, New Mexico, and dispatches trains from there to Gallup, a distance of 145 miles. The Second District man handles trains between Gallup, New Mexico, and Winslow, 127.7 miles. The dispatcher for the Third District is in command, Winslow to Seligman, Arizona—142.7 miles, via the westbound track, and 143.6 miles, via the eastbound line. The Fourth District man works between Ash Fork and Phoenix.

The system of maintaining dispatchers on nearly all railroads is approximately the same as that employed on the Santa Fe. The chief dispatcher has charge of the entire Division. He works from 7 A.M. to 7 P.M. He may have one, two, or three assistants, but he oversees all matters, receiving information from the Divisions on either side of him as to what is coming in the way of

231

A Light Day on the Second Trick of the Albuquerque Division—Third District

PASSENGER — THIRD DISTRICT — WEST
4:00 P.M.—12 M. DECEMBER 1, 1943

TRAIN		DIREC-TION	EN-GINES	NO. CARS	TON-NAGE	DEPT.	TIME	ARR.	TIME	HELP-ER	FROM	TO
2/23 BI Gr. Canyon Limt.	Psgr.	West	3746	11	900	Winslow	11:45 A	Seligman	4:42 P	No		
Main 64080 -1 as 3/23	"	"	3525	10	801	"	1:35 P	"	6:05 P	1331	Winslow	Supai
Main 64736	"	"	3909	13	1105	"	3:14 P	"	8:02 P	No		
Main 64735	"	"	3888	13	1105	"	4:44 P	"	9:31 P	No		
Main 64084	"	"	3862	11	935	"	7:00 P	"	11:45 P	No		
No. 1/3 Calif. Limited	"	"	3749	10	798	"	7:50 P	"	12:46 A	No		
No. 17 Super Chief	"	"	M 11-14A	12	705	"	8:44 P	"	11:59 P	No		
No. 21 El Capitan	"	"	M 12-12A	12	636	"	9:00 P	"	12:15 A	No		
No. 19 Chief	"	"	3775	14	865	"	9:30 P	"	1:40 A	No		
No. 3/1 Scout	"	"	3765	19	1555	"	9:35 P	"	2:39 A	1374 / 3158	Winslow / Ash Fork	Supai / Crookton
No. 2/3 Calif. Limited	"	"	3771	11	860	"	9:55 P	"	3:06 A	No		
No. 3/3 Overflow No. 7	Mail	"	3774	18	1260	"	10:20 P	"	3:35 A	No		

FREIGHT — THIRD DISTRICT — WEST
4:00 P.M.—12 M. DECEMBER 1, 1943

TRAIN		DIREC-TION	EN-GINES	NO. CARS	TON-NAGE	DEPT.	TIME	ARR.	TIME	HELP-ER	FROM	TO
16/43 V	Frt.	West	M-120	66	3437	Winslow	11:25 A	Seligman	7:25 P	No		
8/43 X	"	"	M-122	73	3496	"	12:30 P	"	7:35 P	No		
8/33 V	"	"	M-104	61	3244	"	1:25 P	"	8:05 P	No		
Frwd. 33 Z	"	"	M-128	80	3484	"	3:20 P	"	9:50 P	No		
17-43 Z	"	"	M-101	49	2824	"	4:45 P	"	11:25 P	No		
Frwd. 43 B 9	"	"	M-105	78	3451	"	6:55 P	"	6:10 A	No		
20-43 Z	"	"	M-117	74	3474	"	9:10 P	"	6:20 A	No		
21-43 Z	"	"	M-124	64	3416	"	11:15 P	"	8:05 A	No		

A Light Day on the Second Trick of the Albuquerque Division—Third District

PASSENGER — THIRD DISTRICT — EAST
4:00 P.M.—12 M. DECEMBER 1, 1943

TRAIN	DIREC-TION	EN-GINES	NO. CARS	TON-NAGE	DEPT.	TIME	ARR.	TIME	HELP-ER	FROM	TO
No. 2/4 CJ Calif. Limited	Psgr. East	3898	14	1090	Seligman	2:50 P	Winslow	7:40 P	No	Ash Fork	Williams
No. 8 CJ Fast Mail	"	3768	13	963	"	1:05 P	"	5:05 P	No	Seligman	Crookton
No. 1/24 Gr. Canyon Limited	"	3766	15	1302	"	4:03 P	"	8:37 P	1376	Ash Fork	Williams
No. 2/24 "	"	1399	9	725	"	6:05 P	"	10:28 P	1306 3848 1844	Ash Fork Williams	Williams Flagstaff
No. 20 Chief	"	3784	14	860	"	11:31 P	"	3:16 A	No		

FREIGHT — THIRD DISTRICT — EAST
4:00 P.M.—12 M. DECEMBER 1, 1943

TRAIN	DIREC-TION	EN-GINES	NO. CARS	TON-NAGE	DEPT.	TIME	ARR.	TIME	HELP-ER	FROM	TO
Drag	Frt. East	M-117	67	1537	Seligman	9:55 A	Winslow	4:20 P	No	Ash Fork	Supai
1-GFX-BI	"	M-124	66	3497	"	1:10 P	"	8:05 P	1620	Ash Fork	Riordan
1-PGX-A	"	3880	52	2474	Ash Fork	3:55 P	"	9:25 P	964	Ash Fork	Supai
CTX-CJ	"	M-112	58	2415	Seligman	3:10 P	"	9:40 P	1692	Ash Fork	Supai
Williams Turn	"	1659	43	1517	"	5:30 P	Williams	12:35 A	No		
Drag	"	M-126	84	1996	"	4:45 P	Winslow	10:25 A	No		
1/44-BI	"	M-107	66	3498	"	6:10 P	"	1:05 A	3910	Ash Fork	Supai
6 GFX CJ 7	"	M-125	73	3496	"	9:08 P	"	3:40 A	1692	"	"
1/GFX CJ 6	"	M-116	59	3185	"	10:00 P	"	5:05 A	3848	"	"
Drag	"	M-121	73	2113	"	11:40 P	"	5:25 A	No		

loads, tonnage, and trains. He obtains crews from the engine and train dispatchers, locates helpers, and secures information concerning available motive power from engine dispatchers and reports revealing the condition of such power.

The night chief dispatcher works from 7 P.M. to 7 A.M. He has the same duties and authority as the chief, and usually has one or two assistants. These chiefs occupy an office between the Albuquerque Division's four trick dispatchers—one for each District. They are divided into three shifts, or tricks. The first man is on duty between 8 A.M. and 4 P.M.; the second from 4 P.M. to 12, and the third from 12 midnight to 8 A.M. Altogether there are fifteen trick dispatchers at Winslow. Upon them falls the responsibility for the operation of the trains.

The duties of the trick train dispatcher on the Third District of the Albuquerque Division are probably the most varied of any trick dispatcher's in the country. This district and the Sacramento Division of the Southern Pacific from Roseville, California, to Sparks, Nevada, are, in the author's opinion, the toughest of them all.

On the Albuquerque Division, trains are operated under current of traffic rules with signals. With between 50,000 to 70,000 tons of freight moving in each direction daily, which means from seventeen to twenty-five freight trains each way, besides approximately the same number of passenger trains, not to mention the "Main" trains and wartime extras—all having to whip one of the longest mountain grades in the country—it is only natural that the problems of operation are many and involved.

Temperatures vary on this District to a great degree. I have left Phoenix, on the Fourth District, at 4 P.M. of a day in November with the thermometer registering eighty-five, to find a temperature of twenty-two at Ash Fork at ten o'clock that night; a temperature of fourteen at Winslow at 3 A.M., and at 7 A.M. a temperature of seventeen. Returning to Ash Fork at four that afternoon, the operator "hooped" up a message reporting sixty-five. Still again, while waiting for No. 20 at Seligman at eleven that night, twenty-seven miles west, it was down to twenty-six.

Such variations of temperature increase the difficulties of the train dispatcher. Even when there is no snow, of which there is plenty in this northern Arizona country in the wintertime, these changes are a source of constant anxiety to the man upon whom rests the responsibility of moving heavy traffic.

With steam operation, practically all freight trains are double-headed from Winslow west. These double-headers sometimes cut off at Supai, ninety-six miles west of Winslow, and sometimes run through to Crookton, a distance of 135 miles, depending on whether or not the power is needed back at Winslow, or whether the dispatcher has helpers available at Ash Fork to help the train twenty miles from Ash Fork to Crookton.

All trains stop at Supai to test the air, and freight trains set up retainers for the 3.0 per cent grade, Supai to Ash Fork. Westbound, a "wheel-cooling" stop is made at Daze, after which trains continue to Ash Fork, and there start another 1.5 per cent ascending grade, which is the ruling ascending grade westbound. This grade is almost continuous westbound from Winslow to Riordan, a distance of sixty-five miles. While there are several stretches between Riordan and Williams of 1.5 per cent grade, the track is undulating and trains are able to accelerate considerably for some twenty miles.

Eastbound, trains are double-headed from Seligman to Crookton. Here the helpers are cut off and trains descend a 3.0 per cent grade to Ash Fork, where they again pick up helpers for the 2.0 per cent grade, Ash Fork to Supai. The latter grade in more recent years was established by building the eastward track on the north side of the approach hills to Bill Williams Mountain. After the helper engines are cut off at Supai, trains are handled with one engine to Williams, where double-headers again handle trains over the maximum grades between Williams and Riordan, from which point trains proceed on to Winslow on a downgrade with one engine, making a wheel-cooling stop at Angell, about halfway between Riordan and Winslow.

The handling of passenger trains is much the same as that of freight trains. Double-headers are necessary for many passenger trains, especially in wartime when all trains are heavy and schedules cannot be maintained unless sufficient power is furnished.

The task of providing engines and crews is part of the duties of the trick dispatcher. He has over one hundred crews and engines which he must assign in the handling of trains. He must strictly adhere to the schedules and provisions of the train- and enginemen's organizations. Various classes of men are entitled to certain work, and others are restricted for different reasons, among which is inexperience. He must be familiar with and enforce the hours of service law, which prohibits any man in train or engine service from working more than sixteen hours in any twenty-four-hour period. His failure to have available crews and engines to protect his trains may result in serious delay.

Most important of the duties of the trick dispatcher is that of keeping inferior or slower trains out of the way of superior or faster trains. On the Third District, the necessity of providing for the return of helper engines is in itself no small task.

Every minute of the day and night, the dispatcher must have his finger on the fast pulse of the railroad. Any error of judgment, failure to provide quickly for every contingency, will result in costly delays.

Due to heavy war traffic, it has been necessary to haul approximately a million gallons of water daily into Ash Fork from Chino Valley on the Fourth District to the south. Water must also be hauled to other points on the Third District. The movement of these water trains, the providing of tank cars and motive power and crews become the work of the dispatcher.

The written word cannot adequately describe the difficulties of train operation over this Third District of the Albuquerque Division. The beauty of the country is unrivaled, but there are times when the trick dispatcher finds himself fervently wishing that it had less scenic grandeur and more level track.

Railroad officials, train- and enginemen, track maintenance crews, yardmen, shop gangs—all are deserving of high praise for their untiring efforts to keep the trains rolling. They are the visible cogs in the great railroad machine that, in war or peace, moves mighty caravans down the steel rail. But behind the scenes there is the guiding hand of the invisible man of the railroad, the master strategist, beyond the closed door that bears the words —Train Dispatcher.

CHAPTER XXI

MOUNTAIN RAILROADING ON THE SOUTHERN PACIFIC

Freight-train Operation in the Cascades — C.T.C. in the Tehachapis

The Southern Pacific Lines cross more mountain ranges than any other United States railroad. From Paisano Pass in Texas to Siskiyou Summit in the Northwest, roaring locomotives of the S.P. thread the high rims of the Continental Divide over Steins Pass, N.M., Beaumont Hill, Tehachapi Summit, Santa Margarita Grade, Donner Summit, Dunsmuir to Grass Lake, Cascade Summit, Oregon, and other lofty, lonely mountain passes.

From New Orleans to Los Angeles; from Los Angeles to Portland, Oregon; from Ogden to the Golden Gate—war trains are rolling over the Southern Pacific's vast transportation system. And for hundreds of miles the right-of-way is high-borne mountain iron.

Since the first steel rail was spiked down in an American mountain range, mountain railroading has held the lure of romance and high adventure through the years. For sharp curves and heavy grades constitute a never-ceasing threat to men and trains.

Here we are going to watch both the head- and rear-end operation of heavy freights in the famous Cascades, remembering that the Southern Pacific's Shasta Route is one of the country's most intensively used single-track lines.

A 4,250-ton freight train hangs poised like a mighty dragon in the sky. Some eighty-eight cars are creeping along a shining steel pathway high up in the thin, clean mountain air—a fire-eating monster, breathing smoke and bellowing an iron-throated challenge to the frowning mountain gods.

A Southern Pacific freight is battling toward the summit of the timber-clad Cascades on the Portland Division, between Oakridge and Crescent Lake, Oregon. The ascending grade is 1.8 per cent. The roaring engine on the head end is a great cab-in-front Articulated, an AC-6 or 7, a 4-8-8-2 locomotive designed for freight service on mountain railroad. It has a tractive force of 123,400 pounds, and a total weight of over one million pounds for engine and tender. The cab-ahead design is for the purpose of better visibility and to defend the engine crew against suffocating smoke and gas fumes in snow sheds and tunnels.

Big helper engines are cut into the train—other big Articulateds tirelessly thrusting groaning freight cars upward. Let us go along and see what happens, for it is interesting to see how and where these helper engines are assigned.

Our southbound train has arrived at Oakridge, a helper terminal at the foot of the Cascades, and a cut is made for a helper well back toward the rear of the long train. The head portion is then pulled ahead, and the road engine is spotted for fuel and water.

The lead helper—another AC locomotive—is placed in the train at least seven cars ahead of the rear helper. A third AC, or Articulated-Consolidation, is cut in seven cars ahead of the caboose. This method of cutting in helpers produces the most satisfactory results, and makes for the greatest comfort to crews in those tunnels and snow sheds.

After the helper engines are coupled in, the road engineer, with the co-operation of the rear brakeman, makes an air-brake test to insure that he has control of the brakes throughout the train. The brakes then are released.

Then, with the train orders delivered, the freight is ready to highball. Two curt blasts crack from the dome of the lead engine, and there are echoing blasts from the helpers, saying, in effect, "Let's go!"

The big locomotives then buckle down and go to work. The slack runs out and there is a jerky forward movement of the cars of the long train. The throttle is back, the reverse lever is down in the working corner, and the mountains echo to the growing thunder of these iron-lunged pachyderms of the rail, and 4,250 tons are going over the mountain.

The exhausts have settled to a solid rhythmic chant; drawbars are straining and seven hundred car-wheels lend their voices to the steel chorus.

Always the enginemen are alert to prevent these big engines from "slipping," or losing traction and spinning their drivers, which would break the steady drag and cause the slack to bunch up. Then, when the engine got her feet again, the resulting jerk might easily play hob to draft-gear or cargo.

If everything goes well, the freight finally pulls into Wicopee, twenty miles from Oakridge, and the big engines are ready for a drink. Now comes a ticklish bit of railroading, the problem being to get those Articulateds spotted at the water tanks, for eighty-eight cars make a long, unwieldy train to play with on mountain railroad.

The road engineer eases off on the throttle on the lead engine. The helpers keep working steam, shoving the train along until the head end get close to the upper water column. The helpers are now using their engine brakes to control the movement, the train moving slowly enough to be stopped by the independent brakes of the helpers, and yet not slow enough to stall the drag.

After the road engine is spotted at the upper water column, the engineer applies the brakes throughout the train. He alone, of course, having control of the train line with the automatic brake equipment on the lead engine. As this brake application is noted on the air gauge of the leading helper engine, the engineer of this engine signals the swing brakeman to cut off the helper. After the cut has been made, the helper engineer takes control of the brakes on the rear portion of the train, and backs down to one of the lower water columns, where he spots his engine for water.

The next helper is then cut off, and, in turn, takes control of the brakes on the remaining portion of the train, and backs to a lower water column. When the helper engines are cut off and spotted at the water tanks, the swing brakeman applies hand brakes on the rear of the head portion, which prevents the slack from running out when it becomes necessary for the lead engineer to release the brakes and recharge the brake-pipe.

As soon as the helper engines have taken water, they recouple to the train and hand brakes are released, helper engines holding the slack until air is again tested by road engineer and rear brakeman, once more insuring that all brakes on the train are in control of the lead engineer. Brakes are released then, and when the brake-pipe pressure has become recharged to at least seventy pounds, as indicated by the gauge in the caboose, the rear brakeman signals the engineer of the last helper, and two blasts inform the road engineer at the far-off front that everything is in order and they are ready to go.

The train continues up the grade. At Cascade Summit, the automatic brake-valve and train brakes halt the freight at a point at least eighty-eight car-lengths from the crossover switch. The helpers are cut off and backed away. The lead helper heads into the wye track; the rear helper is switched in behind the caboose and shoves this portion ahead, coupling onto the head section of the train.

Brakes are tested once more, and again released, as the train moves slowly forward at about eight miles an hour until all cars have been inspected, as they move past a brakeman.

The train proceeds then to Crescent Lake. Here the engine is cut off for service and inspection, and the outgoing crew climbs aboard.

REAR-END OPERATION

The train crew is called by telephone, or call-boy, and report for duty. The conductor, who is the ranking employee on a train, first checks to see who his three brakemen are; then assigns them to their positions as rear brakeman, swing brakeman, and head-end man.

The rear brakeman acts as a flagman. The swing brakeman oversees switching and other work en route. The head brakeman rides the engine when the train is in motion, generally, and is under direction of the swing man when switching operations are in progress.

Two heavy-tonnage freight trains operating in
A. T. C. territory on Southern Pacific Shasta Division north of Dunsmuir, California making a
mallard or non-stop meet. The train in the foreground is hauled by an AC Class engine, and the
approaching extra by a 2-10-2 Type Class F-4.
Courtesy Southern Pacific.

All set for #99. The operator at Burbank Junction
Tower watching the famous Daylight cross the
interlocking with engine 4417 4-8-4 Type Class
G-3 after having just lined the railroad for it.
The Los Angeles division to Santa Barbara and
the San Joaquin Division to Bakersfield split here.
Photo by W. H. Thrall, Jr.

Union Pacific 3525, 2-8-8-0 Type, with a westward extra in the Blue Mountains near Motanic, Oregon on the Second Subdivision of the Oregon Division. Photo by R. H. Kindig, U. S. Army.

Santa Fe 3874 and 3822, 2-10-2 Types, double-heading an eastward extra in the early morning down Raton Pass west of Trinidad, Colo. The grade is now only 1.3%. Fischer's Peak is in the background on the First District of the N.M. Division. Photo by Otto C. Perry.

When coming on duty, the rear brakeman checks over the train to see that all hand brakes are released, and gets everything in readiness in the caboose, making sure that it contains the necessary equipment. He puts the markers, which designate the rear end of the train, in place at the back of the caboose.

The conductor checks his watch with the standard clock in the telegraph office, as do the other members of the crew. The conductor examines the consist of the train as revealed by the waybills, which he has picked up at the yard office. He makes note of livestock shipments and/or perishable commodities in refrigerator cars, which may require adjustments of ventilators, and further checks the destination of all cars in the train.

The conductor then gets his train orders from the telegraph office, and sends the engineer's order forward by the head brakeman, together with information about the make-up of the train, such as the number of cars and the tonnage.

When the train pulls out, the conductor and swing brakeman check the train as it pulls slowly past them, noting brake-rigging and other parts of the running-gear that might be dragging, and/or brakes that may not have released. They also check the car numbers against their list, making sure of the correctness of its make-up.

They swing aboard the caboose and wave a highball. The conductor and rear and swing man check the train orders and possible meets, keeping in mind timetable schedules and superior trains that this freight must respect.

The rear and swing brakemen take positions in the cupola, one on each side, thus being in a position to observe the train closely. By day, they watch for dust, smoking journals, sparks flying, which might indicate dragging equipment or a derailed car, or other signs of trouble. They, further, cast an eye now and then behind, watching for fresh marks on the ties, another indication of dragging equipment. They are continually alert as to the position of train order signals. If the order board over the telegraph office is not in the proceed position, a member of the crew takes his place on the steps of the caboose to catch the hoop held up by the operator.

These brakemen, too, watch the indication of block signals.

When passing track workers they keep an eye out for hand signs that might indicate something wrong with the train, like a sagging door on a boxcar or dangerously shifted cargo on flatcars or gondolas.

The conductor, in the meantime, is busy writing up the train in his train book or doing other clerical work. He is equally responsible with the engineer for the identification of all trains met and passed, and must watch carefully the timetable schedules of superior trains, even though they are not included in his orders.

As the train nears a helper station, such as Oakridge, the conductor instructs his brakemen in regard to the helper engines, making certain that they definitely understand the work of placing these helpers, for, in wartime, his crew may lack the experience of the seasoned veterans of normal times.

While the helpers are being coupled in, the conductor goes to the telegraph office for his train orders; then returns to lend a hand at getting things organized for the hard pull over the hump.

In event that the train stops at any point on the main track, the conductor makes certain of flag protection; then starts out to learn the cause of the delay. If it proves to be of a nature that cannot be cleared up quickly, he must, if possible, get in touch with the dispatcher, so that train orders may be changed; thus avoiding unnecessary delays to other trains.

The ascending grade out of Oakridge is 1.8 per cent, and includes three tunnels. The train crew must be on the alert constantly, for on mountain railroad anything can happen. Eighty-eight cars are a lot of train, and that big AC road engine and its three helpers are a lot of motive power, smashing at the ramparts of the Cascades, which dwarf man and all of his works.

The conductor is the train commander. He shares with the engineer the responsibility of definitely checking the identification of all trains met and passed. He must keep a close watch on the timetable schedules of superior trains. He must guess at nothing, take nothing for granted.

Water is taken once and sometimes twice between Oakridge and Cascade Summit, and each time there is that shuffling of the big engines at the water columns. On arrival at the station where helpers are cut out, the conductor must direct the work and again inspect the train.

Crescent Lake is the home terminal of the crew. The conductor here instructs his brakemen regarding the switching out or picking up of cars and the changing of cabooses. He registers the arrival of his train, completes his delay and other reports for the trip, turning them in with his waybills; then writes out his final tie-up time and is ready to go off duty.

Mountain railroading is tough under the best of conditions, but with the Cascade Line crowded with freights laden with the materials of war, in addition to the normal traffic, it is a battle all of the way. Here in the Cascades you can feel the stirring pulse of the Southern Pacific straining for Victory, and know the grim determination of the big engines and the men behind them.

C.T.C. SMASHES A MOUNTAIN BOTTLENECK

Centralized Traffic Control on the Southern Pacific is handling an enormous volume of war traffic over a tortuous stretch of track that formerly was a bottleneck even to peacetime traffic. This portion of the S.P. extends from Tehachapi, California, northward to Bena at the beginning of the great San Joaquin Valley.

The Atchinson, Topeka & Santa Fe Railway also uses the tracks of the Southern Pacific here. Santa Fe traffic, added to that of the Southern Pacific, brings the total number of daily train movements to sixty, including helper movements. This represents a terrific amount of traffic for any single-track line. Consider, then, that the Bena-Tehachapi section extends through rugged mountain territory at a prevailing grade of 2.2 per cent, and it will readily be understood what a serious traffic problem was presented to the Southern Pacific after the outbreak of World War II.

The Bena-Tehachapi section is a forty-eight-mile portion of what is known as the Southern Pacific's San Joaquin Valley Line, which extends from San Francisco to Los Angeles. The tracks, for the most part, are laid along the Caliente and Tehachapi Creek beds, which wind through the Tehachapi Mountains.

These mountains are exceptionally erosive, and when storms smash at them they fairly melt.

Because of the necessity of maintaining negotiable grades, the right-of-way contains a great many sharp curves, horseshoe curves, and the famous Tehachapi Loop, which has a circumference of only 3,975 feet. Frequently an engine and leading cars make the full circle while the rear portion of the train is still in the tunnel under the upper track level.

This stretch of main track has been a problem for a long time, and various solutions have been considered in an effort to find some means of improving conditions. This study included double-tracking and grade revision. But, due to the rugged nature of the country, such measures were regarded as economically unsound.

And then came the war, and the Southern Pacific and Santa Fe's Tehachapi line was deluged by a flood, the like of which they had never seen before. But this time it was cargo for three-shift war plants, and not a wild torrent of mud and water boiling down Caliente and Tehachapi Creeks.

Added to the war load was the valiant attempt these roads made to maintain the usual schedules. Here in the Tehachapi Mountains was a bottleneck that made strong men shudder. Before, the S.P. and Santa Fe had managed to handle the yearly traffic peak, after which they took a deep breath, but now every day was a peak day. Transportation was vital; the supply lines had to be kept open.

Already other bottlenecks on the Southern Pacific had been smashed, as this one must be. There had been a fifty-mile stretch of single track between Stockton and Brighton, near Sacramento, and one over the Santa Margarita grade on the Coast Line. Centralized Traffic Control had relieved the congestion at these points, as it had on the Santa Fe's San Diego line, and on the Union Pacific between Las Vegas, Nevada, and Yermo, California.

In September of 1942, the signal construction forces of the Southern Pacific began the necessary field work. The S.P. and the Union Switch and Signal Company went into a huddle, and forthwith things began to happen—and fast.

The work was so co-ordinated that the installations began to take form with a speed that was amazing. The C.T.C. control machine was shipped and installed in the depot at Bakersfield, and as soon as two or more stations in the troublesome Tehachapis were completed they were placed in operation. And almost at once there was an easing of the congestion.

Great trains of the Santa Fe and the Southern Pacific, long whipsawed by this mountain range and single track, began to spend less time in sidings. Helpers returned more quickly.

The C.T.C. machine at Bakersfield is a standard hookup and similar to those in general use. However, it has some novel features that are of particular interest. In the first place, the machine is mounted on rollers, with all wire connections centering in a detachable plug connector, making it possible to move the machine quickly in case of fire.

Located outside of the depot there is a fireproof cable and emergency connection, by means of which the C.T.C. control machine can be hooked up and the operation of dispatching trains continued without interruption. An additional feature is a row of fifteen telephone ringing selectors, mounted on the control panel, by means of which the dispatcher can call the various operators.

The machine is L-shaped, with a main sector five feet long and a wing sector measuring two and a half feet. Track occupancy lights, which "OS" trains, and all control levers are the same standard arrangement universal on Union Switch and Signal C.T.C. boards.

There are twelve controlled passing tracks located within the C.T.C. territory, and spaced at an average interval of three miles. In flat country and under less severe traffic conditions, it would probably have been considered feasible to do away with some of these passing tracks following the C.T.C. installation. However, in view of the steep grades, the heavy train movement—including helper engines—the necessity of stopping trains to cool wheels, every siding in the Tehachapis is essential.

As with all modern C.T.C. systems, only two code-line wires are employed on the Bena-Tehachapi installation. The remarkable flexibility of the code-line is demonstrated by the fact that

245

the code circuit is superimposed on two dispatcher's wires that were already in existence. The electrical circuits are arranged in such a way that there is a minimum disturbance to telephone communication, the operation of the telephone selectors, and the operation of the duplex telegraph. The derivation of all of these electrical circuits from one pair of line wires represents, of course, a conservation of critical materials.

Because of the extensive number of functions controlled on the Bena-Tehachapi installation, a coded carrier control system is used, similar to the one on the Union Pacific. A conventional direct-current circuit is superimposed upon the dispatcher's line from Bakersfield, thirty-three miles southward to Rowen. From Rowen to Tehachapi, a distance of fifteen miles, a coded carrier is employed. Both of these sections can be operated simultaneously and with no greater coding time than if one direct-current section were used.

At this writing, the installation has been in service but a short time, and there has been no opportunity to make an accurate detailed study of actual train time saved. However, traffic now moves smoothly and without unnecessary delay. Train limits have been increased from sixty-five to as many as eighty cars. This is possible because helper engines can be moved over the road much faster, and, in consequence, more power is available for the handling of heavier trains. The author has personally seen sixteen helpers in one train coming back down the mountain to Bakersfield and knows of cases where as many as twenty-four have been run as one train with copies of train orders for each engine crew.

At one point in the Tehachapis where the constant threat of a landslide in time of storm exists, a slide-detector fence has been installed. In the event of a slide of sufficient proportions to derail a train, a code would immediately be flashed to the dispatcher by means of a red indication light in the bottom portion of the track-model. Further, the wayside signals governing this section of track would be set at stop, thus warning approaching trains in time to prevent derailment.

Much has been written of the magnificent part the railroads have played in the war effort. Both personnel and equipment have been worked to the limit, and troops and war materials have been moved with a minimum of delay. Because of its newness and technical aspects, Centralized Traffic Control is still comparatively unknown to the general public. But no single factor in American railroading has so tremendously increased the track capacity with so small an amount of vital material.

President Mercier, of the Southern Pacific, has estimated that where Centralized Traffic Control has been installed it has increased the capacity of single track from fifty to one hundred per cent. Hence, those murderous bottlenecks have been blasted to smithereens. And so the big, churning drivers of the mighty locomotives roll, and every thundering bark of an exhaust is another cannon shot in support of our fighting men.

CHAPTER XXII

THE NORFOLK AND WESTERN

Roanoke Shops and Engine Terminal

On November 1, 1852, a Virginia & Tennessee locomotive screamed the announcement of the coming of the first train to Big Lick. Big Lick, huddled in a broad valley that was flanked by the Blue Ridge and the Allegheny Mountains, was as shy and bashful as a mountain girl, long sheltered from a wicked world.

Big Lick, as towns go, wasn't much in 1852; the Virginia & Tennessee wasn't much of a railroad; the little, blustering locomotive, with its peanut-roaster whistle, wasn't much of a locomotive. But they all got together, in that brisk fall day in 1852—and another American romance was a-borning. The romance of the country village, the locomotive, and the steel rail.

Big Lick opened its arms to the puffing Iron Horse and its early-day Casey Jones, and they were wed, and lived happily, though noisily, ever after.

Big Lick grew up, and the Iron Horse grew up—grew up a-snorting. Big Lick grew up to become Roanoke, Virginia. The little Virginia & Tennessee Railroad became the Norfolk and Western. The little Iron Horse grew into a roaring Goliath, and shook its iron fists at the mountains and the world, including Hideki Tojo and Adolf Hitler.

The coming of the rails of the Virginia & Tennessee Railroad to Big Lick was the first real step in the development of a bustling railroad city of 75,000 inhabitants.

In 1856, the Virginia & Tennessee had been completed to Bristol, and the long-dreamed-of railroad from Lynchburg to the Southwest became a reality.

You give a young upstart like Big Lick an inch and it will

248

grab for the biggest apple in the basket. In 1881, the up-and-coming citizens of Big Lick raised $10,000 for the purpose of attempting to induce the Shenandoah Valley Railroad to play in their yard. On June 18, 1882, the first train on the Shenandoah Valley, running between Hagerstown, Maryland, and Roanoke pulled into the "Magic City."

That was the year that Big Lick bowed out of the picture, and Roanoke, Virginia, took the spotlight. Today Roanoke owes its very existence to the steel rail that courted it away back there in 1852.

Today the Norfolk and Western operates 2,132 miles of track, with a total trackage of 4,600 miles. Its lines stretch from Norfolk through Petersburg, Lynchburg, and Roanoke, Virginia, to Bristol, Virginia-Tennessee, to Bluefield, West Virginia, and on to Portsmouth, Columbus, and Cincinnati, Ohio. Other lines of the Norfolk and Western extend from Roanoke north through the storied Shenandoah Valley to Hagerstown, Maryland; south to Winston-Salem, North Carolina, and south from Lynchburg to Durham, North Carolina. Innumerable branches tap the fabulous bituminous coal fields of southern West Virginia, southwest Virginia, and eastern Kentucky.

The capital of this great rail network is Roanoke. Here are the Railway's general offices, its principal shops, vast classification yards, and extensive engine terminal facilities. Its huge shops are equipped for the construction and heavy repair of locomotives, cars, and other equipment.

Yes, Roanoke is a railroad city. Its first big industrial construction was the erection of the Roanoke Machine Works, completed in 1883, which became the great, modern Norfolk and Western Shops, employing over three thousand workers. Also, during 1883, the general offices of the Shenandoah Valley and the Norfolk and Western Railroads moved from Philadelphia and Lynchburg to Roanoke.

Another major development in the progress of Roanoke was the building of the Roanoke & Southern Railroad, completed between Winston-Salem and Roanoke in March of 1892. This road later became a part of the Norfolk and Western.

It was in September, 1896, that the Norfolk and Western Rail-

road was reorganized as the Norfolk and Western Railway. So the primitive little railroad that timidly presented itself at the doorstep of Big Lick in 1852 became the powerful railway system that today is the Norfolk and Western.

From great mine fields come the slogging coal trains; from the South, over the Winston-Salem line, come raw materials for the textile industry, leaf and pressed tobacco, potatoes, fruits, pulpwood, oil, furniture; from the Southwest, over the Bristol line, come agricultural and forest products; from the Far West and Midwest come oil and farm products and manufactured articles; from the East, the products of factories, the products of fisheries; from the North more manufactured goods, structural steel, and thousands of the vital items of a Nation at war. A vast amount of war material moves in from every direction, moving from Roanoke to the battle lines of the world.

Roanoke is one of the Nation's greatest classification centers for all kinds of freight. Roanoke is one of the largest furniture-originating cities in the country. Through these great yards move every conceivable item important to life and war—food, clothing, fuel, paper; guns, motorized equipment—and fighting men.

The Norfolk and Western's general offices employ more than three thousand of the 23,000 members of the Railway's great family. Roanoke is the hub of a railroad world of its own.

The yards and engine terminal facilities are rated among the largest and most modern in the world. In recent years, $5,000,000 were spent in expansion and modernizing. The Roanoke terminal, which includes 154 miles of track, can accommodate some 7,400 cars.

To build, modernize, and maintain its locomotives, to make heavy repairs and keep all rolling stock in condition, to sustain it for both war- and peacetime traffic, require a plant covering over seventy-five acres. All new locomotives acquired by the Norfolk and Western since 1926 have been designed and built by the employees of Roanoke Shops. During 1943 alone, these Norfolk and Western workers completed twenty-one new locomotives, six of which were the Class J-1 passenger engines of the 4-8-4 type, designed for later streamlining, and fifteen Class A 2-6-6-4 locomotives, built for either freight or passenger service.

Ten additional Class A engines are scheduled for completion in 1944.

The plant facilities of the Norfolk and Western shops include a pattern shop, machine shop, foundries, boiler shop, pipe shop, erecting shop, freight and passenger car shops, and roundhouse. In addition to all of its construction and maintenance work, these shops have contributed largely to the war effort by the manufacture of a long list of items for the Army, Navy, and war industries. Besides all of this, there rolled out of the Norfolk and Western shops late in 1943 the one-hundredth locomotive of foreign roads to receive heavy repairs.

The Norfolk and Western, also, has sold and leased locomotives to other lines in a considerable number since the declaration of war.

Among the many railroad shops of the country that have accomplished much in their shops in the way of sustaining the activities of Uncle Sam, we find the Norfolk and Western and the New York Central holding high rank. Here, as in their many other outstanding roles, American Railroads have put their shoulders solidly to the wheel.

To maintain its coal-carrying equipment at a high standard, the Norfolk and Western operates a modern assembly line at the Roanoke shops for making heavy repairs to all-steel coal cars. Expert employees here can, when necessary, turn out a rebuilt car every thirty minutes. During 1943, the shops performed heavy repairs on 4,551 cars. Nowhere in the world can you match, or even approach, the teamwork of American workmen and the systematized production-line methods of industry.

The 1940 expansion program included the laying of sixty-six miles of new track, the construction of a score of new buildings, and the movement of 2,600,000 yards of earth in grading operations, with the result that the terminal capacity has been increased more than thirty-two per cent. The present yard facilities include an eastbound receiving yard of twenty tracks, with a capacity of 2,450 cars; an eastbound gravity classification yard and forwarding yard of forty-six tracks, with a capacity of 2,250; a westbound receiving, classification, and forwarding yard of twelve tracks, with a 950-car capacity; a westbound empty yard

WHAT THE RAILROADS HAUL IN WARTIME

Switch list of N. and W. 2/84 as used by retarder operator, Roanoke hump

NO 2/84 EXTRA NO 2148 MAY 16 1944
RECD BILLS AT 1120 AM
TRACK NO 12

1	NW	5558	X 10	WEIGH	
2	NW	10530	X 9	WEIGH	
3	NW	76337	X 40	"	
4	NW	76795	X 40	"	
5	NW	57074	X 38	"	
6	NW	37002	X 38	"	
7	NW	57100	X 38	"	
8	NW	68278	X 38	"	
9	NW	5207	X 38	"	
10	NW	74088	X 38	"	
11	NYC	135909	X 42	HEAVY	
12	BM	71642	X 42	"	
13	PLE	35135	X 42	"	
14	IC	12264	X 37	WHEAT	

34	B4	91455	X 42	"	EXPLO
35	PRR	81660	X 42	"	EXPLO
36	LN	46239	X 42	"	EXPLO
37	LN	61535	X 42	"	EXPLO
38	PRR	65418	X 42	"	EXPLO
39	ITC	6217	X 42	"	EXPLO
40	PRR	65601	X 42	"	EXPLO
41	EJE	60865	X 42	"	EXPLO
42	ATSF	137651	X 42	"	EXPLO
43	UP	182103	X 42	"	EXPLO
44	ATSF	143983	X 42	"	EXPLO
45	CMO	20356	X 42	"	EXPLO
46	OSL	189826	X 42	"	EXPLO
47	GN	49142	X 42	"	EXPLO
48	PRR	80779	X 42	"	EXPLO
49	SP	82822	X 42	"	EXPLO
50	LN	96793	X 42	"	EXPLO
51	CO	4545	X 42	"	EXPLO
52	ATSF	6837	X 41		

WHAT THE RAILROADS HAUL IN WARTIME

Switch list of N. and W. 2/84 as used by retarder operator, Roanoke hump

No	RR	Car No	Code		No	RR	Car No	Code
15	ATSF	116799	X 32 "		53	MDT	16614	X 3 X ROKE FRUIT PROD
16	CBQ	131696	X 18 "					
17	MP	46076	X 15 "		54	LN	8040	X 10
18	OSL	302371	X 32 "		55	SOU	161125	X 10
19	ACY	3103	X 35 "					
20	LN	55932	X 10 "					

SCRATCH OUT THE ABOVE LINE

No	RR	Car No	Code		No	RR	Car No	Code
21	LN	90091	X 42 US EXPLO		56	LN	101400	X 11 US
22	NYC	197159	X 42 "		57	PM	86469	X 11
23	MP	30621	X 42 "		58	LN	7054	X 10
24	CN	480308	X 42 "		59	CO	9912	X 42
25	MILW	13513	X 42 "		60	PRR	567343	X 32
26	SLSF	150805	X 42 "		61	NKP	15732	X 18
27	SAL	16289	X 42 "					
28	BO	385765	X 42 "			SHOP CARS NOT REPORTED AS YET		
29	MILW	271359	X 42 "					
30	CO	87441	X 42 "					
31	NKP	76137	X 42 EXPLO					
32	SP	88105	X 42 EXPLO			THAT IS ALL 1153 AM B		
33	MILW	20981	X 42 EXPLO					

of ten tracks, with a 1,570-car capacity, and an auxiliary yard of eleven tracks, with a capacity of 180 cars.

The yard facilities include a new eastbound car-retarder-equipped gravity classification yard with a double-track hump; two 300-ton automatic car-scales; fourteen electro-pneumatic car retarders, and three brick towers that house the operators of the switches and retarders.

Engine terminal facilities at Shaffers Crossing, Roanoke, were modernized at the time of the yard-improvement project. Locomotives roll into this great terminal from five operating districts —districts reaching out from Roanoke to Bluefield, Bristol, Norfolk, Hagerstown, and Winston-Salem. Expanded facilities here center around a forty-stall roundhouse. The number of locomotives serviced has increased from 80 to 135 daily, and the maximum capacity has not yet been attained.

This is a world where "day never ends." Great road engines trundle in like winded, toil-grimed giants. They are fed, watered, serviced; then grunt away again to pick up their trains and go thundering down the rails of the Norfolk and Western.

On the average of once every ten minutes, a ponderous engine rolls through the assembly-line grooming process, and moves to the "ready" track.

To the layman, a roundhouse is a place of smoke, grime, and mystery. From it emanates sounds of hissing, of blowing, and of pounding. Smooch-faced figures in black, greasy overalls move about. Heads and arms and legs appear from the most unexpected places. In wartime, they may be attached to the male or the female of the species.

A locomotive in a roundhouse assumes frightful and never-before-contemplated proportions, and when you find forty or so of these Gargantuan monsters gathered at their rendezvous you feel yourself growing small.

Vital to engine maintenance at the Shaffers Crossing roundhouse, we find two outgoing engine inspection pits, a washing platform, ash pit, coal wharf, and a recently constructed wye track, where, in case of emergency, these big locomotives may be turned. There is, of course, a turntable at the center of the roundhouse structure.

Light running repairs are made here, heavy repairs being made at the Roanoke shops. Major factors in stepping up the capacity of the engine terminal are the two outgoing engine inspection buildings. These are of brick construction and 163 feet in length. They are called "one-stall" roundhouses. Here minor repairs are made at the same time engines are being inspected and lubricated. This has resulted in appreciably lightening the load on the roundhouse, besides reducing the turnaround time for locomotives.

While providing better facilities for the repair and handling of locomotives, the Norfolk and Western has also installed better facilities for the comfort and convenience of employees. These include new wash and locker buildings, which are complete with the most modern conveniences. There are individual lockers for clothing, circular-stall shower baths, large, sanitary wash basins and drinking fountains. The building has unit heaters, with electric fans for circulating the warm air.

A separate building is provided for engine crews, and includes the headquarters of the chief caller, a register room, and wash and locker rooms.

Having examined briefly the facilities provided for grimed employees when the day's work is done, let us now turn our attention to the big, workhorse road engines, for they, too, are provided with facilities for slicking up.

Here comes locomotive No. 2163, in from pulling a time freight from Bristol. The engineer swings down from the cab, notes the time, and walks to the Engineers' Register Room. Here he makes out a report, indicating any possible repairs needed.

Meanwhile, a hostler climbs aboard the 2163 and moves it to the ash-pit track. The fire is cleaned—or, perhaps, drawn. The ashes from the big firebox are dropped by means of a steam grate-shaking device, which is located on the engine. The bottom of the ashpan has been opened, and a small steel car at the bottom of the pit receives the ashes. This car is then hauled by cable to the top of an electrically operated hoist, which dumps the ashes into a railway hopper car.

The locomotive is then moved to one of the two incoming inspection pits. Here inspectors go over the 2163, checking for steam leaks and worn parts. The tender as well as the engine is inspected by these men, who write their findings on a second report sheet. This report speeds then by pneumatic tube to the office of the roundhouse foreman, who has also received the engineer's report. From these the foreman writes up a third report. On this are listed the repairs required. This report is turned over to the various workmen who make the repairs.

Meanwhile, the 2163 has been taken to the coal wharf, where it is loaded with coal and sand. About twelve hundred tons of coal and twenty-eight tons of sand per day are required to supply locomotives at the Shaffers Crossing terminal. From the coal wharf, the engine moves to the washing platform, and is thoroughly cleaned with hot water and special solvents. The tender tank is filled with water.

If the repair work specified does not warrant moving the 2163 into the main roundhouse, the engine will shuffle away from the washing platform to make its way to one of the two outgoing inspections buildings. It will receive thorough lubrication, and there will be a check of all appurtenances, such as valves, gauges, et cetera, to determine if they are in a satisfactory condition. A further check will be made concerning all necessary supplies.

Having at last been pronounced fit and ready, the 2163 will be moved to a storage track, there to await the call to service.

This assembly-line method of servicing locomotives has stepped up the capacity of the terminal by at least sixty-eight per cent. What we have seen here at Shaffers Crossing, in Roanoke, is typical of the routine that is being employed at engine terminals all over the country. In wartime, the turnaround time of locomotives is constantly being reduced, which contributes largely to those factors called availability and utilization.

To attack and whip problems of this nature is the American way. From the beginning, the Norfolk and Western, and all other railroads of the country, have performed not only the "impossible" but the "miraculous," as well.

To improve its service further, the Norfolk and Western in 1943 double-tracked more than ten miles of its Shenandoah Valley Line; also installed Centralized Traffic Control. The operating territory controlled by C.T.C. extends from Roanoke to Stuarts

Busy "level ends of The N. & W.'s large engine terminal at Shaffers Crossing, Roanoke, Virginia. On account of the war this terminal has recently been modernized and expanded, stepping up its capacity from 80 to 135 engines in a 24-hour period. From left to right the leading engines are: #2145, 2-8-8-2 Class Y-6; #1206, 2-6-6-4 Class A; #2137; #2125, Class Y-6; #2159, Class Y-6A; #603, 4-8-4 Type streamlined Class J. Courtesy N. & W. R. R.

Engine 4192, Class AC8, being lifted from its wheels by a 200-ton capacity electric crane in the new Southern Pacific erecting shop for these locomotives opened for service in 1944 to aid the war effort at Sparks, Nevada. Engine 4260 in the background is Class AC10. Courtesy Southern Pacific R.R.

Norfolk & Western Time Freight No. 85 west of Mountvale, Virginia, on the Norfolk Div. The engine, No. 1206, is Class A, 2-6-6-4 Type. Built in the N. & W. shops at Roanoke. Courtesy Norfolk & Western R.R.

Draft, and from Shenandoah to Bentonville, an aggregate distance of 120 miles, although the farthest switch controlled is located 166 miles from Roanoke. Traffic over both of these districts is directed from Roanoke by means of C.T.C. machines located in the Shenandoah Division dispatchers' offices.

Completion of these improvements made possible an increase of about thirty per cent in the operating capacity of the Shenandoah Valley Line. This constituted a direct contribution to the war effort, for the reason that since early 1942 much of the coal routed eastbound through Roanoke and destined for northern states was diverted from the usual rail-and-water movement, via Norfolk, to an all-rail movement over the Shenandoah Valley Line.

Although not built as a main artery for coal movement, the 240-mile Shenandoah Valley Line handled in 1943 more than 3,750,000 tons of diverted coal from the Southern Appalachian fields to northern states. The enormous task accomplished by the Norfolk and Western in this coal movement was a direct answer to the challenge of Hitler's undersea wolf packs. And again your American railroad proved itself an iron-fisted fighting machine of the home front.

Since that history-making day when the first train entered Big Lick, the Norfolk and Western, of which the little Virginia & Tennessee Railroad was the first and one of the most important units, has maintained a policy of foresight and preparation. Since September, 1939, when the war broke out in Europe, the Norfolk and Western has authorized or expended more than eighty million dollars for additions and betterments to its facilities.

Thus, when war came, the Norfolk and Western was prepared to handle the tremendous burden of wartime freight and passenger traffic. Indicative of this burden is the fact that in 1943 alone N.&W. passenger traffic reached the unprecedented total of 797,961,051 passenger-miles—an increase of about 860 per cent over 1939. Similarly, Norfolk and Western general freight traffic in 1943, including vast quantities of war materials, totaled 4,242,580,320 net ton-miles, or about ninety per cent more than in 1939. Bituminous coal hauled in 1943 was more than 15,229,476,448 net ton-miles, for an increase over 1939 of nearly thirty-eight per cent.

The Norfolk and Western handled this staggering traffic load without car shortages, without congestion, without rail-clogging "bottlenecks." And Roanoke, the Magic City a railroad built—Roanoke, the nerve center of the Norfolk and Western's vast rail network—played a major role in this slugging battle to keep the wheels rolling.

It all harks back to that November day in 1852, when the first train puffed breezily into Big Lick, Virginia; to 1881, when the citizens of Big Lick backed their faith in the railroad with hard-earned American dollars. And today Roanoke stands as a living monument to Big Lick, the history and tradition of which will never die, for it is a bright and glorious page in the annals of another great American railroad—the Norfolk and Western.

CHAPTER XXIII

THE SANTA FE 3776-CLASS LOCOMOTIVES

The 4-8-4 in Wartime – The Chief, of the Santa Fe

This chapter will be devoted to a locomotive whose performance is simply unbelievable—the 3776-class 4-8-4 type of the Atchinson, Topeka & Santa Fe Railway System. This engine, in making one of the two longest steam locomotive runs in America —both of which are on the Santa Fe—is asked to do more, performs better, and takes the hardest beating of any engine anywhere. A broad statement, perhaps, but the behavior of this 3776-class locomotive, as it wheels the famous *Chief* west, La Junta, Colorado, to Los Angeles, California—1,234 miles of mountain and desert—will speak for itself.

Before we ride through at the head end of No. 19, let us pause for a moment to examine the steam locomotive, so ably represented by the all-purpose 4-8-4 of the Santa Fe.

A steam locomotive is more than a machine; it is a personality. No other mechanical contrivance on earth possesses so many human attributes, so closely symbolizes man, who gave it birth. It is almost as though, in the process of its creation, the steam locomotive absorbed certain qualities and characteristics of those worldly mortals who spawned it.

This writer, in 1943, rode over twenty-five thousand miles in the cabs of locomotives on various Class I railroads in the United States, including every type of locomotive built in the past twenty years, and a great many more in the quarter-century preceding the opening of the second World War. It has, further, been my privilege to travel many thousand miles aboard freight and pas-

259

senger trains, with the result that I feel qualified to report something of the enormous task accomplished by the railroads in an emergency created by war.

Space will not permit me to review all of the motive power I would like to include in this chapter. Here I have chosen to write of the great 4-8-4 locomotive. I have ridden all but two of this type in the country, and I feel that these engines provide the finest example of the locomotive builders' art.

The 4-8-4 type locomotive first made its appearance on the Santa Fe in 1927, when Baldwin delivered engines 3751 through 3764. These locomotives, as built, had 73-inch driving wheels, 210-pound boiler pressure, and burned coal. In 1935, at the Albuquerque shops of the Santa Fe, they received one of the finest modernization jobs in America. The steam pressure was raised to 230 pounds. Eighty-inch drivers were installed. The engines were equipped with roller bearings and converted to oil burners. Twenty thousand-gallon tenders were added. These engines are still doing heroic work in handling the *Grand Canyon Limited* and the *Scout*, as well as hauling troop trains.

More remarkable still, these fine 4-8-4 type locomotives run through from Kansas City to Los Angeles, via Wellington, Kansas, Amarillo, Texas, Clovis and Belen, New Mexico, for a total of 1,788 miles *without change*.

In 1938, the Baldwin Locomotive Works delivered to the Santa Fe engines of the 3765-class, the numbers running from 3765 to 3775 inclusive. These locomotives are identically the same as the 3776-class, numbered through 3785 inclusive, which were delivered in 1941, except that the '76-class are built of lighter alloys, therefore weighing a little less, and have tenders with a capacity of 25,000 gallons of water, instead of the 20,000 gallons of the former. Each carry 7,107 gallons of fuel oil.

The 3784 and the 3785 engines are equipped with Timken roller bearing rods, a long forward stride in locomotive construction. Only critical shortages prevented all of the newer 4-8-4s on the Santa Fe from being so equipped. Roller bearings add tremendously to the utilization and the years of service of any locomotive.

The 3765-class engines, as well as the 3776-class, have 300-

pound boiler pressure, 80-inch driving wheels, and a maximum tractive effort of 66,000 pounds. They weigh 281,900 pounds on the drivers, with a total weight of 494,630 pounds.

Now let's look at their performance for a moment. These great 4-8-4s handle trains Nos. 3 and 4, the *California Limited*, which runs in two sections daily, Kansas City to Los Angeles, via La Junta, Colorado; the *Chief*, Nos. 19 and 20; and the *Fast Mail*, Nos. 7 and 8, 1,234-mile runs from La Junta to Los Angeles and return. What's more, they can be turned in three hours for the return trip if it is necessary.

These engines are allowed to run at ninety miles an hour, with a ten per cent tolerance, if the physical conditions of the track permit. There are more excellent high-speed track and more high-speed curves on the Santa Fe than on any other railroad in the United States.

The older 3751-class engines are limited to ninety miles an hour, with no tolerance. The 3765- and '76-class handle fifteen old-style heavyweight cars or seventeen lightweight cars, with trains like the *Chief*, *Fast Mail*, and *California Limited*, westbound, alone over every grade, with the exception of Raton Pass, where the grade is 3.5 per cent. Eastbound, these engines usually are given a helper, with fourteen cars or more, up the 2.2 per cent grade from San Bernardino, California, to Summit on the high rim of the famous Cajon Pass. (Pronounced Ka-hoon.)

They have a helper from Lamay to Glorieta, New Mexico, where the grade is 3.0 per cent, and from Raton, New Mexico, to Wootton, Colorado, with its 3.3 per cent grade.

The regular consist of the *Chief* is fourteen cars, usually composed of two lightweight mail storage cars, a heavyweight working mail car, a combination baggage and dormitory lounge car, four sleeping cars, a dormitory lounge car, one dining car, three sleeping cars, and an observation lounge car, with sleeping accommodations of three rooms. These cars are in the order named in the train. The last eleven cars are always of the lightweight construction type. Two or three cars are added as necessary.

The first sections of Nos. 7 and 8 are always limited to twelve cars. Second No. 8 is not operated every day. But Second 7,

261

which runs daily, will, on occasion, haul as many as *thirty* cars. And what these 4-8-4s will do with that train is unbelievable.

In this book the fact has frequently been emphasized that with fewer locomotives than in the first World War, the railroads have broken all previous records of performance. The answer is larger locomotives, greater speed, greater tractive effort, and horsepower; long-distance engine runs, larger tenders of far greater fuel and water capacity, high wheels, roller bearings, feed water pumps, foam meters, valve pilots, firebar grates; greatly improved lubrication systems, fast servicing en route and quick turnaround at terminals.

The Santa Fe *Chief*, for our money, is the world's finest passenger train, which, incidentally, carries every day more high-ranking Army and Navy officials from Chicago to the Pacific Coast than any other train—men whose affairs demand that they get through on time; men, too, who appreciate good service and good food.

All right, now we're going to climb into the cab of the 3777, coupled at the head end of No. 19, the westbound *Chief*, and ride straight through from La Junta, Colorado, to Los Angeles, California, a distance of 1,234 miles.

Santa Fe engine No. 3460 has brought the *Chief* in over the Colorado Division at 7 A.M., Mountain War Time, and we watch her slipping away to the roundhouse. In the days when she was fully attired in streamlined garments, the 3460, a 4-6-4 Hudson-type locomotive, was known as the Mae West. However, some of her cowling has been removed from over her valve gear, with the result that Santa Fe crews now facetiously refer to the lady as Sally Rand.

The 3460 has traveled at the front of the *Chief* all of the way from Chicago, 991.7 miles. On the last 202-mile lap from Dodge City, she has averaged better than eighty miles an hour.

No. 8, the *Fast Mail* has pulled in from the West, and we highball at 7:10—right on time. The engineer opens the throttle, there is the roar of steam, a cough from the stack, and the big drivers take their first bite at the steel rail. We begin to move —smoothly, easily. The bark of the exhaust quickens, and soon we are swinging into our stride, as the great 4-8-4 hungrily begins to devour the miles. In the cab we are riding as easily as in a Pullman.

From La Junta to Trinidad, the grade is 1.1 per cent for the entire eighty-two miles, and, except when we slow for the order board at Thatcher, the speed is never under seventy miles an hour—better than a mile a minute, and climbing.

To the west, the Spanish Peaks lift their snowy rims against the sky. And there is the beautiful Sangre de Cristo Range, or the Blood of Christ. From La Junta, we have climbed almost two thousand feet. At Trinidad, a helper backs on—an old Norfolk & Western 2-8-8-2 compound articulated, their class Y3, one of the six that the Santa Fe purchased for use on Raton Pass, which, during the war emergency, released twelve of the Santa Fe's 2-10-2 type locomotives for service elsewhere. Everywhere we find evidence of the resourcefulness of the road's officials. In this case the credit goes to Operating Vice-President George Minchin.

Soon the exhausts of the two engines are thundering out their challenge to the Pass. The elevation at Trinidad is 5,990 feet; the grade 3.5 per cent from Moreley to Raton Tunnel, 7,622 feet. Shortly thereafter, just across the Colorado-New Mexico line at Lynn, the helper is cut off, and we drop down to Raton, where our engine takes water and is serviced.

Leaving Raton, we are descending on an average grade of 1.3 to 1.5 per cent for the twenty-seven miles to Maxwell, New Mexico. The speed is breath-taking, as we hold right up to ninety miles an hour. Such running is typical of these engines on the Santa Fe. Often, it seems, they are doing the impossible, as they smash at long sustained grades at high speed, tip over high mountain passes, drift down, to attack a gleaming tangent at one hundred miles an hour.

Maxwell to Azul, seven miles out of Las Vegas, New Mexico, the Second District of the New Mexico Division is uphill all the way, with grades varying from 1.0 per cent to 1.4 per cent. We arrive at Las Vegas at 12:05, to find No. 20, the eastbound *Chief*, awaiting us. This is the regular meeting point for Nos. 19 and 20, the *Chiefs* that have left Chicago and Los Angeles the same day.

The 3777's tank is filled and the engine is serviced, and we pull out at 12:10. From Las Vegas to the top of the hump at Glorieta, a distance of sixty miles, it is a 1.8 per cent climb for all but ten miles; yet these 4-8-4s haul up to fifteen old-style or seventeen lightweight cars over this heavy grade alone, and the job they do is something for the book.

We listen to the cannonading thunder of the exhaust, feeling intimately the surge and power of this workhorse passenger locomotive. The reverse is down in the corner, the throttle is all of the way back, and it seems that the exploding exhaust must certainly take the stack right out of her. How that big locomotive stands up to it only God and the Baldwin Locomotive Works know.

You remember, this is not just an exception, but day in and day out performance. This is a raw, wild world of high mountains and high mesas. Out here on the Santa Fe, there is always one more mountain to cross. This big, strapping engine whips them one by one, and without faltering. You feel that if she hangs together into Los Angeles she should have a long layover, but, instead, she will, perhaps, be turned almost at once and have it all to do over again. Los Angeles to La Junta—La Junta to Los Angeles.

For color and tempestuous beauty, there is no country like this anywhere. More, you have never been out of doors until you have stood on the high plateaus of northern New Mexico and Arizona. The blood in your veins is like wine, and you feel the intoxication of something you cannot describe. You grope for words, for adjectives, and, failing in your search for adequate expression, give this land the adoration of unspoken tribute. You feel that the gorgeous *Chief* of the Santa Fe is whirling you straight across the frontier of the Kingdom of God. The sun is always out and riding these engines up this mountain range cannot help but inspire you.

Now we are heeling to the horseshoe curve at Blanchard, one of the most picturesque on the Santa Fe. This curve was constructed as a means of reducing the grade. We thunder on and up. Ribera, Sands, Ilfeld, Gise, Rowe, Fox. We're climbing the Glorietas to the crashing orchestration of the 3777 . . . 7,437 feet now. Right up in the blue New Mexico sky. On top of the Glorietas at the southern end of the Sangre de Cristo Range.

And then the 3777 screams triumphantly for Glorieta. The exhaust quits. The brakes go on. The big 4-8-4 is panting like a winded bronc. There is a brake test and inspection, for soon we will be dropping down the 3.0 per cent grade to Lamay, through the gorgeous Apache Canyon, along the old Santa Fe Trail.

No. 19 has one hour and thirty-five minutes for the sixty-seven miles from Lamay into Albuquerque. But when the *Chief* is late, the Third District boys whip it in sixty minutes. It is descending grade most of the way, and the ninety-mile-an-hour mark is easily reached.

At Albuquerque, the 3777 is cut off and goes to the servicing rack at the roundhouse west of the station for attention. We have arrived at 3:35—on time. We leave at 3:55. For twenty-seven miles to Dalies, the grade is 1.0 per cent ascending. Dalies is the junction point for the line from Belen.

Dalies to Gonzales now—102 miles—over a grade a little better than 0.5 per cent. This is the top of the Continental Divide, with an elevation of 7,248 feet. East and west the waters flow —to the Gulf of Mexico and the Atlantic; to the Gulf of California and the Pacific.

From Gonzales, the grade is 0.5 per cent descending. What a stretch for rolling, and do they wheel them. The distance from Dalies to Gallup, New Mexico, is 133 miles. Day after day, these engines make it in two hours flat, and they have been known to make up twenty minutes over this district with the *Super Chief*.

I sat in the dispatcher's office at Winslow, Arizona, and watched one cover this 133 miles, Dalies to Gallup, in 124 minutes with *twenty-five* loaded express cars on Second 7. This with one of the 3776-class locomotives you find pictured on the jacket of this book.

We pull into Gallup, the gateway of the Indian country. Zuni, the largest of all the Southwestern Indian Pueblos, is located a short distance west of Thunder Mountain, south of Gallup. From here the traveler may quickly reach the Navajo country, the Hopi villages, Canyon de Chelly, and the Rainbow Natural Bridge. Gallup is the tourists' heaven, and reached by the rails of the Santa Fe. This is the country that gave our train the name it has made famous—the *Chief*.

We arrived at Gallup at 6:50 P.M. The 3777 receives service and water, and seven minutes later the train conductor waves us on. The distance to Winslow is 127.7 miles. We flash past Manuelito, New Mexico; then Lupton, Arizona. Navajo. Adamana. Carriso. Holbrook. Joseph City. The track is practically level the entire distance. For this stretch, No. 19's average time is 62.3 miles an hour. The *Super Chief* and *El Capitan* average 66.6 miles. It is no trick at all for these 4-8-4s to handle their trains on this district in one hour and fifty minutes or better. That is what the dispatcher calls a good run.

Winslow. Nine o'clock. On time. The 3777 is serviced at the pit opposite the enginehouse.

We leave Winslow at 9:10. You will perhaps remember that the last time we were in Winslow, we were riding one of the Santa Fe's big Diesel-electric freight-haulers. We then spoke of the 1.5 per cent grade to Supai. We are now attacking it again, and hard. It almost seems that the 3777 is just hitting her stride. Except in restricted territory, we are cracking off seventy-five miles an hour.

Canyon Diablo. Flagstaff. The Arizona Divide. Beautiful running all of the way. Williams. From here a branch line runs in to the Grand Canyon. We climb on to Supai.

It is here the brakes are tested before we drop down Supai Mountain over a 3.0 per cent grade. Sweeping through Johnson Canyon, through Johnson Tunnel. This is one of the two bores on the westbound main line between Chicago and Los Angeles. Eastbound there are only four tunnels.*

Water is taken at Ash Fork, and a sleeper for train No. 47 to Phoenix is cut out. Lanterns, like fireflies, winking beside the sleeping train. We highball at 12:25, after a fifteen-minute stop. The rail lifts for an average 1.5 per cent to Crookton. The engineer is hitting her hard, and the sharp crack of the exhaust

---

* At certain points, the eastbound and westbound tracks of the Santa Fe follow an entirely separate right-of-way, thus taking advantage of natural gradients.

is talking right back at us. We swing into the arc of a mighty horseshoe curve. Ash Fork, in the valley, is like a diamond-studded brooch against the black, velvet bosom of the night. The air beacon on Bill Williams Mountain throws out its friendly gleam, waving at us and the high-soaring planes from the loftiest point for such a light in the country.

Seligman departure at 12:20 A.M., Pacific War Time. We have moved our watch back an hour. The elevation at Seligman is 5,242 feet; at Needles, 149 miles away, 483 feet above sea level. Dropping down this long, winding grade our average speed is fifty-four miles an hour. The engineer's hand is frequently on the handle of the automatic brake-valve, checking, steadying those swift-running iron feet of No. 19. A beautiful bit of running here.

We whirl past Hackberry, sixty-one miles west of Seligman. If necessary, westbound engines stop for oil here; otherwise they go into Needles. We took water at Ash Fork, and, thanks to the big 25,000-gallon tank on the 3777, will also make Needles for a drink. Kingman. Yucca, Topock. Our flashing drivers sing across the bridge over the Colorado River.

Our whistle shouts at drowsy Needles. We pull in at 3:10. This is California now. Ten minutes for service, and the tireless 3777 picks up the thread of our flashing westward flight at 3:20.

We're climbing again, storming out of the lowlands of the Colorado Basin. For the thirty-one miles to Goffs, the grade is 1.5 per cent, and the new engineer who took over at Needles is really pasting the 3777.*

The sweetest sound I know is the drumming roar of a big passenger engine's exhaust when she's fighting a grade. Tonight I had a front-row seat right upon the queen of them all—this Santa Fe 4-8-4 of the '76 class. I am reminded of another night when I was riding in 19's lounge car on the head end with Second District crews deadheading to Barstow. Instead of going to sleep, they sat there listening to the engine batting the *Chief* up the hill, and really getting a kick out of it. That's the way they feel about the '65- and '76-class locomotives on the Santa Fe.

* For points where crews change see tables of Santa Fe locomotive runs in an earlier chapter.

Just imagine men who work on the railroad every day staying awake for three-quarters of an hour at four o'clock in the morning to listen to an engine working steam.

When Santa Fe men talk about these engines, their eyes light up and their speech reflects deep-rooted pride. "They respond to every touch," an engineman told me. A fireman said, "Just a quarter turn of the feed water pump valve, a touch of the firing valve, one notch on the reverse lever, a slight movement of the throttle, and she's answering with everything she's got in her. Boy, I like to fire 'em!" Attention, Baldwin Locomotive.

It's the truth. They're the nearest to human of all of the locomotives I have ever ridden, except that no human could stand up under the punishment they take.

We are by Goffs at 4:04. The exhaust quickens. This is the great Mohave, studded with dim mountain rims, out there under the eaves of the sky.

The *Super Chief* and *El Capitan* would have had a helper out of Needles, with twelve cars or over; and again, Cadiz to Ash Hill. This to prevent the traction motors from overheating.

What we do on that 1.0 per cent descending grade from Goffs to Cadiz is really to railroad. Cadiz to Ash Hill it is again 1.5 ascending. From Ash Hill to Barstow the grade ranges from 0.5 to 1.0 per cent, with thirteen miles of level track for this last sixty miles. The average time for this 167.6 miles, Needles to Barstow, is 44.7 miles per hour.

That's Calico Mountain out there on the right, hued to make appropriate its name. Daggett rushes to meet us; then the yards of Barstow. 7:05 A.M. On time.

The 3777 again is serviced. We climb aboard. Another crew in charge now—the ninth since we left La Junta.

Our departure from Barstow is at 7:30. We are now on the First District of the Los Angeles Division, and walking down the railroad toward the ramparts of the San Bernardino and the San Gabriel Mountains. Hewn between them is the high cleft that is the famous Cajon Pass. Old Baldy—San Antonio Peak—is tipped with white.

The grade for the 31.5 miles to Oro Grande is 0.8 per cent. Our running time is forty minutes. Victorville, nestling at the edge of the foothills. The nineteen-mile pull to Summit is a 1.6 per cent climb. Thorn. Hesperia. Lugo. Summit station. We stop for train inspection and brake tests before descending Cajon Pass. We leave the haze and tawny coloring of the Mohave and wind down through tumbled hills—a scenic wonderland, and the most photographed spot on the Santa Fe.

In winter these mountains that flank us are blanketed with snow, and often clouds close in until the visibility is zero. We leave Summit at 8:55, dropping down a 3.0 per cent grade on the westbound track. Here, as frequently on the Santa Fe's main line, east- and westbound tracks follow entirely separate grades. Cajon station. The grade eases to 2.2. The east- and westbound tracks parallel one another through Keenbrook, a trouble spot in times of high water in the canyon. Devore. Verdemont. Ono. Then Highland Junction and San Bernardino—locally known as "San Berdoo."

We pull in at 9:40, with ten minutes for service and to take water.

During the emergency directly after Pearl Harbor, the Santa Fe brought twenty-two troop trains over Cajon in fifteen hours with no delay, and at a time when the road was jammed with extra freights being rushed through to the Coast.

The Santa Fe has two lines from San Bernardino to Los Angeles. The Third District, via Riverside Junction, seventy-two miles, with negligible grades, and the Second District, 59.7, with heavy eastbound grades, but only one of 1.5 per cent westbound. Since the United States entered the war, freight constitutes the major traffic handled over the Third District, thus expediting its movement. All fast passenger trains run over the rails of the Second District.

We are out of San Bernardino at 9:50 A.M. The right-of-way is bordered by great orange groves almost all of the way. The whistle screams for frequent grade crossings. We pass the Santa Anita racetrack and crawl through the streets and byways of proud Pasadena, stopping at the station at 11:15. Many passengers detrain. In about five minutes we depart, and, as today is Friday, we meet the eastbound *El Capitan*, which takes de-

269

parture from Los Angeles each Tuesday and Friday, at Broadway, two miles from Los Angeles Union Station.

For the last mile from Mission Tower we are trailing First 3, the all-Pullman section of the *California Limited*, which left Chicago twelve and one-half hours ahead of the *Chief*.

We pull slowly into the world's most beautiful railroad station at Los Angeles, California.

It is the end of the run. The 3777 has laid 1,234 miles behind her.

A mighty engine—247 tons of her—whose performance over those 1,234 battering miles has been phenomenal. We leave her with regret. You do not cross three great states with an engine like the 3777 and not come to feel an affinity for her. She has been warm and friendly; she has been a tower of brute strength when the need was there; she has never faltered, never hesitated, never "slipped" under the burden of starting her heavy train. Her flashing drivers have raced surely and safely down the steel rails at close to one hundred miles an hour at times.

She has crossed the water divide of the United States at 7,248 feet, Raton Pass at 7,622 feet, gorgeous Glorieta Pass at 7,437 feet, the Arizona Divide at 7,335 feet, to stand now in Los Angeles at 264 feet above sea level. She has crossed the Pecos River, the Rio Grande, the Little Colorado, the Colorado, the Mohave. She has been a mighty winged goddess, a speed queen of the rails, whipping time and distance—an engine of the 3776-class of the Santa Fe, roaring through at the front of that famous train of the West—the *Chief*.

The 3777 is cut off and goes to the enginehouse at First Street. Here she will be completely inspected, serviced, and readied for the return trip. She is scheduled to go east with No. 8, the *Fast Mail*, leaving at 10:30 P.M. However, if a shortage of motive power develops, she will leave with No. 4, the *California Limited*, at 6:30.

The R.P.O. and mail storage cars are switched to the mail track for unloading. The passenger equipment is moved to the passenger yards, where it will be cleaned, renovated, and commissioned for No. 20, the *Chief*, leaving the following day.

The dining-car crew, barber, valet, ladies' maid, and Pullman porters lay over until the second day after their arrival on No. 19.

But seldom is there a layover for these big 4-8-4s. Their stamina is unbelievable. We salute them, as we salute the men who built them and the men who run them.

EASTBOUND WITH NUMBER 20

It is 11:56 A.M., Pacific War Time. We have five minutes before the eastbound *Chief* is scheduled to leave the Los Angeles Union Station for Chicago. Our engine is the 3784, which arrived last night on No. 7, the *Fast Mail*, at 10 P.M.

You have been introduced to this 4-8-4 locomotive on the jacket of this book. As we have already recorded, the 3784 and 3785 are equipped with roller bearing rods.

We get the highball from the conductor at 12:01, who in turn has the light from Mission Tower, and move out of the station. As we pass the tower, the 3784 buckles down, and the concussion from the squat stack is hard, furious. It almost seems as though it would tear the flues out of her.

For two-fisted battling performance, the next thirteen miles are probably the toughest assignment of any engine taking departure from its home or originating terminal in the United States.

From Mission Tower to Broadway, the grade is 1.8 per cent; from Broadway to Water Street 1.3. Bear in mind that the speed limit is fifteen miles an hour, and we are running practically on a main street, with a crossing every few hundred feet. It is a slow punishing pull. We cross the Union Pacific tracks at Water Street, and for the three miles to Highland Park the 3776-class engines handle seventeen lightweight or fifteen heavyweight Pullmans up a 2.2 per cent grade without a helper. From Highland Park to South Pasadena, the grade is 1.9 per cent, and from there into Pasadena 2.2.

From Pasadena to Lamanda Park, the grade is 1.9; then level track to Monrovia. However, from that point to Upland, twenty-two miles, it varies from 1.0 to 1.9 per cent. From the very be-

271

ginning, these locomotives are given a taste of what they will have to do, off and on, all of the way to La Junta. In my opinion, this is tops in locomotive performance and unexcelled anywhere.

No. 20 pulls into San Bernardino at 1:40. Five minutes later we are thundering east. Today we have one of the old 1200-class, first of the Santa Fe's Pacifics, for a helper. But if a shortage of motive power had existed, the 3784 would have hauled our present consist of fourteen cars up Cajon without assistance.

At mile-posts 139 and 155 on the Cajon grade we pass through two of the four tunnels on the eastbound main line. Storming up Cajon, we pass freight after freight in the hole for us—long trains, each with its road engine and two helpers—briefly bowing to the rights of the eastbound *Chief*, their crews inspecting us.

Summit is a beehive of activity, with freight trains testing brakes and setting up retainers, and helper engines preparing to scurry down the mountain light, both to the east and west of the pass. Yes, you would know there was a war on.

We are looking across the vast hinterland that is the Mohave. The most fantastic of all trees, the spiked, uncanny Joshua, darts past us. The Mohave's breath is hot; the vistas are tremendous, awesome. We arrive at Barstow at 3:45. Here the engine crews change, the train crew going through to Needles. Service and water, and a highball at 3:50.

The eastbound track on the Second District of the Arizona Division, Barstow to Needles, is two miles shorter than the westbound, and the heaviest grade, extending for twenty-six miles, Hector to Ash Hill, is 1.0 per cent; also from Cadiz to Goffs, thirty-nine miles. Our average speed is 58.5 miles an hour.

At Needles, the engine is again serviced. A new crew to Seligman, a new train crew to Winslow. We leave Needles at 6:45 and immediately attack the 149-mile sustained grade mentioned in the freight Diesel chapter. Hackberry for oil at 8:40 P.M. At 8:45 the exhaust of the 3784 picks up the thread of our flight again, and soon is cracking like a rapid-fire howitzer.

A stretch of 149.7 miles and lifting at from 1.2 to 1.5 per cent, we maintain an average speed of 42.8 miles an hour. And I mean the 3784 is working her passage. You feel the strain, the tireless

The Chief descending the east slope of Raton Pass on the 3.5% grade below Wootton, Colo. This is the sharpest curve on both the east and west slopes of the historic pass. With engine 3779 of the 3776 Class 4-8-4 Type. Photo by Otto C. Perry.

Santa Fe second #8 with 19 cars, 14 of which are D.H.Q. (dead head equipment) returning east after a westbound military move. On many occasions empty cars have to be hauled many miles to be filled with more of Uncle Sam's soldiers and sailors. The engine is #3783 of the 3776 Class and the picture was taken east of Robinson, N.M. on the Second District of the N.M. Division. Photo by Otto C. Perry.

Santa Fe #17, the SuperChief, deluxe all Pullman twice-weekly streamliner from Chicago to Los Angeles, powered with twin unit 4000 h.p. Diesel locomotives, being helped by #926 and 1651 original 2-10-2 Type, up Raton Pass west of Morley, Colo. The grade is 3.5%. These helpers were taken out of storage to do their bit for the Santa Fe war effort. Photo by Otto C. Perry.

thrust of those churning mainrods, the power and the glory that are the heart of the big 4-8-4.

We arrive at Seligman at 10:15. We are now entering a new time zone—Mountain War Time—and set our watch ahead one hour.

A new crew, with Engineman W. J. "Smiley" Jones at the throttle. He will handle the 3784 to Winslow. Smiley Jones, one of the finest fellows and one of the greatest engineers I have ever ridden with. He is known on the Santa Fe for his artistry in running a locomotive and his smooth train handling with the brake-valve.

We climb at 1.5 per cent, Seligman to Crookton, and rush on down to Ash Fork, where a sleeper from train No. 42 from Phoenix is cut into our No. 20.

12:06 out of Ash Fork—five minutes late with fifteen cars. Engineer Jones drops the reverse into the working corner and pulls the throttle out to its last lift, for we are facing twenty-one miles of 2.0 grade, Ash Fork to Supai. The 3784 is tearing the night apart with her hard-hitting thunder. The mighty eighty-inch drivers bite hard at the 131-pound rail. The couplings are straining at our heavy load.

We glimpse the silver blade that is the headlight of No. 19 coming down the mountain on the westbound, and above her a helper coming down light. There is the prickle of lights at Ash Fork under us, sharp and clear in the rarefied air, and off in the west, the glimmer that marks the lights of the helpers at Crookton.

If it were daylight, we could see the smoke of freight trains all of the way back to Seligman. Now there is only the diamond dust in the heavens—the intimate glitter of those low western stars. We are riding close under the arched vault of the sky. This northern Arizona night as usual is magnificent. I have never seen so many stars. It seems as though you could almost reach out and touch them. Nowhere that I have ridden the night trains, nowhere on the oceans where I have fished, have I felt so close to the sparkling dome of the universe.

The operator is out of his office at Daze, inspecting us as we pass. His lantern waves us on. Corva. Sereno. Welch, a newly

273

opened telegraph office for the war emergency. Here we rejoin the westbound track again.

The fireman and Smiley Jones work as a team. The man on the left side of the cab watches the engineer, the water-glass; gives close attention to the firing valve. It requires more brains and judgment to fire with oil than coal, even though oil is much the better fuel. The quick combustion of oil accounts for this. Every time the engineer makes an adjustment of throttle or reverse, the fireman must instantly counter with an adjustment of his firing valve to compensate for the demands of the hard-working engine.

At Supai, we're over the hump, to drop into Williams on a 1.5 per cent descending grade. One o'clock. The locomotive has performed magnificently, and all during the climb the water was never below the halfway level in the glass. We're out of Williams two minutes late, and hammer hard at the 1.5 per cent grade to Riordan.

The crashing stack begins to vomit black smoke, and the fireman takes his sanding scoop, to pour sand, carried in a box on the tender, through the sanding hole in the firebox door. The savage exhaust carries this sand through the flues and tubes, scouring them clean. This performance is repeated every thirty or forty miles on an oil-burning locomotive, and is called "dusting her out."

We slow to throw off mail at Flagstaff at 1:48. From Cliffs to Cosnino, the next two stations to the east, the grade is once more 1.5 per cent for eight miles. However, from there into Winslow the track is level to downhill all the way.

There is a lot of westbound movement tonight, and we meet train after train, including five troop trains. Jones and his fireman have called the indication of every signal, as freight and passenger engine crews do on all divisions of the Santa Fe. Leaving Winona, for the first time, the call is "yellow." Then "red." We hit two guns—torpedoes—and grind to a stop under the peremptory challenge of the red block, after which No. 20 proceeds at a lagging five miles an hour. We stop and extinguish a red fusee. Soon there are the winking lanterns of a flagman. He climbs into the cab, with the information that a freight drag is ahead of us. We crawl up behind the marker lights of a way-car.

Soon there are the whistle blasts of the freight, calling in the flag, shrill and impatient, for they know that they're on the time of the *Chief*. Lanterns swing; there is the clatter of slack running out, and the freight slips away. When the block ahead shows yellow, the whistle of the 3784 trumpets sharply for our own flagman. At Angell we get another red signal. As we stop, the operator "hoops up" an order to run against the current of traffic on the westbound track, Angell to Canyon Diablo. The freight ahead of the one that flagged us down has pulled a draw-head.

They line the railroad and we cross over, running on the westbound to Canyon Diablo, where they are holding a westbound train. We cross back to the eastbound, having lost a precious twenty-five minutes. Smiley Jones snaps the *Chief* down the last twenty-six miles of his run in twenty-one minutes, making up fifteen minutes.

The new engine crew out of Winslow will run to Gallup; the train crew to Albuquerque. We whip the miles to Gallup, arriving at 5:55 A.M. We leave there five minutes late, and with a new engine crew. To Gonzales, at the top of the Continental Divide, the grade is 0.6 per cent, and the same descending to Dalies. We rush on to Albuquerque, and arrive on time, thanks to the nice work of the dispatcher in running us around the freight that had "plugged" us back there at Canyon Diablo.

The 3784 stops at the servicing pit at the Albuquerque round-house. We take oil and water, and highball out of Albuquerque station at nine o'clock. The New Mexico Division engine crew will run to Las Vegas, and the train crew all the way to La Junta.

From Albuquerque to Lamay, the time is fast—ninety miles an hour all of the way if running late. At Lamay, we get a 3100-class 2-8-2 helper for the 3.0 per cent grade to Glorieta. From that point we drop through beautiful country, to lean hard on the great horseshoe at Blanchard and spin the silver-threaded miles into Las Vegas to meet No. 19.

The Second District engine crew takes over. Water and service. As No. 17, the *Super Chief*, and No. 21, the *El Capitan*, run over this division on Wednesdays and Sundays—this being Sunday—we meet No. 17 at Onva and No. 21 at Kroenig's. We go into the hole for them, and lose eight minutes.

From Albuquerque to La Junta, the New Mexico Division is single track, with the exception of the grades from Glorieta to Lamay, and from Raton to Trinidad. With the exception of the El Paso and Coast Denver freight, all of the freight and two passenger trains, as well, run via the Santa Fe Southern District from Newton, Kansas, to Amarillo, Texas, and Clovis and Belen, New Mexico.

Thus, the Santa Fe has two separate railroads. The Southern District eliminates the necessity of climbing heavy grades.

Our No. 20 arrives at Raton on time. The engine is again serviced, and we take water. The new engine crew will go through to La Junta. An old 900- and 1600-class 2-10-2 type back down and couple on. They will help us to Wootton, Colorado, at the top of the 3.3 per cent grade where we emerge from Raton Tunnel.

The blue flag is taken down and we are ready to go, as the car inspector gives us our air-brake clearance. We leave at 2:25. The grimy old Santa Fe–type helpers buckle down, and the 3784's exhaust joins the chorus of shouting stacks. Up, up, up—a thundering tumult from iron lungs an accompaniment for our going. Thirty-one minutes later the 2-10-2s are cut off after a tough eight-mile pull up the pass. We're descending now over a winding grade varying from 2.0 to 3.5 per cent. We consume thirty-nine minutes for the fifteen miles, Wootton to Trinidad.

We get the highball at Trinidad at 3:40, ten minutes late. From Thatcher to La Junta, the speed is over ninety miles an hour all the way over a descending grade. We pull in right on time. And as we come to a stop, three or four car inspectors and other Santa Fe employees make a beeline for our pilot to see how many dead pheasants we have collected. The pickings are poor this trip, for they find only a pair.

The run is over for the 3784. We cannot say enough in praise of her performance, which so often has been astounding. At the roundhouse, she will be inspected, tested, and serviced for her

276

westbound return on No. 19, the *Chief*, at ten minutes past seven in the morning.

No. 20 arrived at La Junta at 5:00 P.M., and at 5:05 this fast-stepping train of the Santa Fe is streaking east toward Kansas City and Chicago behind the 3460-class Hudson, with her great eighty-four-inch drivers singing the eternal song of the rail.

It must be remembered that the runs reviewed here were close to on-time performance all of the way, and the engines were never extended to their capacity over many stretches where, had they been late, time could have been made up.

I have never ridden one of these locomotives that would not steam. They seldom develop hot pins, so thoroughly are they serviced. (I have seen only three.) I have never seen any type of mechanical breakdown, and only two of a minor nature, which were readily repaired by the engine crew at the point of occurrence on the road, the detention being negligible, and I have ridden them thousands of miles over every division on which they are operated.

I have never seen one of these 4-8-4s "slip" when starting, and I remember only two or three occasions when they slipped on a grade, and then because of a very bad rail. It should be remembered that these engines operate over runs involving temperature changes that vary as much as ninety degrees.

I am often asked if I am not tired after having ridden for thirty hours in the cab of these engines. I can truthfully state that I have been twice as tired after being on other locomotives half of the time. But these ride like a Pullman. The big 25,000-gallon tenders carry nicely on their eight-wheel trucks.

From my personal observation, I would say that the only other 4-8-4s in the country that come close to matching the performance of the 3765 and '76-class of the Santa Fe are the Southern Pacific's oil-burning GS-5s and the Union Pacific's coal-burning 820-class, which also have eighty-inch driving wheels and 300-pound boiler pressures, but do not have quite the tractive effort or horsepower.

In October, 1943, the Baldwin Locomotive Works began the delivery of the first of thirty more 4-8-4 type to the Santa Fe.

These are known as the 2900-class. At this writing, as of March, 1944, twenty-two have been delivered. These engines are exactly the same as the 3776-class, with the exception that they are a trifle heavier, as it was impossible to obtain the lighter alloys and, unfortunately, the roller bearing rods, due to war conditions. The only apparent change is a different type of throttle quadrant.

These engines are being used solely in freight service, and are being run through from Argentine, the Santa Fe's great freight terminal at Kansas City, to Clovis, New Mexico, a distance of 652 miles, via Ellinor, Mulvane, and Wellington, Kansas, Waynoka, Oklahoma, and Amarillo, Texas. They have a Red Ball rating of 4,000 tons, and cover this distance in twenty-three hours. They have a drag rating of 5,000 tons with a twenty-eight-hour limit.

I have ridden engine 2900 with 4,080 tons over the Eastern Division, Argentine to Emporia, 106 miles, and the time from Turner Tower at the west end of Argentine Yard was two hours and thirty-four minutes, with no stops. And that is highballing freight.

Like all of these 4-8-4s, these engines are as good in freight service as they are in passenger, and that is saying a lot. As far as the 2900s are concerned, it is a hard job to keep them down to conform to the freight-train speed limits. Our train that night was No. 33, the California-Texas-Oklahoma Fast Freight, and its make-up consisted of sixty-nine red ball cars, sixteen tank, two refrigerator cars, and three deadheads, making a total of ninety. There is nothing quite like these all-purpose-engines, which are every day proving their worth.

The Santa Fe, as this is written, is also beginning to receive the first of twenty new 5001-class 2-10-4s, and also some new freight Diesels.

The new 5001s, like their famous Texas-type predecessors, are one of the finest and most unusual freight locomotive classes ever built in this country. They are the only ten-coupled engines that have driving wheels over seventy inches in diameter. Their

278

drivers are seventy-four inches, and they carry a boiler pressure of 310 pounds.

They are equipped with the longest one-piece engine beds ever built. In service, they operate on the difficult and most important Pecos Division, Clovis to Belen, New Mexico, a distance of 239 miles, and are serviced en route at Vaughn. They are hauling 4,000 tons westbound and 4,800 tons eastbound, with a helper on the 1.8 per cent grade from Belen to Mountainair, New Mexico. This is Red Ball rating. As soon as more of these great engines can be obtained, they will be used to Winslow.

All of the combined effective features of the 3765- and the 5001-class have been included in these two types, and, needless to say, their performance has been of the highest order. The 93,000 pounds of tractive effort of the 5001s, plus the ability to develop tremendous horsepower, has enabled the high-wheel Texas-type locomotive to prove itself superbly on the Chesapeake and Ohio, Kansas City Southern, and the Pennsylvania.

To meet fast freight service demands after the war, the Santa Fe will be in a position to provide the shipper with fast transportation of his goods along its lines. We will see 4-8-4s and 4-8-2s handling fast freight tonnage from Corwith (Chicago) to Argentine, Kansas; 4-8-4s, supplemented by 2-8-4s from Argentine to Clovis; 2-10-4s of tremendous power, together with great 2-10-2s, pulling their long trains from Clovis to Winslow; the big Diesels, previously mentioned, in operation between Winslow and Barstow, and Diesels and 2-10-2s moving over El Cajon to Los Angeles and San Diego; also running from Barstow to Bakersfield, via Mohave and the tumbled Tehachapi Mountains.

Modernized, heavy, high-speed 2-8-2s will haul freight trains over other portions of the far-flung steel network of the Santa Fe System, providing the ultimate in service to the peacetime shipper, as they have served the Government and the shipper in wartime.

Because this chapter has been devoted, for the most part, to the locomotives engaged in hauling the *Chief*, we feel that the concluding paragraphs should be devoted to the train itself.

Besides carrying in its consist three cars of mail, the *Chief*, easily the world's finest train, is, as we have pointed out, always filled to capacity with Army and Navy personnel, high-ranking Government heads, and railroad and war workers whose duti ; demand crossing the country as quickly as possible. Aside from the over burdened transport planes, the railroads provide the quickest and surest transportation.

With the exception of the *Super Chief*—which runs twice weekly—the *Chief* is the only all-Pullman train from Chicago to Los Angeles. There is but one other all-Pullman train from Chicago to the Pacific Coast, the *Overland Limited*, running to San Francisco on a comparatively slow schedule.

The *Chief* covers the westbound run of 2,227 miles in forty-nine hours and forty-nine minutes. The eastbound trip consumes forty-seven hours and forty minutes. The equipment of the *Chief* is exactly the same as before the war. The *Chief*, with the exception of the twice-weekly *Super Chief*, is the only train in the country that boasts three lounge cars. The lounge car at the head end is unsurpassed for its luxury and beauty. The lounge car in the middle of the train has dormitory accommodations for the dining-car crew, as well as providing generous space for the traveler. At the rear end is a well-appointed observation-compartment and lounge. Because of a shortage of equipment in wartime, seat space is on sale in all of these cars.

While the *Super Chief* makes the Chicago–Los Angeles run in forty-one hours and forty-five minutes, she has never won the place in the hearts of Santa Fe men that belongs to the *Chief*. It is Nos. 19 and 20, the *Chief*, that is the pride and joy of the road. Her on-time performance since the war began has been just as fine at is was in peacetime.

In wartime, the dining-car service on the *Chief* and *Super Chief* retains the high standard it established previous to the second World War. In fact, the service on all Santa Fe diners has been maintained at a high degree, considering the difficulties entailed in provisioning a dining car under wartime conditions. Add to that the difficulty in obtaining the crews to man them properly. The stewards have performed wonders, with eight or ten sittings for a meal, and where three would have been unusual in normal times.

Transcontinental travelers riding the *Chief* and *Super Chief* have suffered no discomfiture as there are no crowded conditions in the dining cars. Further, meals still are served out of the diner if desired.

While I do not pretend to be a Lucius Beebe, who is really a connoisseur when it comes to food, it is my opinion that these two great trains of the Santa Fe serve the best food on any dining cars in the United States. The meals are uniformly good; the prices reasonable. My normally moderate appetite tells me that they serve the best chicken salad to be found anywhere in the country. The meats, cold soup, melons, avocados, celery— everything, in fact, is hard to equal.

In praising the high standard of food on the Santa Fe, one must, also, take off his hat to the Fred Harvey System, for you eat food provided by Fred Harvey on the Santa Fe dining cars. However, it is not alone on the diners that the Fred Harvey System is known, but in many railroad stations as well.

The Fred Harvey System maintains dining rooms and lunch counters in twenty-five stations and sixteen hotels along the Santa Fe. They not only have served train passengers who could not get into the dining cars, but have fed thousands of military personnel of both troop and regular trains who would otherwise have gone hungry. They, also, have fed many a hungry railroad man.

Walk into any Fred Harvey restaurant at a Santa Fe station at any hour of the day or night and you will find inviting tables and counters, and food always on hand, pending the arrival of military trains whose coming may have been revealed to the Fred Harvey manager only a few minutes before.

The Fred Harvey hotel service has provided for countless businessmen, war workers, and railroad men. But largely they have ably catered to military men whose duties have brought them to the various cities in which the Fred Harvey hotels are located.

In November, 1943, I was in the Fred Harvey hotels at La Junta, Colorado, and Needles, California. Every room was occupied by Army men, with the exception of a few that were reserved for railroad men, who were getting rest between runs.

Nowhere can you find hotels and eating houses more efficiently managed than those of Fred Harvey. Seldom has it been my pleasure to patronize a more attractive, more charming hostelry anywhere than the La Posada in Winslow, or the Alvarado at Albuquerque.

Countless thousands of travelers are familiar with the famous El Tovar Hotel, of the Fred Harvey System, at the Grand Canyon; many have been guests of the Casa del Desierto Hotel at Barstow, the El Vaquero at Dodge City, the El Navajo at Gallup, the El Garces at Needles, the Fray Marcos at Williams, to name a few—hotels where you will find the color and romance of the great Southwest. Spanish and Indian tradition here—the same that gave to a great railroad the name of Santa Fe; a great train the name *Chief.*

We close this chapter of the Santa Fe by setting the scene in the waycar, or caboose, of an eastbound freight on the Third District of the Albuquerque Division.

There were four of us—the conductor, the swing brakeman, the flagman, and myself. The flagman was an old-time boomer. Down the years he had worked on many railroads all over the country, but had finally put down roots on the Santa Fe. Like most boomers, he had come to regard all railroad officials with supreme disdain. And all of the way from Seligman to Supai, he had been expressing himself in the intensely profane but equally picturesque language of his kind regarding railroads in general and railroad officials in particular.

"You could fire every this-and-so of a big shot," he declared, "above the Super, and the cockeyed railroad would still run!"

He continued to talk in this vein until we met the westbound *Chief* on a reverse curve near Riordan. As the bright gleam of the headlight appeared, there was the customary cry from the high perch of the lookout of, "On the railroad!"

The boys in the cupola always sing it out to let the flagman know when the train is meeting or running around another train. The flagman then goes out on the rear platform to inspect the train being met or passed. This procedure is customary on all railroads, with the result that often a hot box or dragging equipment is detected.

Tonight the *Chief*, as usual, had one of the 3776-class engines, and the big 4-8-4 was really talking. A full Arizona moon touched the fleeting Pullmans, spilled its silvery glow over the world— a world across which flashed the *Chief.* It was a picture you don't forget.

The old boomer gave No. 19's flagman in the observation car a highball with his lantern; then stood watching her markers and rear-end illuminated sign fade away. He turned, entered the waycar, quietly closed the door, put down his lantern, and said in a sober, prideful tone, "Man, there's a train. In wartime or peace the *Chief* is still the *Chief.*"

The conductor, the swing brakeman, and I nodded solemn assent. The *Chief* she is—the *Chief,* of the Santa Fe.

CHAPTER XXIV

WAR RECORD OF THE R.F.&P.

A 1940-43 Summary

The main line of the Richmond, Fredericksburg and Potomac Railroad forms a mighty steel link between Richmond, the capital of Virginia, and Washington, the capital of the Nation. It further links the Baltimore & Ohio and Pennsylvania Railroads on the north and the Atlantic Coast Line and Seaboard R.R. to the south with 116.5 miles of main-line track.

It is sometimes called the "Bridge Line," for the rails of the Richmond, Fredericksburg and Potomac cross many rivers, including the Potomac, Bull Run, the Rappahannock, the Mattapony, the Chickahominy. Mighty engines roar through—the Governors and the Generals—pulling the war trains. Famous streamliners like the *Silver Meteor* and the *Champion* flash down the rails.

Born when the Nation was young, the Richmond, Fredericksburg and Potomac has given faithful service over a period of 110 years. Granted a charter on February 25, 1834, it has continued in operation under its original name, and without reorganization, to the present day.

The Richmond, Fredericksburg and Potomac—the biggest little railroad in the country.

Frequently damned, seldom praised, and, in normal times, always taken for granted, the railroad system of the country in wartime is instantly recognized as the bulwark of National Defense. For without adequate and dependable rail service it would be impossible to mobilize and train a mighty army. In the hour of deadly peril on December 7, 1941, the railroads of the Nation were in a position to answer instantly the call to arms.

284

Here we are going to present a summary of the Richmond, Fredericksburg and Potomac's activities from prewar 1940 through 1943, that we may better understand the enormous task successfully accomplished by this road.

1940

In 1940, the war in Europe was building its frightful crescendo. The German military might was in high gear, and America stood on the sidelines, awed and horror-stricken. In that year, passenger traffic on the R.F.&P. increased twenty-six per cent and freight traffic ten per cent, but these increases were in line with the trend of the times. Revenue passengers numbering 1,510,595 were carried in 13,967 trains; 4,563,981 tons of freight were hauled, requiring 7,050 trains. The daily average of passenger trains was thirty-eight and of freight trains nineteen, for a total average of fifty-seven trains per day for the year.

The program of track improvement, including the use of heavier rail and stone ballast, maintained its upward trend. All in all, things moved along soberly and with a normal pulse. The outlook was regarded as encouraging.

1941

The year of 1941 was marked by a substantial increase in the activity of an expanding Army, Navy, and Marine Corps. Uncle Sam leisurely removed his coat and began the rebuilding of the big military camps of 1917-18, together with the construction of new ones. The result was a growing freight traffic.

The United States training center at Fort Belvoir and the Marine Corps establishment at Quantico were enlarged. An area of some eighty thousand acres in Caroline County, designated as the A. P. Hill Military Reservation, was acquired by the Army for large-scale maneuvers. Training here began in March of 1942. The Government began the construction of thirty miles of railroad, connecting with the R.F.&P., to serve the Naval Proving Ground at Dahlgren.

There was a growing activity at such centers as Camp Lee,

Fort Eustis, Camp Pickett, and at Hampton Roads, Virginia. In the South Atlantic states of North and South Carolina, Florida, and Georgia camps were astir. The Parris Island Marine Base and Fort Jackson; Fort McPherson, Fort Stevens, Fort Oglethorpe, Camp Wheeler, Camp Gordon; Fort Bragg, Fort Benning, Camp Stewart, Camp Blanding. Eventually the number of posts, camps, and flying fields in these four South Atlantic states was raised to more than 150. Tennessee, Alabama, Mississippi, and Louisiana came into the picture with some seventy such training centers.

Forming a vital link between the South and the densely populated area to the north, the Richmond, Fredericksburg and Potomac began to feel the ever growing weight of the traffic movement. New training technique necessitated the frequent movement of men and equipment. In the year of 1941, the R.F.&P. handled a total of 281,287 troops for whom special train or car service was provided.

The total number of revenue passengers carried in 15,622 trains was 2,537,531, an increase of sixty-eight per cent over 1940. The total travel even then was fifteen per cent above 1918, the peak passenger year of World War I. Freight traffic accelerated to 6,599,612 revenue tons, or forty-five per cent above 1940. The freight traffic, represented by 9,463 trains, exceeded the peak of the first World War by thirty-seven per cent.

During this year of 1941, the program of laying all main-line tracks with 130- or 131-pound rail was completed. The R.F.&P. purchased ten all-steel Pullman parlor cars, which were converted into coaches. Seven all-steel coaches were modernized and air-conditioned.

And then, with Old Man 1941 preparing to make his exit from the scene, the gods of Shinto unleashed their War Demons, and Pearl Harbor was baptized with blood.

1942

America was at war! The future was dark and unpredictable. The United States, a potentially mighty nation, still shuddering from the murderous assault of a once-fawning, oily-tongued "friend," stood bewildered and angry, like an overgrown country bumpkin, bitten by a poisonous snake, which he had imprudently fondled.

The war trains had already begun to roll. The railroads were ready. Because of enormous expenditures for better equipment and improved track since the termination of Federal Control in 1920, together with the effectiveness of the carriers' national organization, the Association of American Railroads, rail operation was vastly more efficient and successful than anything attained under the United States Railroad Administration in the first World War.

Today the railroads are moving a staggering amount of traffic without serious delays or congestion. This is due to the complete co-operation of the military branches of the Government, together with the aid of organizations like the regional Shippers' Advisory Boards, established under the auspices of the Car Service Division of the Association, which maintains a Military Transportation Section in the Army's Pentagon Building. This department assists the military branches in the routing of troops and further aids the railroads in supplying the necessary cars.

The close co-operation between the railroads and the Government involved the establishment of emergency rates, storage-in-transit arrangements, et cetera, as found necessary for Government War Traffic. Requests for such rates or arrangements are made to the Association of American Railroads and are promptly considered by its Traffic Department, acting under the advice of the Traffic Executive Chairman's Committee, which is composed of the chairmen of the several territorial freight traffic organizations. When necessary, the advice of the Chief Traffic Officers representing all railroads is sought. When approved, the new rates or other arrangements are made effective through quotations by the Association to the Government departments concerned.

In December of 1941, the President, under his emergency powers, established the Office of Defense Transportation, with the late Joseph B. Eastman as Director. This organization has been most helpful, especially in the conservation of equipment, through such methods as the heavier loading of freight cars, the reduction of circuitous routing, limitation of diversions and reconsignments, the prompt loading and unloading of freight, the diversion of traffic from routes that were becoming congested and the scheduling of petroleum products in solid trains of tank cars to the Eastern Seaboard territory. The Interstate Commerce Commission and the various State regulatory bodies have co-operated with the Office of Defense Transportation and the railroads in every way possible in making effective the emergency measures found necessary.

Thus, through preparedness and marked efficiency on the part of the railroads, the wholehearted co-operation of all governmental agencies and the shipping public, the country has escaped Federal operation of its transportation system in this its greatest national emergency.

Beginning late in 1941, the withdrawal of all Atlantic coastwise shipping, due to sinkings by German submarines, an enormous volume of traffic that ordinarily moves by water was tossed into the laps of the railroads, particularly the R.F.&P.

In 1942, passenger traffic increased 110 per cent over 1941; 18,860 passenger trains—of which 2,099 were troop trains—carried 5,326,883 passengers; 15,683 freight trains hauled 11,758,693 revenue tons, with 215 trains carrying only military impedimenta. This was an increase of seventy-eight per cent over the previous year.

The main-line passenger traffic was made up of 1,075,302 troops, 1,213,978 servicemen and -women on furlough, and regular passengers to the number of 2,803,172.

The daily average of all trains was ninety-five.

The total trackage of Potomac Yard was brought to ninety-five miles by the construction of 11.5 miles of new track. Five new 4-8-4 Baldwin passenger locomotives were purchased and placed in service late in the year; also two 1,000-horsepower Diesel switch engines. An order was placed for ten new freight locomotives.

Locomotives destined for the reconquered territories of Soviet Russia shown on New York Central flat cars. Built for 5-ft. gauge and standing on rails on the car they reach a height of 17 ft. 2 in. above the rail. 2-10-0 Types are also handled in this manner. In the same train other locomotives of standard gauge are destined for use of the U. S. Army abroad. Courtesy New York Central R. R.

Richmond, Fredericksburg & Potomac #573, one of eight 2-8-4 Types recently delivered to that road by the Lima Locomotive Works. The train is the northbound Potomac merchandise at Summit, Virginia. These engines, the first with a two-wheel engine truck ever owned by this road, have proved a great addition to the R. F. & P.'s magnificent motive power fleet. Courtesy R. F. & P. Railroad.

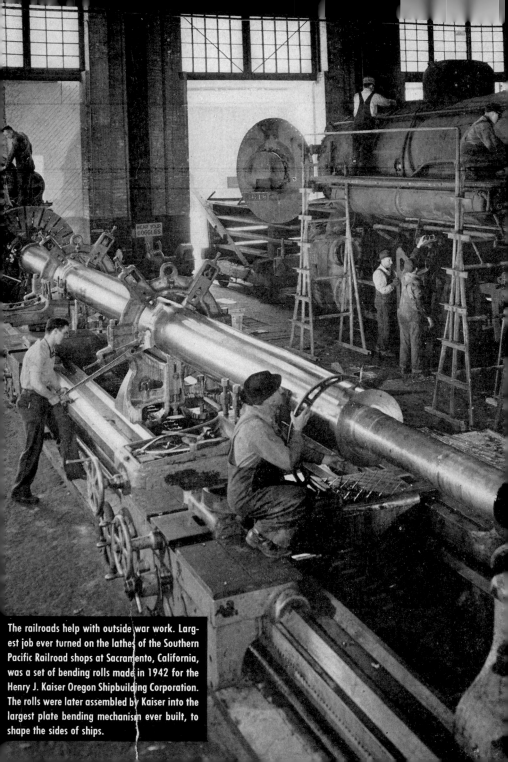

The railroads help with outside war work. Largest job ever turned on the lathes of the Southern Pacific Railroad shops at Sacramento, California, was a set of bending rolls made in 1942 for the Henry J. Kaiser Oregon Shipbuilding Corporation. The rolls were later assembled by Kaiser into the largest plate bending mechanism ever built, to shape the sides of ships.

Illinois Central Extra #1494, 2-8-2 Type, with a trainload of tanks and trucks belonging to a U. S. armored division on the Louisiana Div. between Canton, Miss., and MaComb, La. Courtesy of U. S. Army.

Rio Grande Main running as passenger extra 3506 east with 25 cars of ski troops, 5 of which are out of sight around the second curve, drifting down the 1.8% grade below Cold Creek, Colorado. The locomotive is one of the road's earliest 2-8-8-2 Type Class L-95 with auxiliary water car. This is on the Moffat Tunnel route. Photo by Preston George.

1943

Main-line passenger traffic boomed; 20,898 passenger trains were operated in 1943; 2,363 troop trains carried 1,487,237 troops; 2,649,295 furlough passengers traveled on the trains of the R.F.&P., and 3,699,878 other passengers. The total number of revenue passengers stood at 8,395,493, an increase of fifty-eight per cent over 1942.

In each month of 1943, except January and February, the number of passengers exceeded the total of 581,190 carried in the entire twelve months of the depression year of 1933, while in August, 1943, the 774,790 passengers carried exceeded the entire passenger travel for the year 1934. The peak day of April 22 saw 33,324 passengers riding, or more than rode the R.F.&P. for either the full months of June or August in 1933.

The freight traffic in 1943 was above a million tons in each month, and the total for any three months exceeded the entire tonnage hauled in the depression years of either 1933 or 1934. The peak was reached in May, when 50,355 cars hauled 1,271,040 tons of revenue freight.

The total freight tonnage moved over the rails of the Richmond, Fredericksburg and Potomac in 1943 was 14,111,257 tons, an increase of 209 per cent over 1940.

Let's take a look at some of the consist of these freight drags, much of which in normal times moves by boat. There is citrus fruit and phosphate rock from Florida, sugar from Cuba, bananas from Central America, tank cars with petroleum products from Louisiana and Texas. There's newsprint paper from Canada; cotton, cotton fabrics, pulpboards, naval stores, leaf tobacco, molasses from the South; fertilizers, canned goods, asphalt, and burlap from the North—which is just skimming the vast list of commodities hurrying through in bulging freight cars.

The War Production Board permitted the railroads to build a limited number of locomotives and freight cars, but no material was available for new passenger equipment in 1942 or 1943, except that the Defense Plant Corporation arranged for the construction of 1,200 Troop Sleepers and 400 Kitchen Cars for troop trains. These were put in service late in 1943.

So crowded were passenger trains late in 1942 and in 1943 that the Office of Defense Transportation, the Association of American Railroads, and the railroads themselves were forced to appeal to the public by radio, press, and magazine advertisements to refrain from riding the trains unless it was urgently necessary.

Because of the desperate need for sleeping cars for long-distance troop movements, the regular winter train service between New York and Florida—some of which had operated for more than fifty years—was discontinued after the 1941-42 season.

Additions to Potomac and Acca Yards were completed in 1943. Ten powerful 2-8-4 locomotives for fast freight service were received from the Lima Locomotive Works and placed in service in February and March, at which time renting of road locomotives from other lines was discontinued. The last 4-8-4 Baldwin passenger engine ordered in 1942 was received in January. Two more 1,000-horsepower Diesel switch engines were placed in operation in the yards at Acca and Richmond. Three secondhand Articulateds were purchased from the C.&O. for handling trains on the hump in Potomac Yard, together with several rented switch engines. In 1944 four 4-8-2s were purchased from the N.&W. and ten more 4-8-4 Governors with 20,000-gallon tenders ordered from Baldwin.

The daily average of trains operated in 1943 was 57 passenger and 46 freight, for a total of 103. On April 21, a maximum of 131 trains were run.

In 1943, freight traffic on the Richmond, Fredericksburg and Potomac was three times that of World War I, and passenger travel nearly four times the peak of that in 1917-18.

Now let's take a look at the astounding traffic growth as a whole over a period of three years, 1940 through 1943:

	1940	1943	Increase 1943 over 1940
Revenue Passengers Carried	1,510,595	8,395,493	456%
Passenger Miles	146,194,180	816,480,183	458%
Tons Revenue Freight Hauled	4,563,981	14,111,257	209%
Ton Miles	437,292,251	1,436,765,553	229%
Trains Operated–Passenger Service	13,967	20,898	50%
Trains Operated–Freight Service	7,050	16,616	136%

	1940	1943	Increase 1943 over 1940
Total Trains Operated	21,017	37,514	78%
Mileage of Passenger Trains	1,531,460	2,281,047	49%
Mileage of Freight Trains	739,210	1,721,344	133%
Total Train Mileage	2,270,670	4,002,391	76%

Thus we find that in 1943 passenger travel was 5½ times and freight tonnage 3¼ times the figures for prewar 1940, which was accomplished with an increase of only seventy-six per cent in total train mileage. The increase of 458 per cent in passenger miles over 1940 was carried with only 94 per cent more passenger-carrying car-miles, indicating the crowded condition of the trains. Two hundred twenty-nine per cent more ton-mileage was hauled in 1943 than in 1940, with an increase of 136 per cent in loaded freight-car-mileage, reflecting the heavier loading of cars.

The following graph indicates the traffic growth from year to year:

Tons Revenue Freight Hauled:

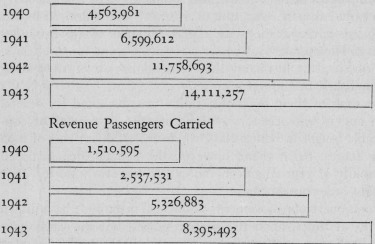

1940	4,563,981
1941	6,599,612
1942	11,758,693
1943	14,111,257

Revenue Passengers Carried

1940	1,510,595
1941	2,537,531
1942	5,326,883
1943	8,395,493

The year of 1944 opened with moderate increases in both passengers carried and freight hauled, but it is quite probable that some reduction in the training program along the Atlantic Seaboard and a return of tonnage to water routes may hold the figures for the year below the totals of 1943.

Traffic through Potomac Yard in the years 1942-43 greatly exceeded, of course, all prewar years. 1,422,244 cars—loaded and empty—were cleared through the Yard in 1943, an increase of eight per cent over 1942 and ninety-six per cent over prewar 1940. The peak movement was in May, 1943, when 266,166 cars were handled.

Adding to the problems of the Yard, it was found necessary to relieve the overburdened Washington Terminal passenger facilities of troop movements to and from the C.&O., the Southern, and the R.F.&P. and route the trains through Potomac Yard.

The Richmond, Fredericksburg and Potomac's tracks and equipment have been maintained in remarkably good condition despite constant use, the density of traffic, the lack of materials, and the shortage of experienced men.

Wartime railroading, even in good weather, is an onerous job, but when the weather turns sour that is the time when the stuff railroad men are made of reveals itself. In October of 1942 torrential rains seriously damaged the tracks north of Fredericksburg, and employees of the R.F.&P. did a valiant job of restoration.

In early February, 1943, the most severe sleet storm on record paralyzed communications and signals for about twenty-five miles north of Richmond. This writer was on the scene for three days, and observed at first-hand the tremendous job of restoration accomplished by the repair crews.

On each of these occasions, traffic was disrupted for several days, and it was necessary to hold up the movement of considerable freight in both directions, as well as divert part of it to other routes. Right there, however, the R.F.&P. demonstrated the ability of your American railroad to perform miracles, as it brought order out of chaos.

Occasional troop movements of unusual magnitude have drawn heavily, at times, upon the motive power, but the yards have been kept open, and somewhere, somehow, the traffic was kept moving. How it was done only God and the Richmond, Fredericksburg and Potomac know. The daily average of forty-six freight trains in the year 1943, or the equivalent of one long freight drag each way close to every hour of the day and night, speaks of an operating efficiency that is almost unbelievable. Add to these workhorse freights, fifty-seven fast-wheeling passenger trains, and you know that the boys are railroading on the Bridge Line.

Because of conditions beyond control and weather that at times has been vile without comparison, it has been impossible always to maintain passenger-train schedules, but the Richmond, Fredericksburg and Potomac reports that in the main the traveling public has been most gracious and understanding.

Probably no railroad in the country has been called upon to carry so greatly an augmented volume of traffic, in proportion to available facilities.

"The record of outstanding achievement accomplished," declares John B. Mordecai, Traffic Manager, "was possible only through the loyal and unfailing effort of the 4,000 men and women, from top to bottom, who make up the personnel of the road."

The accomplishment is the more remarkable when it is borne in mind that by the close of 1943 some 595 experienced men had been furloughed to the armed forces of the Nation.

Thus we find the Richmond, Fredericksburg and Potomac taking its rightful place with the mighty—the biggest little road in America, and at its head a great railroader, a great leader, a grand gentleman, and a real American—President Norman Call.

CHAPTER XXV

REMEMBER THE RAILROADS

Rio Grande – Illinois Central – Roller Bearings – Marker Lights

In these pages, we have reviewed in part the wartime operation of a few of the great railroads of America. It is, obviously, impossible to include in one book all of the lines that have joined the greatest battle of transportation in the country's proud history.

We have attempted to picture a general cross-section of American Railroads at war. Each and every railroad in the United States has been confronted with seemingly insurmountable difficulties and problems. Each and every railroad has met and overcome operating problems of a nature that no written word can adequately depict.

Let us briefly examine one such typical example. It concerns the Denver and Rio Grande Western. The high steel of the Rio Grande spins its shimmering length through and across a raw world of breath-taking grandeur—the Colorado Rockies. From the pioneering days of the Colorado narrow-gauge lines to the present time, railroading here on the tumbled roof of America has presented difficulties of a sort to dismay and discourage any but the most determined and courageous.

In line with all other American railroads, the Rio Grande has accomplished the successful movement of an enormous increase in war traffic over that of peacetime years. For instance, during 1942, the road handled 105 per cent more freight and 61 per cent more passenger traffic than in 1929. This was accomplished with an ownership of 9.4 per cent fewer freight cars, 29.4 per cent fewer passenger cars and a reduction of 0.6 per cent in locomotive tractive pounds.

The foresight of the management of the Rio Grande in spending millions of dollars to improve the property and plant in the depression period brought its reward, not only to the railroad, but in furthering the war effort, as well.

The Denver and Rio Grande Western forms an important sector of one of two great central transcontinental routes. Delays and operating difficulties have occurred, but the Rio Grande has, through infinite courage and resourcefulness, managed to keep the war trains rolling.

At a time when the road was struggling with its greatest burden of war traffic, a disastrous fire in Tunnel 10 of the Denver & Salt Lake Railway, the Moffat Road, blocked one of the Rio Grande's two main arteries, for this line is also used by the Rio Grande's through Western traffic between Denver and Orestod, Colorado.

The fire in Tunnel 10 caused the roof of a 300-foot section of this 1,570-foot, wood-timbered bore to collapse, choking the tunnel with smoldering debris and molten rocks. Here, in the black, smoke-choked, heat-ridden bowels of the mountain, men fought valiantly to subdue the flames—men of the Rio Grande, the Salt Lake Line, and Denver firemen, three of whom gave their lives.

Shoulder to shoulder, railroad men of the Rio Grande and the Moffat Road worked to reopen the line—worked under fearful handicaps and difficulties. *Forty-three days* after the start of the fire, on September 20, 1943, the heat was still so intense, the carbon-monoxide fumes so deadly, that work had to be halted temporarily.

Heroism, ingenuity, and heartbreaking toil at last whipped one of the toughest jobs railroad and construction men ever faced anywhere, and on December 1, at 4:53 P.M., Denver & Salt Lake train No. 1 rode the rails again, there in Tunnel 10.

In the meantime, it was necessary to route Rio Grande trains over the Royal Gorge Route, by way of Pueblo and Tennessee Pass, a 175-mile detour, and one that entails grades of as much as 3.0 per cent to the westward of the Pass. Some traffic was diverted to other transcontinental lines, but there still rolled across the Colorado Rockies every last possible ton of freight, every passenger car, the Rio Grande could haul.

Yes, then and now, the Rio Grande has its hands full, but

they are big, brawny, capable hands—hands that in wartime are knotted into the fists of a mighty iron warrior.

THE ILLINOIS CENTRAL

The Illinois Central Railroad, in 1944, has reached the ripe old age of approximately ninety years, although some of its component lines were built as early as 1836. The system operates over 6,800 miles of line in fourteen states, from the Great Lakes to the Gulf and from Chicago west to the Missouri River.

Among United States railroads, it ranks fourteenth in mileage, ninth in freight and passenger revenue, and has 500 connections with 130 railroads. It owns 1,500 locomotives and 50,000 cars, of which over 1,000 are passenger, baggage, mail, and express cars. It employs 30,000 persons. It is the largest coal-carrying railroad located wholly west of the Appalachians. It originates more cotton and handles more bananas than any other road, and it is the second largest road in volume of meats and packing-house products originated. Their strawberry move is very large and they too have carried their share of the oil traffic.

The Illinois Central operates 456 modern electric suburban trains in and out of Chicago, with an average of over 100,000 passengers per week-day travel.

On May 17, 1936, the Illinois Central inaugurated the Diesel-electric train, the *Green Diamond*, running between Chicago and St. Louis, which was among the first streamliners in America. It established on October 1, 1936, the MS-1 as the world's fastest long-distance freight train, covering 506 miles, Chicago to Memphis overnight.

In the war year of 1943, the Illinois Central handled its largest volume of traffic, for a total of 56,640,571,000 gross ton-miles. This traffic was handled with a decrease of 2.3 per cent in freight-train miles, compared with 1942, and a decrease of 10.1 per cent compared with 1929, and was accomplished by increasing the tonnage handled by each train, which was 2,716 tons per train in 1943, 2,461 tons in 1942, and 1,755 tons in 1929, representing increases of 10.4 and 54.8 per cent respectively.

What the Illinois Central has accomplished in wartime has

been on a par with the stupendous achievements of other American railroads, and is something to think about—and remember.

The manpower shortage has proved to be one of the major problems, with the lack of trained employees often becoming acute. However, the Illinois Central, like other roads, has attacked the situation with the usual American vigor and resourcefulness. The road turned to women, and to youths in the sixteen-seventeen year bracket. Classes in telegraphy were sponsored in local high schools. Other classes were established in Chicago, Carbondale, Illinois, and Memphis, Tennessee, for the training of youngsters for service as firemen, brakemen, and switchmen.

At the close of 1943, approximately 3,800 women, and 1,500 boys between the ages of sixteen and seventeen, were in railroad service. And what the women and these kids have accomplished, how they have adapted themselves to the job of helping to win the war, is something to stir admiration in even so hard-shelled an old codger as the Railroad.

On the battle fronts, the 715th Railway Operating Battalion, which was organized and officered by Illinois Central men in 1942, has, and is, fully maintaining the high tradition of American men.

ROLLER BEARINGS

The part that roller bearings are playing in keeping war traffic moving occupies a prominent place on the Honor Roll of the railroads. That there has not been a greater application of roller bearings to railroad equipment since the opening of hostilities has been due to acute material shortages.

However, when the war is won, roller bearings will play a prominent part in the building of swift peacetime fleets of both fast freights and faster luxury streamliners of the rail. For the trains of tomorrow, this writer feels safe in prophesying, will give America the finest transportation this world has ever seen.

The application of roller bearings to all classes of railroad equipment is in its infancy, but even today the records reveal amazing performance where they have been applied. Timken Roller Bearing freight car tests show a saving or reduction of eighty-eight per cent in starting resistance. Milwaukee Railroad passenger tests show a reduction of ninety per cent resistance in starting. Pennsylvania Railroad tests show the starting resistance of a roller bearing freight car was only 1.5 pounds per ton, against a starting resistance of forty-three pounds per ton for a friction bearing equipped car.

We have had occasion to observe at first-hand the performance of crank pin bearings and lightweight side-rods as applied to such locomotives as Santa Fe engines 3784 and 3785, which have averaged 2,000 miles more per month than sister engines built at the same time but equipped with friction bearings.

There are at the present time approximately 260 locomotives in the country equipped with Timken lightweight reciprocating parts. The application of light weight parts and roller bearings is one of the most important improvements in design for steam locomotives in the past decade. One Chief Executive has told us that his railroad would not have been able to handle the increased war traffic if they had not converted a large number of their existing locomotives to roller bearings in the years immediately preceding World War II.

Applications have been worked out, we are informed, whereby roller bearings can be applied to almost all existing locomotives, tenders, and passenger cars, with only minor changes to frames.

Of the large number of new steam locomotives and tenders on order at the present time, a large majority are to be equipped with roller bearings at such time as the necessary alloy steels are available.

With roller bearings, availability goes up; maintenance costs go down. The New York Central has decreased liability of delays on engine trucks so equipped ninety per cent. Locomotives on the Chicago and North Western, equipped with Timken bearings on driving axles and trailers, are giving one hundred per cent service, and have run up three-quarters of a million miles without difficulty. The N.&W. engine crews and officials are keen about the performance of the Class J engines.

In America, there are always men of vision hammering at the door of tomorrow—men who believe in themselves, the products of their hands, and the future of the country. Back in the early

1930s, the Timken Company built a steam locomotive completely equipped with roller bearings. This company was convinced that what roller bearings had done for the automobile they would do equally well for railroad rolling stock. You can call it a sales campaign, or you can call it inherent Yankee determination to overcome obstacles, for there were obstacles, a lot of them.

The railroads were skeptical, and roller bearings cost more. Old Man Depression was in the saddle. The railroads were spending money, plenty of it, but they were not in the mood to experiment to any great extent with new-fangled notions.

So Timken built this locomotive to demonstrate the correctness of their thinking. The engine operated on fourteen railroads, coast to coast, and it is now in service on the Northern Pacific Railway, with over one million miles to its credit.

How the problem of applying roller bearings to freight cars will be worked out, we do not know. However, we believe such bearings will become standard on modern passenger cars. As concerns motive power, the application of roller bearings seems to offer the railroads the largest return on any single investment they can make, as they prepare to give to America the trains of the future.

MARKER LIGHTS

Marker lights indicate the rear of the passing train. Here we light them and set them in their brackets, for this is the last car.

In 1943, I rode over forty thousand miles on the railroads of the United States. Twenty-five thousand miles of this distance was covered in the cabs of locomotives, as I mentioned in the chapter on the Santa Fe 3776-class engines. Up there, with the wind in your face, the thunder of the exhaust, and the song of the wheels in your ears, and your eyes looking down the steel rail, you live in a world apart. And yet there you are close to America—close to its teeming cities, its villages, its deserts and plains, its mighty, majestic mountains, its wild life. You acquire a better realization of its bigness, its almost limitless resources, its spirit.

It is not necessary to attempt here to summarize the wartime accomplishments of the American Railroads. We have reported facts and figures, together with our own observations, in the foregoing chapters.

We abhor statistics, of which there are many in these pages, but in recording the achievements of the railroads they are the necessary brush strokes that materially aid in creating the final picture of Railroads at War. They give depth and perception to the canvas—the Fourth Dimension that provides a more intimate perspective. We have attempted to arrange them in a manner that would be easy to read and understand.

One thing that the public as a whole does not realize is the fact that, where in World War I the military personnel were transported in day coaches, with troop trains limited to a speed of thirty-five miles an hour, in the second world conflict, the men in the armed forces, so far as possible, moved in standard Pullman or Tourist sleeping cars, and at speeds comparable, very nearly, to that of the crack passenger trains.

Among the really phenomenal tasks accomplished by the railroads during World War II has been the movement of a vast number of "high and wide" loads, with close to a one hundred per cent safety record. The job of loading and hauling on flatcars landing barges, boats, tanks, trucks, big naval guns, together with a great many other heavy and outsize pieces of machinery and equipment, has in itself presented many problems, not only involving the loading and securing of such freight, but of checking heights and overhangs against the dimensions of tunnels, cuts, and bridge structures.

Enormous has been the number of shipments of explosives, hauled countless thousands of miles, and these loads are under the alert and watchful eye of the railroads always. I rode a train made up of twenty-nine carloads of bombs and thirty-two cars of small ammunition westbound over Raton Pass, Trinidad to Raton, on the Santa Fe, with two engines on the head end and two on the rear. The time for this 3,500-ton train of some seventy cars over the 7,600-foot 3½ per cent grade Pass was two hours. Because of its consist, the Trainmaster rode the train.

Officials all over the country are riding the trains—troop trains, mixed "Main" trains, prisoner trains, hospital trains—concerned with the safe movement and prompt delivery of such trains at their destinations.

Often the railroads receive no advance information concerning the consist they are to handle, and are required to accept and transport unusual cargos of valuable merchandise that should be moving by express instead of freight. For example, I was in Omaha in the Union Pacific offices one morning when they received a boxcar from a foreign line at Council Bluffs.

This car contained airplane instruments consigned to Portland, Oregon. The valuation was $992,000! Almost one million dollars' worth of intruments of watchlike precision, jolting around in a boxcar. The Operating Department was stunned. They doubted that the valuation figures were correct. But they were.

The Union Pacific gathered up this unwanted child from its Omaha doorstep and tenderly started it on its way to Portland, which was all they could do about it—except to send an official along with it to see that no harm befell those precious instruments. This man filed a report at every division point, which was telegraphed to the Operating Vice-President, who never let it out of his mind until the "escort" at last wired that the car had been delivered to the consignees in the Rose City.

The shortage of locomotives, cars, manpower, and materials for maintenance places the railroad under a constant and increasing strain, for the equipment is wearing out. Every day the burden becomes greater.

Never has there been a time when railroad men of long-training and experience were more urgently needed, and it seems to this writer that those now left on the job should be allowed to remain where they are. I feel that no group of men is of greater importance to the Nation than the railroad men—from the president and operating vice-president right on down the line. General managers, traffic managers, division superintendents, trainmasters, yardmasters, train dispatchers, engine and train crews, shopmen, and trackmen—every last one of them is a vital cog in the railroad machine.

What's more, you do not have to coddle and pamper your railroad man to keep him on the job. You do not have to give him a morning and afternoon recess, serve him coffee and doughnuts, entertain him. There is little "absenteeism" on the railroad. Just so long as he has his health, your railroader works.

I have seen an operating vice-president on one of our largest railroads on the job forty-four out of forty-eight hours. I know a superintendent of passenger transportation who did not hit the hay for three days over a holiday weekend. Officials all up and down the line are in there pitching night and day. On the line, railroad men are relieved after sixteen hours, as required by law. They then get ten hours rest. For any time under sixteen hours, they get eight hours rest. But, remember, they may have to spend two or three hours getting to and from the job.

I have heard men in "Defense" industries boast of how little work they "could get away with." Your railroad man, on the other hand, boasts of what he has accomplished. You don't find railroad men sleeping or shirking on the job. You find them working full time, and then, perhaps, staying awake, just for the joy of listening to an engine like one of those Santa Fe 3776-class locomotives working steam on a grade. That's your American railroader.

He's keeping open the supply lines to Berlin and Tokyo.

Another major job accomplished by the railroads, and one about which we hear little, is the able manner in which they have protected bridges, tunnels, shops, yards, and other property from possible acts of sabotage. The safeguarding of vital areas has assured the delivery of essential supplies destined for our armed forces overseas. Guns, ammunition, and men must go through. There can be no delay to a train that is "keeping a date with a convoy."

Distances are great; trains are heavy; men and engines grow weary, but war transport rolls on.

The steel rail, creeping westward, the driving of the Golden Spike at Promontory, Utah, on May 10, 1869, the building of our Railroad Empire was, primarily, a military necessity. The American Railroads today are a military necessity, and this war could not have been fought if the railroads had failed to meet their responsibilities.

Your cruiser, aircraft carrier, battleship—all would have remained "red earth" in the Iron Range without the railroads to move the ore to the blast furnaces, to haul the coal for the fires of industry, to rush the steel to the shipyards and war plants.

Too much credit cannot be given the Office of Defense Transportation, the Interstate Commerce Commission, the United States Army Rail Transportation Corps. These organizations have ruled well and wisely. Always in the high places we find such men as the late Honorable Joseph Bartlett Eastman, who, at the time of his death on March 15, 1944, was the Director of the Office of Defense Transportation.

Under war conditions, the general public has suffered some inconvenience, it is true, but it has been small, after all, compared with the sacrifice made by our fighting men.

If you could not always get a seat or a berth on a train, remember that the requirements of the Military Service came first always. The railroads have, further, made every effort to provide men and women on furlough with transportation at all times. Remember that the Richmond, Fredericksburg and Potomac in one year transported 2,649,295 servicemen and -women on furlough—men and women going home, many for the last time.

If you could not get into the dining car, if you could only get a sandwich instead of a full meal, remember that it was because the Dining Car Service was first concerned with the feeding of the men in uniform. Remember that men on the battle line are often huddled in the mud and slime of shell and fox holes with no food at all for hours on end.

In one war year, the New York Central served 3,000,000 extra meals on its dining cars. In a kitchen only 6 by 13½ feet, chefs on the Central have averaged more than a meal a minute.

The railroads, too, have provided much in the way of extra service. For instance, in the Grand Central Terminal, New York, we find a "Nap Nook," with comfortable steamer chairs for the convenience of travel-weary servicemen.

A neon sign in the Union Station at Omaha, Nebraska, displays this greeting: "Service Men's Center—Everything Free." Railroads serving the Union Station here have installed air-conditioned quarters, with a recreation room, shower baths, canteen, and First-Aid station in charge of Registered Nurses. Local concerns and townspeople have contributed complete equipment and supply refreshments. Volunteer workers give their time.

These are small things, perhaps, but they reflect the human side of the great railroad carriers, engaged in the grim business of war transportation.

The going has been tough, and the public has been forced to accept many inconveniences. Some have grumbled and complained and magnified petty annoyances, but, on the other hand, the vast majority of travelers have exhibited infinite patience and a good-humor that reflects the sportsmanship of your average American.

When the war is over, the railroads, having performed the transportation miracle of all time, will devote the same energy, ingenuity, and fertile resourcefulness to the development of trains that will make travel a pleasant and thrilling experience. Already the preliminary plans have been drawn. There will be offered to both coach and sleeping-car passengers the most commodious and attractive accommodations in railroad history. The coach sleeper will come into its own. Upper and lower berths will become but a memory, while in their place we will find roomettes, even more luxurious than those of today, and at a cost of very little more than your present lower berth.

Motive power will develop, and the pace will be fast and safe.

Remember the prediction of Horatio Allen, pioneer locomotive builder—"The man is not living who can tell what the improved breed of locomotives will accomplish in the future."

Remember then, when the war is won, that Victory was bought with the blood and courage of American fighting men. Remember, too, the service of the railroads. The same dependable, unfailing kind of transportation they have provided for our Government in wartime will, in the same measure, be rendered to the shipper and the traveler of America in peacetime.

Rio Grande #5, the Exposition Flyer, detouring via Tennessee Pass when Tunnel 10 on the Denver & Salt Lake was burned out in November, 1943. The helper #1501, 4-8-2 Type Class M-67, and the road engine 1706, Class M-64 4-8-4 Type, are working hard up the 1.42% grade west of Malta, Colorado. Photo by R. H. Kindig, U.S. Army.

Rio Grande Extra 3617 West climbing the 2% grade on the D. & S. L. west of Denver as it heads toward the Moffat Tunnel, with a consist of heavy machinery, oil and merchandise for the west coast. #3617 is a 2-8-8-2 Type Class L-132, and one of the D. & S. L.'s 200 Class 2-6-6-0 Type is cut in just ahead of the rear end. Photo by Preston George.

Note the roller-bearing rods on Santa Fe engine 3784, 4-8-4 Type, running 80 miles per hour near Laguna, N.M. on the First District of the Albuquerque Division with #20. Photo by Otto C. Perry.

Easter morning, 1944. #19, the Chief, descending Raton Pass just west of Lynn, New Mexico. The tower at that point and the helper that assisted #19 up the pass and has just been cut off may be seen in the distance. Photo by Otto C. Perry.

INDEX

305

308

312

313

314

Union Switch & Signal Co., 13, 20, 21-2, 245
Union Tank Car Co., 76
United States Railroad Administration, 287
Upland, Calif., 271
Utilization (locomotives), 7, 44-52, 120

Valley, Nebr., 166
Vauces, Ohio, 169
Vauclain, Samuel M., 114
Vaughn, N. M., 58, 59, 96, 97, 279
Verdemont, Calif., 269
Vermilion Range, 112, 113, 116
Victorville, Calif., 268-9
Vincent, Calif., 38
Virginia, 220
Virginia Air Line, 133
Virginia, Minn., 116
Virginia & Tennessee R.R., 248, 257
Vulcan, 153

Wabash River, 100
Walapai, Ariz., 147, 148
Wakpala, S. D., 212
Walkerford, Va., 225
Wallbridge, Ohio, 218
War Production Board, 77, 289
Wasatch Range, 154
Washington, D. C., 63, 127, 128, 129, 151, 153, 284
Washington, Mass., 106, 107
Washington Sub-Division (C.&O.), 133
Watsonville, Calif., 42
Wave, Calif., 38
Waynesboro, Va., 133
Waynoka, Okla., 55, 58, 59, 95, 278
Welch, Ariz., 273-4
Wellington, Kan., 55, 57, 58, 59, 95, 260, 278
Wellton, Ariz., 28
West Albany shops (N. Y. Central), 108
West Breakwater Yards (Cleveland), 125
Western Ave. Roundhouse, 205
Western General Division (C.&O.), 221
Western Maryland R.R., 133
Western Military Bureau, 39
Western Pacific R.R., 80, 142
Western R.R., 106
West Hamlin, W. Va., 225

West Huntington Belt Line, 222
Westinghouse locomotive, 213-5
West Newberry, Pa., 104
West Springfield Yards (B.&A.), 108, 109
Wheat transport, 190-1
Whipple Mine, 141
Whiskey Island, 125
Whitcomb, W. Va., 225
White Oak Sub-Division (C.&O.), 140
White Sulphur Springs, W. Va., 225
Whitesville, Ky., 168
Wichita, Kan., 53, 55, 57, 59, 95
Wickenburg, Ariz., 57
Wicopee, Ore., 239
Williams, Ariz., 144, 146, 235, 266, 274
Williamsburg, Va., 227
Wilmington, Del., 6
Winding Gulf Branch Line (C.&O.), 134
Winding Gulf coal field; 135
Winona, Ariz., 143, 274
Winona, Minn., 210
Winslow, Ariz., 54-7, 59, 142-5, 231, 234, 235, 265, 266, 272, 275, 279, 288
Winston-Salem Line (N.&W.), 250
Winston-Salem, N. C., 249, 254
Winton Co., 80
Wisconsin Dells, 209
Women workers, 129
Woodland, Calif., 28
Wood River, Nebr., 65
Wootton, Colo., 261, 276
Worcester, Mass., 106, 110
World War I, 3, 6-8, 64, 78-9, 112-3, 170-1, 200, 229, 286, 290
Wyoming, 192

Y-3 locomotives, 263
Yakima River, 216
Yampai, Ariz., 147, 148
Yards: Chesapeake & Ohio, 64, 140-1; New York Central, 108-10; Southern Pacific, 33-4; see also names of yards
Yermo, Calif., 9, 11, 22, 244
Young, Rear Admiral William B (quoted), 8
Youngstown, Ohio, 119
Yucca, Ariz., 147, 267
Yuma, Ariz., 28; Yard, 33

Zephyrs, 6, 210
Zuni, 265